68

BAD DAYS IN BASRA

My Turbulent Time as Britain's Man in Southern Iraq

BAD DAYS IN BASRA

My Turbulent Time as
Britain's Man in Southern Iraq

Hilary Synnott

I.B. TAURIS

LONDON · NEW YORK

Reprinted in 2008 by I.B.Tauris & Co Ltd
6 Salem Road, London W2 4BU
175 Fifth Avenue, New York NY 10010
www.ibtauris.com

In the United States of America and Canada distributed by
Palgrave Macmillan, a division of St. Martin's Press, 175 Fifth Avenue,
New York NY 10010

First published in 2008 by I.B.Tauris & Co Ltd

ISBN: 978 1 84511 706 1

A full CIP record for this book is available from the British Library
A full CIP record is available from the Library of Congress

Library of Congress Catalog Card Number: available

Designed and Typeset by 4word Ltd, Bristol, UK
Printed and bound by TJ International Ltd, Padstow, Cornwall, UK

Contents

Acknowledgements

IT WAS THE persistent encouragement and cajoling of Iradj Bagherzade of I.B.Tauris that caused me to attempt to write a book about my experiences in Iraq, and the advice of him and Abbie Fielding-Smith, my commissioning editor, which led it to take on a lighter, rather than an academic, form. I was further encouraged by Dr Toby Dodge, a colleague at the International Institute for Strategic Studies and himself a distinguished historian of the country, and by Andrew Rathmell, who has spent a great deal of time in Baghdad since the occupation in 2003 in an advisory capacity and has written learnedly about the situation which followed on from it. To all of them I am most grateful.

But I doubt that I would ever have managed to complete the task, and certainly not in the timescale involved, without the generosity and hospitality of the Master and Fellows of Clare College, Cambridge, who were kind enough to award me the Eric Lane Fellowship for the Summer Term of 2007. The relative tranquillity of the University allowed me to concentrate on the task at hand to an extent which would have been impossible elsewhere; and various discussions with students and Fellows proved invaluable in marshalling my thoughts.

Others provided moral and advisory support: Dr Brendan Simms of my own college, Peterhouse, encouraged me to lighten up the draft, and his suggested title for the book, *Bugger Basra*, greatly tempted me; Glen Rangwala of Trinity, Cambridge, who has also written about Iraq, offered some invaluable expertise; Chris Catlin, journalist, author and old friend, shared some tricks of the trade and urged me on; Robert Wilson reminded me of many political complexities; and Jeremy Greenstock cast an experienced eye over the draft. I must also thank Dr Celia Duff, Fellow of Clare, and the *British Medical Journal* for their kind permission to reprint an extract by Dr Duff about the state of public health in Basra. The Foreign and Commonwealth Office, too, played its part: by politely requesting only a very few amendments to the manuscript for reasons which were both prudent and sensible; and by enabling me to pursue a career which, while sometimes trying, was never dull. The spirit and zeal of the multinational team with whom I worked in southern Iraq, too many to name and including some brave Iraqis who have since been killed, more than made up for the immense frustrations surrounding our efforts; they prevented this book becoming solely an angry narrative of failure.

My two older brothers, Anthony and Timothy, published experts in their own, very different, fields, were kind enough to encourage rather than engage in sibling criticism, despite never having allowed me to recount my 'When I was in Borneo' naval reminiscences of the early 1960s. They have both been greater sources of inspiration and example than they realise. To our late father I owe some old-fashioned ideals which I have strived to live up to.

Finally, special thanks must go to my wife Annie, who did not marry a diplomat, who refused ever to accept the label 'diplomatic wife', still less 'Ambassadress', but who nonetheless stood by me and kept me going through some cumulatively difficult times. Without her I might have taken a very different and less-fulfilling direction.

Hilary Synnott
Goodworth Clatford

List of Plates

Acronyms

ACPO	Association of Chief Police Officers
CJTF-7	Combined Joint Task Force 7
CPA	Coalition Provisional Authority
ACPO	Association of Chief Police Officers
CPA(South)	The CPA's southern branch office
DFID	Department for International Development
FCO	Foreign and Commonwealth Office
GT	Governorate Team
IGC	Iraq Governing Council
KBR	Kellogg Brown Root
MOD	Ministry of Defence
MND(SE)	Multinational Division (South East)
ORHA	Office of Reconstruction and Humanitarian Assistance
RMP	Royal Military Police
SCIRI	Supreme Council for the Islamic Revolution in Iraq
USAID	US Agency for International Development

Prologue

If you do not break them, they will break you; yea and bring all the guilt
of the blood and treasure shed and spent in this kingdom upon your head
and shoulders.

Oliver Cromwell, as attributed by John Lilburne, *c.* 1649.

IN THE LATE summer of 2004, the British Foreign Secretary, Jack
Straw, held a party in Lancaster House, an opulent building a
stone's throw from the forbidding austerity of St James's Palace,
in central London. The occasion was intended to thank those
civilians who had tried to stabilise and reconstruct Iraq after the
main combat had finished in the spring of the previous year.

I had worked closely with many of the guests in circumstances
which had sometimes been difficult, sometimes exhilarating and
sometimes comical. I was glad to see them again. And I
appreciated Jack Straw's thoughtfulness in recognising the civilian
contribution and providing the opportunity for us all to gather
together as a whole. But I had mixed feelings. Ultimately the outfit
in which I and my colleagues in Iraq had worked, the Coalition
Provisional Authority (CPA), had been a failure. No amount of
congratulations about individual efforts could disguise the fact
that this neo-colonial organisation, which had assumed
responsibility for the governance and administration of a country
of some 26 million people, had been wound up after scarcely a year
of troubled existence.

I was gossiping with some old friends when Jack Straw affably
pulled me aside for a chat. He would be saying a few words to
round off the party, he said. Did I have any thoughts for him to
include? Much as I liked him – he had been exceptionally
supportive when I was in Basra and also in the difficult period after

9/11 when I had been High Commissioner in Pakistan – I wished that he had given me a bit of notice; the issues were important. My mind was full of competing ideas and a jumble of memories of my time in Iraq, where I had been a bizarre blend of ambassador – to the Iraqis and to the Americans – and quasi-colonial governor of four Iraqi provinces. What could I say that would not be either an optimistic platitude or unhelpfully despondent? I did not want to be negative. I still hoped that, despite the trend, Iraq might one day come right; but it did not look promising.

All I could think of was a previous forecast by Prime Minister Tony Blair – that history would judge. I blurted out something to the effect that history might well be the judge, but that it was too soon to be sure that the judgement would be what we wanted. Straw moved on.

He had registered the point. A few minutes later I heard him announce: 'History will be the judge, and I am quite sure that the judgement will be positive'. Then he warmly thanked us all. Nice, but not quite what I had had in mind. I turned back to the party.

When Queen Victoria first visited Lancaster House, now the Foreign Office's main venue for impressive entertainment, she was recorded as saying to her hostess in a majestic put-down: 'I have come from my house to your palace'. However, those who had served in Iraq were not over-awed by the gilded grandeur of their surroundings. They were used to palaces. Saddam's main palace had housed the CPA's Headquarters in Baghdad. One of his summer palaces in Basra had been the base for British civilian operations in southern Iraq, after deteriorating security conditions had forced a move from more dangerous and uncomfortable premises the previous October. But the Lancaster House palace had the advantage of functioning toilets, a free flow of sparkling wine and the prospect of going home at the end of the day.

The guest list for Jack Straw's party ran to 622 names. What we had in common was our direct or indirect participation in the CPA, which had been set the confident goal in mid-2003 'to establish a secure, peaceful and democratic Iraq that will stand against terrorism and no longer threaten America, the region, or the world', which was supposed to fulfil it in practice, and which had been prematurely wound up a few months before the party.

We were a mixed bunch. A couple of hundred were employees of the Foreign and Commonwealth Office and the Department for International Development who had served on the ground in Iraq. Their average age was conspicuously young. Old stagers such as myself and some of the expensively hired contracted consultants stood out as exceptions. Another couple of hundred were advisers and civil servants who had provided support from the UK. Others included 30 police officers, officials from other government departments and military people who had been closely associated with the civilian effort.

Jack Straw, Hilary Benn, the Development Minister, other ministers and senior officials circulated benignly. They seemed pleased that southern Iraq, where the main British effort had been concentrated, was turning out relatively well. It was clear that other parts of Iraq were not. Some British Ministers were rashly or, according to one American commentator, 'slyly' taking credit for the contrast. As violence in central Iraq had increased, they could not resist implying, or even declaring outright, that the management of the South was a model for others. But these Ministers had little or no appreciation of the complexities and magnitude of the task. Nor had they collectively been prepared to devote the human, financial and technical resources to enable the civilian arm of the Coalition to even begin to provide order and governance to a country in which the entire state apparatus had imploded. Self-congratulation and implicit criticism of American methods had done nothing to encourage American paymasters to provide the South with resources themselves, as I had quickly found out.

Many of the guests therefore shared my own mixed feelings. Perhaps the CPA had been doomed from the start. Perhaps it was inevitable that it would not be able to fulfil its arrogantly ambitious goal. Conceived in a hurry, formed a month after the ground combat had finished and expected to continue for several years, its demise was announced only six months later and it was wound up six months after that. Intended to settle Iraq down to allow the rapid withdrawal of armed forces, its infant bureaucracy had failed to make an impact.

The Coalition's civilian administrators had now left, to be replaced by a more conventional diplomatic and development cooperation relationship with Iraq. But more than 150,000 foreign troops had had to remain in an environment in which violence, criminality, sectarianism, insurgency and terrorism were spinning out of control. Although Iraq had become nominally fully sovereign and the foreign forces were present at the request of the Iraqi authorities, many of the country's citizens still regarded these forces as occupiers.

In the years that followed, the situation in the country as a whole, and in the South, went from bad to worse. External civilian reconstruction efforts ground to a virtual halt, leaving the field to the military and to high politics and attempts at statecraft. The Americans engaged in successive changes of policy, practice and tactics to try to salvage the situation so as to allow and facilitate a weak Iraqi government to exercise authority, while encouraging, cajoling and threatening them to do more. Meanwhile, the British and other Coalition partners in the South reduced their force levels, and in some cases withdrew altogether, amid increasingly bitter American accusations that 'the Brits have lost the South' – as if the rest of the country was any better.

Now, some four years after I left Basra, with only an occasional return to Iraq, I have increasingly detected a seductive line of argument that the Iraq experience was a worst-case anomaly – that we should not have got ourselves into that maelstrom against a background of such ignorance and so poorly resourced, and that the like will not occur again.

There is of course some force in this. It is certainly to be hoped that when political leaders again decide to engage in 'a continuation of political activity by other means', in Clausewitz's famous definition of war, there will be a clearer prior assessment of the nature of the political activity which should take place after the 'other means' are halted; that there should be a better understanding that the ultimate object of war – a form of political activity – should not be limited to military victory as an end in itself, but should be the promotion of peace.

This argument is sometimes conveniently developed to suggest that, because the situation was unique, there is little need to adapt well-tested existing structures to try to meet challenges which are unlikely to arise again. But such an extrapolation would be wrong-headed and dangerous.

From my own close experience of the nature of the civilian structures for management, supply and control, and having seen that they did not stand up to many of the tests to which they were exposed in Iraq or in the preceding Afghanistan campaign which continues to this day, I believe that many changes are still needed.

I take this view because, in the light of recent post-Cold War experience and the current international climate, it seems more, not less, probable that the international community will be presented with challenges stemming from fragile states which directly or indirectly affect their interests. This has proved to be the case in Bosnia, Kosovo, East Timor, Sierra Leone and Afghanistan. There have been some successes, but often the balance between military and civilian engagement has been seriously out of kilter.

More difficult than the learning of lessons, the lessons need to be applied. Some of them may be difficult, awkward and expensive. Some may challenge existing balances of power and influence between well-established and proud government departments. And there are few political or promotional prizes to be gained from preparing for contingencies which cannot be precisely defined and which may never arise. But failure to meet the challenges is costly in lives and money – blood and treasure – as recent experience has so clearly demonstrated. The enormous disparity between the human and financial costs of military and civilian efforts in recent campaigns, the fact that the Army have increasingly been drawn into essentially civilian functions, and the overstretch repeatedly emphasised by senior British military officers, suggests that the current balance of effort and engagement is very far from being either equitable or effective.

This book is therefore intended in part to encourage the processes of necessary change. The illustrations in it arise from the peculiarly British role in attempting to stabilise and reconstruct Iraq's four southern provinces – where both the military commander and, in my case, the civilian Regional Coordinator, were British. But the judgements and observations draw also on my 30 years' experience as a diplomat, in which some half of my career was concerned with developing countries with large Muslim populations, together with more than ten years' prior service in the British armed forces.

If what follows includes criticism of decisions, systems and structures, this is not intended to reflect badly on the dedication and effort of individuals. And if there are invidious comparisons between the effectiveness of the British Armed Forces and the shortcomings of the British Civil Service, this should not suggest that the latter should become more like the former. I have no doubt that the Forces have their own defects, about which I am not well placed to comment. And, as this account shows, many admirable public servants, dedicated to the concept of altruistic Crown Service, could not humanly have done more to meet the challenges with which they were faced.

Nearly five years after the start of the Second Gulf War, some of the heat and anger about the early mistakes may have dissipated, and it may now be easier to engage in cool assessment about the lessons to be drawn from these mistakes. But, despite the extensive analysis of the key political decisions, the dust has far from settled. There remains much to know about and to be learned from the interplay between the policy-makers and the civilian and military practitioners. This book attempts to fill some of the gaps and to convey the atmosphere of the time and place.

Bad Days in Basra

Map of Iraq

PART ONE
THE ASSIGNMENT

PART ONE

THE ASSIGNMENT

Chapter 1

'It's a Bloody Mess'

I had believed these misfortunes ... to be due mainly to faulty leadership, or rather to the lack of leadership, Arab and English.

T.E. Lawrence, *Seven Pillars of Wisdom.*

ANNIE AND I were painting the sitting-room ceiling when the phone rang. The Permanent Under-Secretary at the Foreign and Commonwealth Office (FCO), Sir Michael Jay, was on the other end. He asked after the roses. We had always been friendly, but I knew that no serving Foreign Office mandarin rings on a working day for an idle chat. I grabbed a pencil and paper, sat down on a dustsheet-covered armchair and tried to avoid getting paint on the telephone.

I drummed my fingers impatiently while Jay came to the point. The Coalition's senior civilian in southern Iraq, the Danish ambassador to Syria, Ole Wohlers Olsen, would be leaving Basra early. The Prime Minister had decided with the Americans that it would be best to have a British person to replace him, to facilitate cooperation with the Army in the region, which was under British military command. My name had 'come up'. Would I like to go to Basra and take the Dane's place? Jay said that he realised that I was in my last ten days before retirement, but I seemed to be the man for the job. If I agreed, he said, it would be nice if I could get to Iraq by the end of July, two weeks later.

My first instinct was to decline there and then. I knew that there had been unsuccessful trawls for senior volunteers for a somewhat different job a few months earlier, while I was still British High Commissioner in Pakistan. Word had reached me that no serving or retired diplomat had wanted to 'work for Rumsfeld'. Having spent 15 of my 30 years as a diplomat abroad, I had been looking forward to life back in my own country. I had planted some more apple trees in the garden and had made plans. Whatever the urgency, I saw no need to give a definitive response on the phone straightaway.

After a pause, I told Jay that I would think about it. He did not press me and punctiliously added that, in fairness, he should make clear that he would be asking another possible volunteer as well. I asked who it was he had in mind. He gave me a name and observed that, since the person concerned was currently the Governor of Bermuda, it was possible that he would not feel able to accept. I doubted that that was a judgement which called for decades of diplomatic experience. I would have been astonished that the other man, though eminently qualified, would have agreed to exchange his plumed hat and canapés for a tin helmet and military rations.

To sweeten the pill, Michael added that, since my wife could obviously not accompany me to Basra, she could if she wished stay in Kuwait at government expense. I had never before heard of such an arrangement. There were no Foreign Office procedures which would allow for it. They must be desperate, I thought. Not that there was any question of Annie giving up her work in England to languish in a Kuwaiti hotel.

As soon as I put the phone down, I rang the Head of the Foreign Office Iraq Policy Unit, a steady and exceptionally sensible middle-ranking officer who seemed to carry the entire burden of the British civilian contribution to the Iraq issue on his own shoulders. He already knew that I was being approached.

I asked what was going on. He replied immediately: 'It's a bloody mess'. He went on to explain that Ambassador Olsen was frustrated by what he regarded as his impossible situation. A few days earlier, during a spot of leave in Denmark, he had given an interview to the press and had not unreasonably complained that the Americans had not given him and his team in Basra sufficient support. It was unlikely that he would return from his leave.

The British military chiefs, I learned, were meanwhile incandescent about the inadequacies of the civilian operation in the four southern Iraq provinces, which fell under their military authority: unless the civvies, who were their 'ticket home', got their act together, they would be stuck. According to the military chiefs, the Foreign Office were being 'pathetic'.

The Americans meanwhile wanted more input from the Brits, the sole other 'occupying power' as designated by the relevant United Nations Security Council Resolution. John Sawers, a senior Foreign Office official who was the Prime Minister's representative in Baghdad before Sir Jeremy Greenstock's arrival in September, had said that what we needed was a 'King of the South', to take overall charge of policy and operations there. The 'King' should report jointly to the recently appointed Coalition Administrator in Baghdad, Ambassador Paul Bremer, who was in effect the 'Emperor', and to the British Prime Minister. His task would be to coordinate with the Army on the ground, with the Foreign Office and the Department for International Development (DFID) in London, with Bremer in Baghdad and with all the Iraqis in the provinces.

All this was recounted crisply and frankly on the telephone. I got the message. It was indeed a 'bloody mess'. The task sounded impossible. Somebody had to take it on, but it did not, perhaps, have to be me.

*   *   *

Four months before this conversation, in early March 2003, I was a guest at a stand-up buffet supper given by a prominent political figure in Pakistan, a strong opponent of the Pakistan military President, General Pervez Musharraf. Despite Musharraf's support for the Coalition in the Afghanistan campaign after the destruction of the World Trade Center in September 2001, Pakistani opinion was united in its opposition to the American approach to Iraq. Pakistanis were appalled at the possibility of military action should the debates in the United Nations, which were then under way, fail to satisfy the USA. Several European Union countries, especially France and Germany, were similarly horrified at the prospect and were actively lobbying against them. Since the British Government had been identified accurately as being supportive of the US Government, I had been under strong personal attack myself. Many of my Pakistani friends and my fellow European diplomats had no hesitation in letting me know their views, without mincing their words.

I was sipping a lime juice and soda when the French Ambassador pulled me to one side.

'Hilary', he said, looking earnestly into my eyes, 'we have known each other for three years now and I think we can be honest with each other'.

The Ambassador's English accent was not as good as his Urdu, which was flawless. I looked earnestly back and waited for what might come next.

'Tell me, mon ami, cher collègue. There are occasions, hein, when an ambassador is not comfortable with his instructions, n'est-ce pas?'

'Yeees', I ventured, cautiously.

'I wonder if this is not one of those occasions?'

The earnest look into my eyes continued, inescapably. I decided that I should respond brightly.

'Actually, mon cher ami, it is not. I think that we're doing the right thing. And, while I can understand that some might disagree with the way we and the Americans are going about this, what I can't understand is how your government thinks we should all deal with Saddam and his deadly weapons in practice. Don't both of our governments have a responsibility to uphold all these binding Resolutions by the UN Security Council?'

I had no doubt that if I had revealed any hesitations to my French colleague about my instructions, an exultant report would have reached Paris within hours and could well have been used further to undermine the official British position. I would not have blamed my friend for this; we were both professionals in our trade and I would have done the same had the positions been reversed.

But I had meant exactly what I said. I had seen some of the communications between London and Washington about the intelligence communities' concerns about weapons of mass destruction (WMD) in Iraq. And I had read the Prime Minister's personal foreword to one of the British Government's dossiers on the subject which had referred to a capability of launching weapons within 45 minutes. The British Parliament had voted, albeit with a slim majority, in favour of military action in order to eliminate the risk of the use of such weapons. I had no reason to doubt the accuracy of my Government's assertions, and on that basis I believed the cause to be just and expedient.

I had an additional reason to support such a position; one which was never put to the British Parliament. I believed that, after the massive contribution which the USA had made to the security of Europe in the two World Wars of the twentieth century, we owed it to the Americans to support them in their time of crisis after the atrocities of 9/11.

The French Ambassador continued. He appeared to accept that he could not penetrate my diplomatic armour, because it was actually part of my skin. So he shook his head sadly and told me that the French Government would veto the draft.

Frankly, I did not believe him. I knew that, spurred on by the British Prime Minister Tony Blair, the US Government had reluctantly agreed to try and secure agreement to yet another resolution in the United Nations Security Council. The British Representative to the UN, Sir Jeremy Greenstock, was master-minding one of the most important lobbying exercises in the UN's post-Cold War history. If the new draft Resolution was to be adopted, we needed a majority among the 15 members of the Security Council and no vetoes from any of the five Permanent Members, who, in addition to the USA and UK, included Russia, China and France. Pakistan was one of the non-permanent members of the Security Council whose vote might tip the balance. The French Ambassador, whose government opposed the draft resolution, and I were pressing the Pakistanis in opposing directions.

I had seen the reporting telegrams from the British Ambassador in Paris and from Jeremy Greenstock in New York. It was clear that the French were negotiating very hard and had referred to the possibility of a veto; but I could not believe that they had yet made a decision. A veto would be a profound snub to their American and British allies in NATO and, in the case of the UK, their partner in the European Union. But, more significantly, it would let Saddam off the hook and lift the pressure on him to reveal, as we hoped, the location of the WMD and hence avert an invasion. I therefore believed that the French would continue to negotiate and leave a final decision on a veto until the last possible moment. Surely their government would not reveal their intentions beforehand to those diplomatic missions not directly engaged in the UN discussions?

I was wrong, on two counts. Very soon thereafter, the French made clear that, were the draft to come to a vote, they would indeed veto it, causing the draft to be dropped. And it subsequently emerged that it was most unlikely that Saddam had any WMD to reveal. There was no sound basis for Blair's '45 minutes' claim.

But in March 2003, when my conversation with my French colleague took place, I was not a direct player in this contest; like many other British heads of diplomatic missions, I was part of the lobbying process. I was also more than preoccupied with the Pakistan-related aspects of the military campaign under way in Afghanistan, to the west; and with the serious tensions with India, to the east, which were only just starting to ease following the terrorist attack on the Indian parliament in December 2001. So I had plenty of other matters to concern me apart from my professional differences with my French colleague.

When the US- and British-led invasion of Iraq started, on 20 March 2003, my Pakistani friends and contacts were horrified. The animosity against the USA and Britain was palpable. I had heard the blast on St Patrick's Day morning, 17 March, a year earlier, when a suicide bomber in a nearby church had killed several

Americans and wounded others, including a member of my staff. Constant security threats and several physical attacks on our High Commission building had caused us to be protected like a fortress. Our movements had been severely restricted ever since the start of the campaign in Afghanistan in October 2001. Former friends would no longer talk to me or did so while ramming an accusing finger into my chest. They were now turning from me because of the position taken by the government which I represented. The armour provided by my ill-founded confidence in our cause was a great psychological help, but I was glad that the three turbulent years of my posting in Pakistan were soon coming to an end.

I was particularly relishing the prospect of leaving the constraints of diplomatic life abroad. I had had quite enough of the Foreign Office and what I regarded as an over-preoccupation with administrative matters at the expense of policy advice and execution. I had therefore decided to leave the Diplomatic Service early, at the age of 58, a couple of years before what was then the statutory retirement age.

I had joined the Royal Navy some 40 years previously as a 17-year-old and been accepted into the Diplomatic Service 11 years after that. So, after so much Crown Service, working for the nation rather than for any political party of the day, I was looking forward to no longer having always to act on instructions. I wanted, at last, to do what I chose to do. I told my former colleagues that I intended to cultivate roses, brew my own cider and, with the help of a pot-still acquired in Italy, perhaps distil some of the latter, as an 'aromatic perfume', since home distilling of alcohol, even for personal consumption, is quite illegal in Britain.

* * *

The task in Basra sounded horrendous. It would involve reporting both to Blair and to Bremer. Every principle of management advised against split reporting lines since these could lead to divided objectives and confusion. And I was very familiar already with the tensions between the Development Ministry, DFID, the Foreign Office, the Ministry of Defence and the British

Army. Attempts to coordinate between these powerful and entrenched bureaucracies promised to be painful.

But most importantly, my experience over the previous few years suggested that the traditional role of ministerially led Cabinet Committees, which thrashed out inter-departmental differences and forged a common policy to be executed by officials, had all but broken down. Instead, a small team within Number 10 Downing Street attempted to fulfil such a function itself, giving broad policy direction but all too often based, it seemed, on inadequate study of the consequences. While a cabinet committee under the Foreign Secretary's chairmanship did exist, it met on an ad hoc basis and only fortnightly. As I was to find out, it had little to do with the practical issues in Iraq. This left lots of room for in-fighting between senior officials of government departments, which in some cases had effectively become rivals. Under Clare Short's tenure in DFID particularly, it was no secret that she sought actively to distance her Department from the Foreign Office and regarded the activities of the Ministry of Defence as being often profoundly at odds with DFID's objective of 'the eradication of poverty'.

Despite these misgivings, I told the Foreign Office that I would ponder on the idea. I made some more enquiries, making full use of all my old contacts. The description 'bloody mess' still seemed entirely appropriate. Did I really want to preside over that?

Within days, however, the likely terms of reference had changed. John Sawers reported from Baghdad that Bremer, now with a couple of months' experience in the country, had decided that he did not want any 'King' on his patch, even if tribute were paid to him. He wanted to keep all the levers to himself. While he would accept the presence of a Regional Coordinator covering the four southern provinces, he intended to create additional Coordinators in each of the 18 provinces who would report direct to him.

My actual role therefore seemed likely to be very different from what had originally been suggested. And the British Army's fears about the inadequacy of the civilian contribution, even though their expectations were based on over-optimistic and unrealistic assumptions, proved to be correct. But, despite all the evident uncertainties, Annie did not object when I mused that I would kick myself for the rest of my life if I did not have a go. I might not know what I was letting myself in for, but it was bound to be challenging and different. So I started more methodically to brief myself, though still without commitment. I declared my agreement the day before what was to have been the date of my early retirement and so remained a British diplomat for a bit longer.

With my appointment as the Coalition's civilian coordinator in the South, coupled with the British command of the Coalition's military presence there, the four southern provinces seemed like some sort of British fiefdom – but one which, for all the pretensions of those politicians who sought reflected credit, was still entirely dependent on American resources for its lifeblood.

The urgency of my appointment did not allow for any traditional pre-posting briefing. I concentrated on the FCO, the Development Ministry and the Secret Intelligence Service. I judged that I would do best to get military briefing on the spot, where there was no shortage of military folk. I therefore reserved calls on senior officers in the UK for one of my visits back and when, having seen the situation myself, I might having something to say which interested them. Somebody suggested that I should receive pre-posting safety and security training at an Army establishment at Chilwell, near Nottingham. However, I did not want to use up that time, and the pressure from the Foreign Office and the Army to get out to Iraq was becoming intense.

My initial impression from my calls, which were also informed by lengthy telephone conversations with Janet Rogan, one of the very few British Diplomatic Service officers in Basra who was holding the fort after Olsen's departure, was that civilians in Whitehall had little idea of what was actually happening on the ground in the civilian arena. No one had expected that the UK would suddenly have to take a civilian lead in the South, in effect supporting and mirroring the British military presence there. Instead there had been some vague expectation that the Americans would sort things out. The Army in London were far better informed than their civilian counterparts, a result of their frequent face-to-face discussions with senior British officers in Baghdad and

Basra by means of a video link – a facility which did not exist for the civilians in the South and which, despite many promises, never materialised. Janet Rogan also told me that there were no secure civilian communications between Basra and Whitehall. I was yet more surprised that the Whitehall mandarins had no inkling that the briefings they received were based on emails through Yahoo and Hotmail or on open telephone conversations. Had anyone been intercepting such communications they would not have been surprised at the demise of the Coalition Provisional Authority in Iraq a year later.

My interlocutors in London disarmingly acknowledged the information vacuum. They agreed that it was regrettable. This, they added for good measure, was one of the reasons why they hoped that I would agree to get out there very soon. On the basis of what I had learned over the previous few days, I could see their point.

But I had other concerns of my own and was reluctant to drop everything at once because the British Government of the day had got itself into a pickle. In the couple of months since our return from Pakistan, I had got as far as signing up contractors to extend the kitchen, rewire the electrics and re-plumb our whole house. I was committed contractually and had intended to keep a close eye on progress. Our two dogs, rescued in Pakistan and still in quarantine in France, needed visiting and exercise.

The compromise was that I would get myself out to Basra by the end of July, as had originally been proposed. I would stay initially for one week, make an assessment for Ministers and senior officials, and draw up appropriate recommendations which could be followed up before my return to Basra a month later. This would be less inconvenient personally and it made operational sense, such was the knowledge gap in London, to offer a situation report and argue my on-the-spot judgements personally.

I remained concerned about the vagueness of my task. It seemed that Ministers simply wanted someone in Iraq on the ground at once and were less concerned about what I should do once I got there. Certainly they had no guidance or policy instruction to give me. I therefore asked for written terms of reference.

This seemed to come as a surprise to Whitehall administrators. Such arrangements are not usually made for Heads of Mission whose broad duties are well established by years of precedent. I insisted that I was not going to be head of a diplomatic mission, British or otherwise, but that I would be a seconded British official working to an American boss to head up part of an international effort under the leadership of the US Defense Secretary. I needed to know what my government, at whose request I was going, expected of me.

I got my way, but was little the wiser. My mission statement, to use contemporary FCO jargon, was crafted by the head of the Iraq Policy Unit and quickly approved by the hierarchy. It ran to half a side of A4 paper and entailed giving 'leadership and direction' to the work of the CPA in the four southern provinces; and it also required me to give a political context to the work of the military commanders in the South. I would be 'accountable directly to Ambassador Bremer'.

But there was also a covering letter, marinated in subtleties. From a Whitehall perspective, it read, despite Bremer's decision to create 18 provincial Coordinators who reported directly to him, 'the UK Supremo in the South concept still holds'. But, the letter explained, this could not be expressed explicitly since my terms of reference had to be approved by Bremer. In addition to being accountable to Bremer, I was to report also to the FCO and to Jeremy Greenstock on a back channel. The CPA's Director of Operations in Baghdad, also British, was responsible for establishing the provincial teams. He expected that they would not in fact be operational by the end of August, as Bremer had planned (he was more than right). I was therefore to exercise an active coordinating role until the situation evolved. In the best tradition of British pragmatism, we were all to 'play it by ear'.

My tour was to be for six months, at least initially, which was the same as the tour length for the British Army and the British commanding generals, who had just changed over. I would arrive just a month after a new general. But he, unlike me, would have the benefit of a full supporting staff and experienced Chief of Staff already in place, a sizeable personal back-office, and full military administrative and communications materiel. It was understood that my length of tour might be reviewed at some point, but I offered no hostage to fortune by implying that I would be open to any extension; I would keep my powder dry.

On the day I was due to leave, I was summoned to see the Prime Minister at Number 10 Downing Street. I turned up at the famous front door about five minutes before the appointed time and was greeted by a young diplomat, seconded to Number 10, who had made a brilliant contribution as part of my team in Pakistan. I noticed a British MP sitting in another room with a politician from the Kurdish part of Iraq and assumed that I would be in for a long wait. But within minutes of the appointment I was called into one of the small rooms on the ground floor, where Blair held his informal meetings, to be greeted warmly.

Blair was accompanied by his Chief of Staff, Jonathan Powell, and by the Head of the Joint Intelligence Committee, John Scarlett – later to be appointed head of the Secret Intelligence Service – while my former colleague from Islamabad took a record of the meeting. I had met Blair several times in the past, most recently during his visits to Pakistan after 9/11 but on other occasions also. I had seen him enough to know that the cheerful, eager-to-please persona portrayed in some of the media did not exclude a steely focus on serious policy issues.

In a 20-minute meeting, Blair set out his approach to the challenges in Basra and promised me every possible support. Since this was a private meeting, I refrain from going into detail, but it was made clear that Blair wanted rapid and visible progress over reconstruction in southern Iraq, and that I was expected to be the catalyst for this objective: a task which was 'of great importance to the government and the country'.

I was immensely boosted by being enjoined to telephone Blair personally if I had particular problems. I responded that it was unlikely that I would do so, but that it would be invaluable to be able to refer to such an assurance.

Fortified by this encouragement, I hurried with my single suitcase from Downing Street to the Gatwick Express to catch the overnight plane to Kuwait, from where I was to be driven across the desert to Basra.

Chapter 2
How it all Started

Hasty generalization is a logical fallacy involving inductive generalization based on insufficient evidence ... basing a broad conclusion upon the statistics of a survey of a small group that fails to sufficiently represent the whole population.

Definition drawn from a text book on Logic.

WHAT FOLLOWED THE fall of Saddam Hussein's regime in Iraq was quite unexpected. It had not been anticipated; it had not been planned for; and, as soon became clear, it proved unmanageable.

Those who had initiated the operations in Iraq in 2003 knew little about the country. Traditional political, commercial, diplomatic, media and social links had eroded over the previous decades of Ba'athist rule, and had been virtually extinguished during the 12-year regime of international sanctions which commenced with Saddam Hussein's invasion of Kuwait in 1990. Heavy reliance was placed on the testimony of exiles who had agendas of their own and who were adept at manipulating their paymasters. The decision-makers and their strategic policy advisers had no idea of the limits of their knowledge or the extent of their ignorance.

Just four days before the invasion, the US vice-president, Dick Cheney, told the press: 'I really do believe that we will be greeted as liberators. I've talked with a lot of Iraqis in the last several months myself'. This was subsequently corroborated by Condoleezza Rice, then Bush's National Security Adviser, who revealed her belief that, after the defeat of the Iraqi Army, ' ... the institutions would hold, everything from ministries to police forces'.

Such judgements also informed the US Administration's financial projections. Cheney and Deputy Secretary of Defense Paul Wolfowitz had stated publicly that the cost of reconstruction would be largely covered by Iraqi oil revenue. By April 2003, the White House had requested only $2.4 billion for post-war rebuilding.

As became abundantly clear, such assumptions proved to be spectacular misjudgements. But, as a result of them, the implosion of all the governing institutions in the country with the removal of Saddam Hussein's controls came as a complete surprise to the key decision-makers; as did the discovery of the parlous state of Iraq's infrastructure, run down and chronically ineffective as a result of neglect, underinvestment, lack of maintenance, unavailability of spares, obsolescence and damage from successive wars.

Such plans as had been made, which are described in Chapter 10, were not designed to cope with what actually happened.

On 20 January 2003, President George W. Bush signed National Security Presidential Directive No. 24, which gave control of post-war Iraq to the Department of Defense. Just seven weeks before the start of the war, the Pentagon had put together a group of soldiers and civilians, under the leadership of retired Lieutenant General Jay Garner, called the Office of Reconstruction and Humanitarian Assistance (ORHA).

Garner and his team, who reported to the Commander of US Central Command, General Tommy Franks, were meant to administer Iraq after the end of hostilities. ORHA was still forming itself when its 169 members of staff deployed into a hotel in Kuwait on 16 March. That same day, Cheney confirmed that 'we need to be prepared to provide humanitarian assistance, medical care, food, all of those other things that are required to have Iraq up and running again. And we are well equipped to do that'. But the demands upon the Coalition's military and civilian resources proved to be infinitely greater and more varied than humanitarian assistance, food and medical care.

*　　*　　*

The challenge of state-building and transformation had no parallel since the collapse of Germany and Japan after the Second World War; but other comparisons with those efforts some 60 years earlier are weak, and much weaker than were perceived in 2003. While planning for the end of the Second World War started in 1941, four years before the end of the conflict, the US Pentagon was put in charge of the operation just four months before the formation of the CPA. Recognition of the real needs and planning for them commenced only after the main conflict was over and Saddam's government had fallen.

The success of the Coalition's combat operations designed to topple Saddam Hussein was also a great surprise. What the British historian John Keegan has called 'The 21 Day War' started on 20 March 2003. The television photographs of American soldiers toppling Saddam's statue in Paradise Square in central Baghdad were seen all over the world. Like Kennedy's assassination, Princess Diana's death in 1997, and 9/11 in 2001, hundreds of millions of people would remember what they were doing that day – 9 April 2003. Baghdad had been occupied and, like his statue, Saddam's regime had at last been overthrown.

The military campaign had been expected to last 125 days, which included an anticipated 30 days to take control of Baghdad. The war of manoeuvre having been completed more than 100 days early, it was then that the real problems started.

The Coalition armies, operating with minimum numbers of personnel, were hard pressed and insufficiently resourced to deal with such undeniably security-related tasks as looting, custody of ammunition dumps and border controls. They had no wish to take on additional tasks which they considered should fall to civilians.

Nor, in the case of the US Army, were they very familiar with the demands and techniques of civil administration. They therefore resented it when ORHA, which had established a low-key presence in Baghdad on 18 April and had started to set up subsidiary offices as best it could elsewhere, proved unable to deal with the civil governance tasks with which it was faced. In the absence of sufficient human and financial resources of its own, ORHA's requests for military help simply made matters worse. It was clear that it was not going to work. ORHA was wound up in May, after only four months of controversial existence, and Garner returned to the USA. The still-born organisation was formally 'transitioned' or subsumed into the CPA on 1 June 2003.

The head of the CPA, Ambassador L. Paul Bremer III, known to his friends as Jerry, arrived in Baghdad on 11 May 2003. While ORHA's objectives were vague, the CPA was given an extraordinarily wide remit – essentially to take full authority for the governance of the country. Put together from virtually nothing, it was made up of personnel from 17 participating countries under American leadership. It had become the civilian arm of the Coalition, alongside a military force to which 33 countries contributed a total of some 170,000 troops, of whom the vast majority, about 136,000, were American. Although no end-date was specified when the CPA started, it was expected to remain in being for at least two years, until the end of 2005.

Unlike ORHA, the CPA was not under military command. Its boss, now with the official title of Administrator, was answerable to the US President but reported to Donald Rumsfeld, the Secretary of Defense, not the Secretary of State, Colin Powell, who usually led on matters of foreign policy or development assistance. It was Bremer's task to oversee, direct and coordinate all US Government programmes and activities in Iraq, except those under the command of the military commander of the US Central Command. The CPA was to exercise powers of government and was formally vested by the president with all executive, legislative and judicial authority necessary to achieve its objectives, with the formal proviso that it should be consistent with relevant UN Security Council Resolutions and the laws and usages of war.

The President's and CPA's goal for Iraq was declared to be 'to establish a secure, peaceful, and democratic Iraq that will stand against terrorism and no longer threaten America, the region, or the world'.

Thus, the CPA was essentially conceived to be a wartime organisation, concerned with security, within the context of the unfortunately named American Global War on Terror. This military and war-orientated strategic approach to the stabilisation of Iraq coloured the CPA's entire operation. The reconstruction of the country, which had been crippled by decades of Ba'athist centralised tyranny, eight years of war with Iran, 12 years of international sanctions, two 'Gulf Wars' and wholesale looting, was seen as a means to that primary goal of counter-terrorism rather than an end in itself.

Empowered to take exceptional measures where deemed necessary, Bremer set about doing so. These tended to reflect his professional background. He had been a specialist in dealing with terrorism: he had no wider expertise in developing countries. He would point out to officials wrestling with intractable issues that he was 'The Law', that is, the ultimate arbiter of what was necessary and of what would happen. The Law, however, was one thing and may have been relatively easy to lay down. Law and Order was a much more difficult challenge.

However, there was an inextricable linkage between the security environment, progress over governance, and reconstruction and public perceptions. A permissive security environment was necessary but it was not sufficient for long-term stability. Each of those four elements could reinforce or undermine the other. None of them could be neglected.

The CPA's organisation reflected the fact that the improvement in the well-being of the disadvantaged population did not figure in the CPA's main declared goal. Nowhere in its management structure, which was divided into policy and operational activities, was there a directorate with responsibility for human security and the livelihood and employment of the Iraqi people as a whole. Under Rumsfeld's overall charge, the CPA presented itself, through its mission statement, its organisation and often by its actions, as being more concerned with enforcing law and imposing order than with eliciting stability by improving the Iraqis' condition and by attempting to win over hearts and minds.

On his arrival in Baghdad in mid-May 2003, Bremer was confronted with a near breakdown in relations between the civilian and military components of the Coalition, despite the fact that General Tommy Franks had been in command of both. Bremer had to take swift and radical measures across a broad front. Determined to stamp US authority on the country and eradicate any vestige of Saddam's noxious and all-permeating regime, his very first decisions included the dissolution of the former security apparatus, including the entire Army, and the removal from their positions of the top layers of the Ba'athist official hierarchy. These decisions, which came to be heavily criticised, had far-reaching consequences which were clearly not fully appreciated at the time.

On the political side, Bremer, with assistance from the senior British civilian representative in Iraq, concentrated on identifying members of an Iraqi Governing Council, which was established in mid-July. The reconstruction effort initially focussed on engaging big foreign contracting companies, almost exclusively American, to assess the needs and to provide remedies. But there were also important organisational arrangements to be made since, without adequate advisory, management and executive structures, many of the challenges stood no hope of being met.

Garner had set up ORHA into three groups, on a regional basis. An American retired brigadier general, Buck Walters, was the Coordinator for Group South, while other Americans dealt with the north and central regions.

However, the American and British Governments were keen to demonstrate publicly that the Coalition in Iraq extended beyond those two countries. The Coalition would be strengthened politically and the 'ownership' of its endeavours would be widened if other countries shared some of the senior positions. Since a British general had been put in charge of a multinational military division in the four provinces in the extreme south, it made sense to have a separate civilian administrative region which also covered those same provinces. Garner's original three groups were therefore expanded into four: the Kurdish areas in the North; Baghdad, which covered the Sunni heartland and housed CPA's headquarters; the South Central Region, based in Hillah; and the South Region, based in Basra.

The Danish Government stepped forward to fill the South Region, and in May the Danish and British Foreign Ministers selected Ole Olsen, who was concurrently the Danish Ambassador to Syria. Olsen was an Arabist of long standing and spoke the language fluently. Married to an Algerian physician, he was himself a Sunni Muslim – although southern Iraq was overwhelmingly Shia.

Unique in having a Regional Coordinator who was not American, the South always seemed to be different from the rest. In the early days, a British official described it as 'the bastard red-haired godchild of the CPA' – hardly a term of endearment.

As I was soon to discover for myself, conditions in Basra were a far cry from those which a head of a diplomatic mission might have been accustomed to, and not only in terms of physical discomfort. Resources, command and management structures and the most basic materiel were all absent. It seemed hard to get anyone in Baghdad or in capitals of the countries making up the Coalition to understand, to respond or to do anything practical to improve the situation.

Small wonder then that, on returning to Denmark on leave in early July 2003, Olsen allowed some of his frustrations to emerge. A Norwegian newspaper reported that Olsen had complained that the Americans had not provided any personal security to himself or his staff and contrasted his situation with other parts of Iraq: he had expected more support from Baghdad. On 28 July his official resignation was announced. I left London for Basra the next day.

Chapter 3
Arrival

Better forty years of oppression than one day of anarchy.

Arab proverb.

MY PLANE ARRIVED in Kuwait airport at 6am on 30 July 2003. I was met, after a largely sleepless night, by Janet Rogan, a talented British diplomat with Kosovo experience, and Ed Botterill, a fresh-faced and enthusiastic young Army officer whom the Commanding General in the South had thoughtfully provided to head up my office, in the absence of anyone else. I had waited around in the busy concourse for over an hour before being met, and during that time I had watched the strange mixture of passengers arriving in the country, many of whom were clearly destined for Iraq. I was a bit concerned in case something had happened to my greeters, but I was glad that I had not commented on their delay. When I reached Basra I was to realise how much they must have relished having a good night's sleep in a comfortable Kuwaiti hotel themselves: sleep did not come easy in the CPA base.

As I left the airport, a bottle of blackcurrant squash, which Annie had put in my luggage no doubt to keep scurvy at bay, was examined carefully in case it should contain alcohol. This was clearly a stricter place than Pakistan.

Once outside, Janet introduced me to a stocky, shortish man of middle years, with a pepper-and-salt moustache and wearing a khaki outfit patched with loaded pockets. He might have been on a fishing trip were it not for the strange bulges around his clothing. He took off his Aviator Ray-Bans, enveloped my hand in his and squeezed. It was then that I realised that I had mistaken his bulk for portliness. He had a barrel chest with hands to match. As I was to discover later, his seemingly large girth was due to the large number of weapons and ammunition concealed about his person.

Revealing an American accent, he told me that he was in charge of my personal protection team. He waved an introduction to his five younger and taller colleagues, and explained that they were all members of the Naval Criminal Investigative Service – the NCIS. I thought this an odd title for a supplier of bodyguards and was to discover later that there was a television drama series devoted to their exploits. I was also surprised to find myself with such a large team, and two armoured vehicles, to look after me. No one had mentioned this in London, still less had they offered to supply me with protection themselves. It seemed a bit over-dramatic. My predecessor had publicly complained about alleged American unconcern for the safety of civilians in the South. This force must have been a consequence.

The tallest of the group, standing at 6 foot 8 inches, looked to be straight from central casting or perhaps a slimmer relation of the then Governor of California, Arnold Schwarzenegger. The sides and back of his head were close shaven; black, gelled hair on top was about an inch long. This was a style favoured by the US Marines, of which Tom Fergusson, like his father before him, had been a proud member. He was my personal protection officer. When I was out and about, he was seldom more than a few inches from my right shoulder, which allowed his right hand, his preferred shooting hand, maximum freedom of action. I was protected even when I tried to sleep in Basra, since the whole team occupied a room opposite mine, accompanied by their armoury of varied weapons.

The greetings and the initial relationships were conducted with the utmost formality on their part. When on duty they communicated between the two vehicles by means of throat mikes and earpieces from which clear plastic spiral tubes trailed disconcertingly. They seemed uncomfortable if I chatted to them and preferred to answer in monosyllables of which the most frequent was 'Sir'. This was going to have to change, since our lives were to be linked together.

We headed north across the desert on a multi-laned, modern highway for 60 miles. Slowing down, we hit a rougher, newly laid road which took us across the sand bunds and ditches over which the British and American forces had entered Iraq four months earlier. After the briefest of pauses, we were waved through a border post guarded by some American soldiers. This was my first visit to Iraq. Fifteen years earlier, I had caught a glimpse of another checkpoint into Iraq, well to the north-west of this one, when I had been posted in Jordan. But then I had been touring in the Jordanian desert and was about to stop for the night to camp and enjoy a barbecue.

This re-introduction to the country, however, was not promising. As we crossed into Iraq onto another good road – this time one of Saddam's highways which allowed his Army to move quickly down to the South should it be needed there – a sandstorm blew up. The visibility deteriorated sharply and we eased down from exceptionally high speed to simply very fast.

I paid little attention to the state of the weather as I was engrossed in Janet's account of all the problems and deficiencies which were waiting to greet me. But the light became darker and the visibility got worse. Jeff, the driver, tried the windscreen wipers, which proved definitely unhelpful. An affable remark from me, intended to reassure, was greeted with silence.

What was happening was that the polythene film, which the team had just put on the windscreen on instructions from their head office to give further protection from possible enemy assault, was being remorselessly sandpapered by the flying grit. It never recovered. Throughout the next six months my images of Iraq as I travelled round the South were blurred and unfocussed. This seemed to be an appropriate symbol of the wider situation.

After a couple more hours of driving, we reached the outskirts of Basra city, passed through some flimsy corrugated iron gates and pulled up outside a scruffy former government office building.

I had intentionally worn a tie with my shirt and sand-coloured long trousers on my arrival in Basra. I knew that all the civilians would be more sensibly dressed in short sleeves or T-shirts since the daytime temperature was now in the upper 40s Centigrade and rising. My choice did not, however, stem from some old-fashioned attachment to formal dress code or a wish to emphasise my status. Rather, I wanted everyone to know very quickly that I had arrived and who I was.

I walked past some uncharacteristically overweight Gurkha guards and entered the former Electricity Accounts building that was to be my new home and office, shared with over a hundred others. It did not quite come up to its grand designation: Headquarters CPA(South). As I passed by muttering benign greetings, I noticed that people were asking each other who was this tie-wearing stranger who was clearly no military man. Everyone was to know soon enough.

My Danish predecessor, in the best Scandinavian egalitarian tradition, had established a routine of meetings with the entire staff every evening. That was fine when his team had initially numbered no more than a dozen or two. In the early days, as Jay Garner's ORHA transitioned into Jerry Bremer's CPA, the building was inhabited on the top floor by the British Military Police, on the second floor by the Army's Civil–Military Operations Centre, and the nascent CPA organisation was confined to the bottom floor. But numbers were swelling and circumstances changing. There were now more than 60 living in increasingly cramped accommodation, with more arriving daily, and a large body of support staff. The Military Police had gone, replaced by a contingent of Gurkhas who formed our static guard and who lived in tents in the former car park. The British Army maintained a presence with us, but many of them commuted daily to and from the much more comfortable quarters in the main headquarters at the airport, about 15 miles to the north.

Daily meetings in such numbers were not sustainable, nor would they be an efficient use of everyone's time, and I knew I would have to change the arrangements. But I wanted first to make sure that everyone understood the purpose of changes before I introduced them; and it would be useful if my team could form an opinion of me and for me to get a feel for them. So, on the first evening, I met everyone and delivered what I hoped was an encouraging peroration. I went round everyone who was packed into a third-floor 'recreation room' and asked for significant reports, comments and questions. The various team leaders gave brief accounts of where they stood, in the knowledge that I would be talking to each of them in detail later. But generally the participants seemed to want to hear what I had to say, rather than to talk themselves, and to decide what to make of me.

Having heard their reports and asked a few questions, I offered some observations of my own, conscious that I was of an older generation than almost all of them. I gave some details of my professional background and emphasised my personal commitment to helping Iraqis get their country back on its feet, and to helping my new team in their own efforts to achieve this. I made clear that I had been sent upon the personal authority of the British Prime Minister who was himself committed.

My multinational audience seemed to welcome these words as an indication of an overdue interest in their activity. They no doubt also expected rapidly enhanced practical support. The first element was undoubtedly well-founded; the second less so.

It was after 11pm, having arrived in Kuwait that morning at 3am UK time, that I was first shown where I was to sleep, on the top floor of the building. I was privileged in being the only member of CPA staff with a room of his own. This arrangement proved to be fortuitous. My predecessor had been accompanied by his wife (London had made clear that there was no question of that in my case), and it was simpler for me to take his room than to devise something more egalitarian. I did not object.

The room was furnished with a wooden bed with a brightly coloured polyester blanket, a small Ikea bedside table imported by my predecessor and a rush mat. Fluorescent strip lights were suspended from the ceiling, on either side of an electric fan which had a fault in its bearings so that it swung round drunkenly and emitted a clanking sound. The walls had recently been re-painted an off-white colour of which there was much evidence on the pink and white marble-chip flooring. A curtain of sorts had been draped over a pole fixed above a window which overlooked a corridor. It was in this corridor that smokers habitually gathered for a night-time chat next to a French window overlooking the town. Nice for them, less so for me. There were no sheets, towel or soap: no one had thought that I might need them, while I had unwisely expected some sort of basic hotel accommodation which would include such necessities; and no chair, table or desk. Washing facilities were yet to be found. The lavatories were out in the yard, two floors down and then some. My heart sank.

Feeling very tired and not a little depressed by what I had heard and experienced already, I wondered whether I had not really been very foolish in agreeing to this assignment. My years in submarines had included greater discomforts, but at least the boats had been equipped for the purpose and gave you a good meal. Also I had been over 30 years younger in those days. With an effort to put such thoughts behind me, I hoped I might find some sheets in the morning.

After over 24 hours of travelling, experiencing a sandstorm and listening to concentrated briefing, I felt in need of a shower. Intending to use my shirt as a towel, I made for the unisex bathroom down the corridor. This had previously been a set of lavatories for employees of the Electricity Accounts Authority, and was furnished with three plug-less sinks and four cubicles containing squat-type bowls made of chipped porcelain. Because the city's water supply had broken down during the conflict, alternative arrangements were necessary. Some unpainted copper tubing disappeared into the roof above each cubicle while, at head height, the lower end of each tube was furnished with a red plastic shower head bound on with wire. A stopcock regulated the water flow. On the outside of each door was a sign which declared: 'This is not a toilet. Use the facilities outside'; that is, two floors below. On the inside another sign ordered users to conform to 'ship's routine': 'Strip off; tap on; wet down; tap off; soap up; rinse off'. Impossible to conform: I had no soap.

I hung my clothes over the top of the cubicle, usefully indicating a presence inside since there was no lock, placed my feet on either side of the former lavatory aperture, and turned on the water. It was scalding hot and I let out a yell of surprise. By this time someone else had come into the bathroom and was brushing his teeth. Hearing my discomfort, he patiently explained to me that the water came from a steel tank on the roof and heated up after a day's summer sunshine. It was therefore best to take a shower after about 1am or in the early morning. It was not possible for everyone to do both because the water would run out, as I discovered later for myself when still at the 'soap up' stage of the ship's shower routine.

Despite my fatigue, I hardly slept. I got up several times in the night to turn off the clanking fan, only to have to switch it on again as the heat became intolerable. I felt no more refreshed in the morning. I reported to Annie that the conditions reminded me of the two-star campsites in Corsica in the mid-summer season, but without the wine. I was recalling our joint experience of the mid-1970s. Since then the campsites had improved. In Basra conditions were to get worse before they got better.

Next morning I got up just before 8am, later than intended, and, having missed breakfast, found everyone already at their work. I had arranged a meeting with my senior staff at 9.30, but found that, once in my tiny office, I had nothing to do because I had no telephone and no computer. A bookcase, another Ikea import, contained some sand-dusted stationery and basic office materials. Some printouts of CPA Orders were stacked forlornly on one of the shelves. The most recent was a month old, when my predecessor had left. I flipped through them but was unable to take them in.

My only assistant was Haytham, an irrepressibly cheery local Iraqi, who wiped off from my Ikea desktop the dust imported by my ineffective air conditioner. Not being an Arabic speaker, I drew on my rusty stock of Arabic greetings to exchange a few sentences with him. Our inability to converse with each other by the spoken word did not seem to matter. He quickly and accurately assessed the situation and produced a plastic cup full of double-strength black coffee. Welcome as it was, it would not be enough to replace the fluids being evaporated by the intense heat of the room. I resolved to get hold of some oral rehydration salts.

I had inherited a team of seven section heads, whom I instantly dubbed the Seven Pillars of Wisdom. They were of several nationalities and of varying ages, backgrounds and experience. Their sections were similarly diverse. The smallest, which dealt with political affairs, was perhaps the most important since at that time it was in the closest touch with Iraqis and was the litmus test of the mood around us. The largest covered finance and nearly every aspect of reconstruction in which the CPA intended to engage. Linked to the reconstruction task was a section dealing with contracts and accounting, without which no construction work could proceed, and which was to prove one of the most intractable problem areas. Our military liaison team was headed by an Army brigadier who reported jointly to me and to the British general in command of the Army in the South. A US Army reservist colonel led on matters affecting the three other provinces outside Basra. A senior police officer from Northern Ireland dealt with all civilian aspects of law and order: police, the judiciary and the courts. A British Army major, soon to be replaced by a senior Danish journalist, handled press releases and public relations.

After an initial mutual briefing session, I had separate sessions with each in turn and asked them to draw up a note describing their section's strategies and capabilities. Most had been so preoccupied with dealing with incessant and pressing day-to-day challenges that this request required them to go back to first principles. Some had never managed a team of staff before and so had no previous experience of such a requirement. The results, when I started to receive them over the next few days, proved very variable.

I learned that, thanks to a recent large injection of staff from the Army and the attachment of reservists from the Territorial Army, who brought their civilian skills with them, there had been real progress over the previous month, though from a very low base: an interim City Council had been established in Basra; a ferry service linking to Dubai had just started; it was hoped that Basra's international airport would start operating within a month; and there was now a greater knowledge about a wide range of technical issues, including power generation and distribution, health, education, customs and finance.

I also learned that, apart from the problems of organising the CPA(South) operation itself, the biggest single issue was the relationship with Baghdad. Basra felt isolated: short of money, people and guidance. They needed help, but their requests to Baghdad were either being ignored or turned down peremptorily. No one wanted to lodge complaints, not least because they had seen what had happened to my predecessor. Baghdad gave the impression that the South should look after its own problems, yet it had no means to do so.

Each of the Seven Pillars carried an enormous weight of responsibility. It seemed to me that the organisation had reached a stage where the nature of the tasks ahead could begin to be identified. This was an advance on the state of almost total ignorance of conditions on the ground which existed when the Coalition forces first arrived in the South. It was clear that none of the Pillars was yet strong enough for the load which I needed them to carry: we needed more people. However, I was greatly heartened that all the section heads – volunteers every one – were in good spirits, highly motivated and determined to do the best they could.

For my part, I needed to establish harmony with my British Army counterpart; and I needed to forge a constructive and fruitful relationship with Baghdad. But first I needed some soap and a towel.

* * *

I also desperately needed to acquire a feel for the mood of the city and of the nascent political sentiment. I was fortunate in being able to call on the advice of a member of the FCO's Research Department, Robert Wilson, himself an experienced Arabist, who had worked on Iraq issues for much of the previous decade. Tall, studious and measured, Robert had built up a series of relationships with former exiles. He knew all the considerable numbers of significant Iraqis who had fled to the UK. As I often witnessed, they would greet him as an old and respected friend, share confidences with him and seek his advice.

Robert was probably the Coalition's most knowledgeable political observer on the ground at this time. His insights enabled me to look behind the confident assertions with which I was generally faced. I always regretted that Baghdad did not draw on this knowledge more methodically and give it greater weight on those occasions when we were consulted.

In early August 2003, on Robert's advice, I decided to pay my respects to the elderly and venerable cleric Sayyid Ali al-Musawi, who presided over the largest mosque in Basra. I had several motives. I wanted first of all to take the measure of the man personally. I had met many Muslim clerics in Pakistan, India and, before that, in Jordan. Some of them, powerful personalities in their own right, had important political roles as well as being religious leaders. Some were deeply corrupt and had increased their influence further by using the more secular instruments of bribery or extortion. Others, who practised a conservative interpretation of their faith, could be even more threatening to moderate governance precisely because they came to their positions by truly democratic election processes, were incorruptible and would not be diverted from their pressure to introduce Sharia Law. Others again were honest, moderate and well-meaning. What would be the case in Iraq?

In Pakistan, as elsewhere in the Islamic world, the main weekly prayer meeting on Fridays was the occasion for all sorts of influential messages to the faithful. They might be religious homilies, calls for peace and harmony, or political speeches and rabble-rousing. It was of course abundantly clear that Saddam's regime would not have tolerated any such political role. There could be no alternative source of power and influence to his own instruments. Any deviation would be reported up the line by his security apparatus. And over time plenty of clerics were simply murdered, including the father of young firebrand cleric Moqtada al-Sadr, Ayatollah Muhammad Sadiq al-Sadr, who had been assassinated in 1999.

The question in my mind, now that Saddam had been deposed, was to what extent any of the clerics would be tempted to use the pulpit for essentially political purposes. More positively, if we could win over religious leaders to believe that we, the Coalition, were trying to help, we might be able to persuade them to use their sermons to induce their congregation to be supportive, or at least not obstructive. Sayyid Ali's mosque could accommodate 12,000. It could be an important outlet for messages of moderation.

An appointment was duly made and my less than discreet motorcade of three armoured vehicles pulled up outside the mosque early one afternoon. Waiting to greet us was one of Sayyid Ali's sons. He was confident, affable and spoke perfect English with an American twang. We took off our shoes and were ushered to some seats, where we sat and looked about us at the empty building. I felt almost overwhelmed by the size, opulence and strange beauty of the vast space. The walls and ceilings were clad in white marble into which were embedded elaborate patterns of mirrored glass, which reflected and refracted the bright afternoon sun.

After a short pause, Sayyid Ali himself joined us, walking slowly with the aid of a stick and accompanied by two assistants. The initial courtesies were protracted. Once these were completed, more assistants brought tables loaded with pastries, cakes decorated with acidic pink and green icing sugar, nuts, dates and dried fruit. Another round of courtesies were then in order as we were offered sweet tea in small glass jars and pressed to consume the supply of food which greatly exceeded any possible demand.

Conversation was difficult. Not because of any awkwardness or aggression on the part of Sayyid Ali, but because his remarks were brief and entirely unexceptionable. I explained what I believed to be the purpose of our presence in Iraq: to liberate the country from the tyranny of Saddam and his security apparatus, to help its citizens find their feet again, and to promote peace and security.

Sayyid Ali applauded these aims. 'Peace is good' he said. In response to concerns about the future and the risk of dissent or violence, he again said that he believed in peace. As to the themes of the sermons on Fridays, these, he said, advocated peace. No, he did not approve of those who did not themselves favour peace.

We progressed no further and learned little from him of the trends and currents of opinion in Basra: it was not his role to concern himself about such matters. He was, he assured us, solely a religious figure, although he also thought it important that his mosque should offer help to such of the poor who needed it.

The conversation reminded me of a similar attempt to glean political intelligence 20 years earlier when, during my posting to Jordan, my boss had decided to call on one of the most influential Bedouin tribal leaders. The Sheikh received us in his tent in the desert, where we sat in a line of armchairs, set side by side. My ambassador, an Arabist by training who had spoken the language for some 25 years, made increasingly desperate attempts to start a conversation, ranging from inconsequential small talk to comments and questions about significant recent events. The responses on the Sheikh's part were limited to repeating, at intervals of about one minute, 'Ahlayn. Ahlayn' – 'Welcome. Welcome'.

It was only after we had consumed our huge helpings of sheep's heads and hot yogurt embedded in saffron rice and pine nuts, which we did without speaking at all, that the Sheikh made a remark to his principal guest.

'With some more practice', he declared, 'you may come to speak our language quite well'. I was glad that the seating arrangement did not allow my boss to spot my delighted smirk.

We learned rather more from Sayyid Ali's son, who showed us round the mosque once we had taken our leave of his father. Surprisingly, in view of the extent to which Saddam had persecuted the Shia in the South, he said that there were very few demands on the mosque for help in the form of food or financial help. Basra, he said, offered plenty of work for the local people, who were generally prosperous or, at least, not indigent. The mosque's main focus for social welfare, therefore, was to be a hospital, financed by funds available to Sayyid Ali from unspecified sources. The building was currently under construction, but it would eventually need equipment and supplies.

My operational conclusion from this pleasant encounter was that, other things being equal, Sayyid Ali would be disposed to be a force for the good and that he personally was most unlikely to wish to have his mosque used for propaganda against the Coalition. But I was less certain about the extent to which he would actively resist any such tendency by other clerics who preached at that mosque. I resolved to offer a sizeable sum to enable the hospital to receive some modern equipment. Other hospitals in Basra, which we were also trying to support, had been looted and damaged, so there was no doubt that such facilities were sorely needed. If such a gesture were to help maintain the mosque's support for the Coalition, as well as bring humanitarian benefit to Iraqis, then so much the better.

But Sayyid Ali was interesting for another reason. He was leader of the Shaikhi school of Shia Islam and was perhaps the religious leader who was closest to the Shia of eastern Saudi Arabia, which may have been the source of some of the funding for his costly new building. Not only would he have silently resented Saddam and his Sunni henchmen, he would also have felt little sympathy for his co-sectarians in the Shia north, symbolised by the centres of Najaf and Karbala. At that time, such attitudes were quite widespread among the southern Shia. Even if many followed the guidance of their religious leaders in those holy shrines, the southerners saw themselves as different from those further north.

Some time afterwards Sayyid Ali sent me a present of some of the famous Basra dates, which he said were grown on his own palms. I put the box in my Private Secretary's office, which adjoined mine, for visitors to dip into. A couple of days later I was interviewed by an attractive young American woman from a press agency. At the end of the meeting, as I escorted her out, I asked if she would like a date. My caller swung round with a horrified look on her face. I pointed to the box on James Roscoe's table. She shook her head and hurried on. James dissolved into mirth and broadcast the story with embellishments for months afterwards.

Chapter 4
Baghdad:
The Green Zone

A palace and a prison on each hand.

Lord Byron, *Childe Harold.*

IF MAKING CONTACT with key political figures in Basra was important, no less pressing was the need to find out the thinking in the Coalition's headquarters in Baghdad and to make an impression there. I therefore paid my first visit after just three days in the country.

The previous day I had met Major General Graeme Lamb, the highly experienced and effective General Officer Commanding Multi-National Division (South East), MND(SE), who politely but straightforwardly had let me know what he hoped and expected from the civilian side. Once again I heard the 'ticket out' refrain. The Army had done what they could to repair the region's broken infrastructure, but their real job was to maintain security. They were prepared to help us in a transitional period, but expected us to take over all civilian tasks as soon as possible. When we had done so, and they had provided a secure environment, then most of them could leave and we could get on with administering the country.

I had also met the excellent Swedish UN representative in Basra, Oma Almgren, who had offered every possible assistance in what we both readily agreed was a shared task. However, I knew that I had to find out Baghdad's policies and priorities before I could set directions for my team in the South. It was clear from my few days in Basra and from my discussions with Graeme Lamb that I would need more resources. I particularly needed to know where I stood with Bremer, the CPA's administrator and my boss. What role did he expect from me and what instructions or guidance could he provide? What support could I expect from him? I needed more information about whatever central planning might exist and how the Baghdad bureaucracy worked in practice. I knew that I would need a lot of help and guidance from others if we were not to waste time re-inventing wheels; and I needed money, people and skill if we were to make progress. On each of these aspects I had little reason to be optimistic from what I had heard in London and in Basra.

Most of all, however, I needed to make an impact on Bremer and his staff so that Baghdad would become disposed to help and feel confident that we could make a contribution to the greater effort.

The dawn flight from Basra Airport to Baghdad in the cockpit of an RAF Hercules was both a novelty and a respite. I had travelled often in military aircraft, but never had I experienced the steep rates of climb and descent and the corkscrewing motion which were necessary precautions against possible rocket attacks from the ground. After my nights in Basra, which were too short and included too little sleep, and once I had persuaded the two pilots that they did not need to entertain me with their chat over the intercom, I slumped into a refreshing nap. I awoke with the changed engine note to see Baghdad and its waterways hurtling towards us. We landed with a bump after our spiralling descent.

Tom Fergusson, my ever-present bodyguard, and I were briskly whisked off to an armoured vehicle, instructed to don body armour and helmet, and briefed by contracted British protection personnel on procedures if we were to encounter difficulties. All this was in stark contrast to the relatively relaxed situation in the South where, on my first evening, I had dined in a local restaurant downtown. The previous day, I had even engaged in some tourism by going round the historic ruins of the almost mythical Ziggurat at Ur, as part of a visit to the massive US military base at Tallil, near the city of Nasiriyah.

I quietly did exactly as I was told and found myself outside Saddam Hussein's notorious Palace, now the CPA headquarters, after a hair-raising half-hour's high-speed drive from the airport to the centre of Baghdad. Glancing up at the massive stone helmeted heads which still dominated the roofs of the Palace, I went through the enormous ornately carved doors to find an ants' nest of activity: service personnel dressed in military fatigues and scruffily dressed civilians were scurrying about on multifarious missions. I took a deep breath, metaphorically squared my shoulders and realised that, within such a maelstrom, it would not be easy for me to rise above the waves, to make an impression, and to gain attention and support.

Andy Bearpark, Bremer's Director of Operations and my most senior British contact in the CPA, was not one to scurry or engage in fruitless haste. With enormous experience of development and crisis management, he had served in Kosovo and had survived the experience of being one of former Prime Minister Margaret Thatcher's advisers in Number 10 Downing Street. He made no secret of his bemusement at the extraordinary situation which surrounded him and the shortcomings of the two-month-old CPA bureaucracy. Constantly being summoned to meetings with Bremer which took crucially important decisions after only minutes of discussion, he was under no illusions about the differences between deciding to take action and achieving the desired results, but he agreed that there was no option but to try.

On the operation in Basra, Bearpark was characteristically blunt and honest. The South, he said, was not working adequately. I had no reason to argue. I had seen that for myself in the space of three days. I had been given a similar message by the Foreign Office, gently, and by the Army robustly; and my own team of multinational civilians clearly needed help.

David Oliver, a former US Navy rear admiral and nuclear submariner, and Bremer's Finance Director, was even more blunt. He said simply that the South was not working at all. He intimated that there had been too many complaints and not enough action.

As for funding, Oliver patiently described the gap between the needs, which he had recently tried to quantify, and the financial resources available. I realised that I would have a hard struggle to wrest any cash from Baghdad for what Tony Blair had instructed me to do, and there was no sign of any significant funding coming from the UK.

Oliver also told me of plans to withdraw from Iraq all the current banknotes with Saddam's picture on them and to replace them with new ones. Four hundred and twenty tons of new notes were due to be delivered to Basra later that month. It was only when I subsequently spoke to the British Army that I appreciated the risks and complications of such an endeavour.

I spent the rest of the day sniffing around the labyrinthine Palace to assess the mood of the place and identify the levers of power and influence. The senior British officer in Baghdad, Major General Freddie Viggers (described to me as Vigorous Viggers), was full of constructive sympathy for our plight. He promised to provide us with a secure communications link to the British Army headquarters, which meant that I would no longer be faced with a two-hour round trip if I needed to talk about confidential issues. The communications system and an operator arrived the following day.

I bumped into other personalities whom I had encountered in previous stages in my career and who also proved helpful. It was strange now to meet them in such a peculiar environment. The US diplomat Robin Raphel, whom I had known when we were both posted in Delhi and then when she led on South Asia in the US State Department during the Clinton administration, was in charge of the Trade Ministry. The US diplomat in charge of the Foreign Ministry, Susan Johnson, was the wife of the Pakistani Ambassador to Beijing who had been government spokesman when I was in Islamabad. The small British team, under the temporary leadership of my diplomatic colleague David Richmond, between the departure of John Sawers and the arrival of Jeremy Greenstock, was well plugged-in, without illusions and informative.

The messages I received were consistent: Bremer was highly praised for his confidence, decisiveness and vigour, but his style of working and of decision-making was difficult for others. The top management team was of varying effectiveness. Lower down, there was a shortage of expertise, especially of languages and of Arabic and Islamic culture and traditions. There was a preponderance of appointees who were familiar with American politics but little else. The average age of the civilian volunteers was unusually young. I found this disturbing not because I doubted their ability and drive, but because it suggested a dearth of middle and senior managers with solid experience of development and developing countries who might have been able to direct youthful energies into optimally profitable directions.

An American commentator later wrote of some of these young staffers as 'ordinary, overconfident, mildly presumptuous college graduates – freshly scrubbed Americans of the sort who inhabit Washington, DC, nestling up to power'. The description fitted my recollection. To make matters worse, many of them emulated the top boss's style, but without the benefit of his experience.

One of the major shortcomings of the administration, I learned, was the phenomenon of 'stove-piping'. This is a management-speak term which conveys the idea of isolated furnaces of activity, with no communication between them, delivering their separate products to a single recipient. It would be unfair, I thought, to lay the deficiencies of such a hastily assembled and, frankly, chaotic bureaucracy, in which few if any of its components had worked together before, entirely at Bremer's door. They seemed mostly to be an inevitable product of the circumstances in which the CPA was conceived.

Overall, I judged that the CPA headquarters in Baghdad suffered from similar shortcomings to those in the South, but on a higher plane and a larger scale, albeit with the benefit of a very much more comfortable, if more insulated, environment.

My mood was not improved the next morning at my first meeting with Bremer. Having stood outside his office for some minutes after the appointed time, I was ushered in by a young aide. I found Bremer with his head lowered over paperwork at his desk. When he had finished his perusal, he stood up, greeted me correctly with a power handshake and we both sat down. He stretched out his trademark desert-booted feet on top of a coffee table beside me.

Bremer's opening remarks warned me to ensure that there was no repetition of the briefing to a delegation of US Congressmen who had recently visited the military headquarters in Basra. On reaching Baghdad, they had apparently subjected Bremer to a cross-examination about the problems which the British Army had brought to their attention the day before. In fact, said Bremer, it would not happen again because he would himself ensure that CoDels, as they were called, did not visit the South again.

I was not concerned whether this unusual style of greeting amounted to an attempt to dominate his interlocutor at the outset or simply reflected Bremer's customary style of dialogue. I had been subjected to plenty of similar gambits in my career and it would not affect my own approach. I therefore let the observation, which was none of my concern, pass and made my pitch, with no small talk.

I put forward three pithy operational objectives: to improve the two-way communication between Basra and Baghdad; to prioritise our work in the light of a better knowledge of our combined objectives and resources; and to improve our security and conditions to allow an orderly pattern of work over the long term – the South was in a transitional phase which I was keen to complete swiftly. I added that Prime Minister Blair had told me personally that he wanted progress in the South and that I was to call on him if necessary. I was nonetheless, I emphasised, a member of the CPA rather than solely an instrument to advance direct British interests.

Bremer assented to this in a manner which suggested that there was no other option: the implication was that there could be no doubt that it was he, not the British Prime Minister, who directed CPA staff in Iraq. He was content with my priorities, and in the ensuing discussion I recognised his ability to deploy charm if he chose.

Encouraged, I suggested that, in pursuit of the first priority, which we evidently shared, we might meet at least monthly – a greater frequency could have been unrealistic owing to the pressure of engagements and the real difficulty of travel. Bremer responded positively and at once declared that such meetings should henceforth include the other three Regional Coordinators, from the Kurdish region, Hillah and Baghdad itself. It was important, he declared, that he knew what was going on in the provinces; he therefore proposed to call for weekly political reports. This pledge consoled me that Basra's poor communication with Baghdad might not be unique.

Bremer's main message, however, was that the emphasis for his and the CPA's attention would be Baghdad, not the provinces. Baghdad, he said, was the key to the Iraq problem: settle Baghdad and the rest of the country would fall into line. I could see why others had dubbed him 'The Viceroy', in the manner of Lord Curzon of India.

This visit to the Baghdad Palace, one of many, provided the first evidence for me of the very different mode of operation between the USA and the UK in matters relating to Iraq. The differences in civilian management styles seemed also, so far as I was able to judge over the next six months, to be reflected between the respective military arms. Of course the scale of American operations was out of all proportion to the British effort. But I was struck by the centralisation of American authority and the degree to which managers involved themselves in detailed instructions which were expected to be carried out to the letter. Nor was it apparent to what extent such decisions reflected consultation with interested parties or experts. It was not clear to me that possible problems and setbacks had been talked through in advance or that feedback would be expected or welcome.

The contrasts between the US and British communities in the CPA seemed to run deeper than the different characteristics of individuals involved, and to apply to the entire approach to activity and planning. My diplomatic career had not included any posting in the USA so I could not, and still cannot, judge whether these differences reflected US administrative culture in general: I had not 'learned American'. But I suspect that they were also a consequence of the CPA's painfully brief existence as a bureaucracy: no one was an expert in this sort of endeavour, so it was easier to let the bosses decide as they thought best.

Nevertheless, I was particularly surprised and dismayed in my first encounters in Baghdad by the lack of interest in the political and social situation in the four southern provinces, and by Bremer's declared intention to concentrate exclusively on Baghdad. Henry James had observed in the nineteenth century that 'All England is a suburb of London' – a notion which is deeply offensive to English country folk. Bremer appeared to regard all Iraq as a suburb of Baghdad.

As an absolute newcomer, I was in no position to second guess this lapidary judgement. I assumed that it was based on intelligence material to which I had no access. But I had seen the importance of local factors in other countries, and I was astonished that no reporting arrangement from the provinces had been established before my call on Bremer. I reminded myself that the CPA leadership had enormous and immediate problems on their doorstep and that there were chronic difficulties over electronic communications all over the country. No doubt, I hoped, matters would quickly improve as the many projects underway started to take effect. Such hopes were never to be realised.

On my return to Basra airport that night, I joined Graeme Lamb for a substantial meal in the communal military dining hall and briefed him on my impressions and, such as they were, the results of my trip. Freddie Viggers would get me secure communications; Andy Bearpark would get me more funding and arrange for expert security advice about our premises. Beyond that, the way forward presented real risks of confusion and duplication of effort. Close functional links would be essential. Graeme and I decided to meet formally at least once a week, together with Oma Almgren, the UN representative; and we would have more ad hoc meetings where possible.

My next priority, I decided, was to do something about our working conditions. We had to have more space if we were to house the experts needed to accelerate reconstruction. Our present building was vulnerable to every form of attack. And the sanitary arrangements threatened to poison us all before long.

*   *   *

My second visit to 'The Bubble', as the Baghdad Palace had come to be known, was a month after the first. By this time I was more of a known quantity and received much encouragement and countless offers of support. The occasion was the first meeting of Regional Coordinators which Bremer had promised to set up when we first met.

I observed my counterparts with interest. Two, based in the Kurdish region and Baghdad itself, were retired US military officers, a grade or more junior to the American Divisional Commanders in their regions and a fair bit older even than myself. The Northern Coordinator, who made a point of emphasising how peaceful and quiet his region was, shared responsibilities with two fire-eating American generals; the Baghdad-based Coordinator had several more generals on his doorstep as well as Bremer himself. Neither Coordinator was in the business of making waves.

My remaining opposite number was very different: a much-travelled, Arabic-speaking US diplomat in his mid-forties. But, unlike most diplomats I had come across, Mike Gfoeller sported a cowboy hat and a handgun on a belt round his waist. I rather envied these accessories. They suggested panache and seemed to make an impressive statement. However, I reflected that the British Army would be horrified if I tried to copy such an example. No CPA civilian in the South, apart from the Territorial Army reservists who were no longer technically civilians, carried weapons. Mine would have to remain the written and spoken word. And I could think of no appropriate headgear, since a bowler hat was out of the question.

I was also jealous of the fact that, being based at Hillah, which was close to Baghdad without being in its pocket, Mike could easily travel there and work the CPA bureaucracy – extract funds and publicise his successes – while I and my team were dependent on unreliable and infrequent air transport, and had to put aside at least a couple of days for any visit. Mike was clearly Bremer's favoured Regional Coordinator and no doubt deservedly so. Liaising closely with the Divisional Commander in his region, who had enormous resources at his disposal, he seemed to be working wonders. I was nonetheless a bit piqued to listen to lavish praise for Mike's success in, for example, setting up democracy workshops which Bremer had visited, when Bremer had so far seen nothing of our own burgeoning operation in the South.

Bremer did visit us shortly thereafter. Accompanied by the Iraqi Governing Council's Minister for Water and Abu Hatem, a tribal leader from Maysan Province in the south-east whom Bremer called the Lord of the Marshes, he descended by helicopter in a cloud of dust in our car park. A flock of American cameramen came too. After I had briefly greeted him, we all dashed off at high speed to a bridge over one of Basra's stagnant canals to be filmed against this admittedly photogenic background, confident that the encompassing stench would not be apparent on American television screens.

To my surprise, Bremer announced to all the world that work would begin on cleaning the canal within the following four days. He introduced me to the cameras as the man who would make it happen. The American interviewer, delighted by my accent and the chance to present an 'English Knight' to his audience, allowed me a lengthy spot which I used to my best advantage.

Yes, I declared, I was very glad that we would soon be cleaning the canals, as Ambassador Bremer had promised. It would certainly be of great benefit to the lives of the people of Basra and, I said clearly to the cameras, I knew that Baghdad would immediately be sending us funds to ensure that this happened since the project had the Administrator's personal endorsement.

No funding arrived for this purpose; nor was there any guidance from the Americans in Baghdad who shadowed the Water Ministry about how, if at all, we might fulfil their boss's public promise. On the contrary, I was warned that a contract had been placed with an American contractor for major canal works which would restore the original system of sluices and allow the ebb and flow of the tides in the Shatt al-Arab waterway to flush them through. If we were to set about cleaning them up before this, we would not achieve anything because they would remain stagnant repositories of effluent from the adjoining buildings. I was told that since we would simply waste our effort and CPA's expenditure, there was no question of any extra funding for this purpose.

If I was disappointed with my failure to lever Bremer's opportunism to acquire more resources, my Baghdad counterparts were more philosophical. Such occurrences happened every day. Everyone knew and had come to live with the mismatch between Bremer's urgent expectations and the practical realities.

My principal military adviser, a brigadier seconded from the military headquarters who was also in charge of military operational support, had told me of one of his early encounters in Baghdad. MND(SE) had been allocated a large tranche of money with an instruction to spend it quickly. The brigadier had pointed out that the Iraqi government offices in the South had collapsed, so it was proving impossible to come up with sensible projects instantly: the plan would not work. His unfortunate interlocutor, who looked exhausted, agreed but said that there was no option; if it did not work, he had said sadly, then Bremer would 'smash someone's face in'.

Despite this, I found myself instinctively on Bremer's side in such matters. To me, witnessing a palpable deterioration in security and wholesale unemployment, what mattered was to get people working and show improvements on the ground. Nugatory expenditure on such projects was secondary and paled into insignificance compared with the massive costs of maintaining and running the Coalition's military presence.

I was conscious too that, just days after our first Regional Conference and ten days before Bremer's visit to Basra, President Bush had announced a new allocation of $87 billion of funding to support operations in Afghanistan and Iraq; $24 billion of this was expected to come to the CPA. If so, I wanted an equitable share of it; I could not expect anything approaching this magnitude from the British Government.

It was during this same visit to Basra that Graeme Lamb and I were able to sit down with Bremer for some serious discussion. To the intense irritation of Bremer's aide who had made the arrangements, a mysterious, locally-based American official managed to infiltrate himself into the discussion too, making us four in all. For my part, I was keen to use the opportunity to impress Bremer with how much had improved in the CPA's civilian presence in the South over the previous six weeks and to convince him that it was in the CPA's, and therefore his, wider interest to build upon this; we needed, as usual, more resources of every kind. To my surprise, the American spoke up in support, echoing my own political assessments. Graeme Lamb, who did not regard himself as being in Bremer's chain of command, was content to keep his own counsel.

But Bremer had a different agenda. While he heard me out politely, the issue uppermost in his mind at that time was oil smuggling. The Iraqis had developed highly sophisticated smuggling techniques during the long period of UN sanctions which were proving hard to penetrate. Having been filled up with crude oil from the southern oilfields, trucks would peel away from their convoys and make for the banks of the Shatt al-Arab, where their cargo would be transferred to barges. These would make their way south, where they would unload onto tankers waiting for them on the high seas. The Coalition had launched a crackdown, and the main stage for this was in the British area of operations. Perhaps Bremer had heard rumours of difficulties or delays. He asked Graeme Lamb somewhat sharply where we stood.

Graeme, who knew exactly where we stood, described the situation and referred to some of the considerations with which I knew the Army's legal branch had been wrestling, including those affecting the possible arrest of a tanker when outside territorial waters and issues of admissible evidence for subsequent prosecutions. It was necessary, said Graeme, to work within the law. Bremer's memorable response took me back to the Old West and Mike Gfoeller's hat: 'I am the law' he snapped.

In one sense, Bremer may have been absolutely right, in that he was the personal instrument for the execution of the responsibilities of the occupying powers. The CPA's mandate amounted to a severe limitation on Iraq's sovereignty. But international legal responsibilities and norms were surely not to be ignored. Did they not supersede the rights even of a superpower? The revelations from Abu Ghraib, some months later, were to make this clearer than it might have been in September. Graeme and I changed the subject.

At the end of the month I was in Baghdad again, for another coordinating conference, which this time included the Divisional Commanders and such leaders of the CPA provincial teams as had by then had arrived. Bremer was not able to attend this, so Jeremy Greenstock stepped in to encourage focus. He summarised with a list of follow-up items which was to prove too comprehensive to be executed. The first set of operational conclusions emanating from this consultative process was seemingly ignored.

By this time my team was sending reports to Baghdad at the end of every week which described what we had been doing in each of our specialist sectors, from politics to fixing water supplies. These reports ran to over a dozen pages and were usually quite detailed. If they were read in isolation, the sheer volume of activity and the extent of change might reasonably have been interpreted as progress. They amounted to sets of 'metrics', which official spokesmen liked to use to show that things were going pretty well. Our report for 1 October 2003 suggested that there had indeed been a step change forward as the effects of more resources and more experts started to kick in. But the superficial impression given by the reports could also be misleading. As we increased our visibility of the problems, so it became clear that, despite our progress, we were not keeping pace with the demand. Nor could we be certain that we would ever succeed in doing so.

I assumed that the other regions were sending similar reports up to Baghdad and that the nerve centre of the CPA must have had a reasonable idea of what was happening out in the provinces. I was therefore very surprised when, in early November at one of my face-to-face meetings with Bremer, he lamented that he never heard from the CPA provincial teams, of which he was the direct line manager. It seemed that, despite our efforts to keep him informed, neither our reports nor any summary of them were being passed on to him. I had established that our reports had reached Baghdad. But the no-doubt well-intentioned filtering systems in Bremer's outer offices had the unintended consequence of thwarting one of the major purposes behind Bremer's decision to create the provincial teams in the first place: he was not getting the feedback he needed.

* * *

The Green Zone, which has been so richly described in Rajiv Chandrasekaran's book *Imperial Life in the Emerald City*, attracted an endless stream of visitors from the provinces. The Rashid Hotel, in which I stayed several times, was a source of appetising food and, at its ever-crowded bar each evening, of mutually reinforcing high and alcoholic spirits. Its 14 floors of rooms were home to 700 CPA staff. It had a disco, which was apparently very popular, and a selection of souvenir shops, which got larger each time I visited. My military adviser and I dined in its grand restaurant one evening with David Richmond, then the senior British diplomat in Baghdad. After the Basra chuck wagon that had been our source of nutrition over previous months, it seemed like real luxury – an enormously welcome interlude.

It was on one such visit that an impeccable source close to Bremer's Chief of Staff confided in me a story which he was unable to keep to himself. A certain woman had somehow acquired passes in several different names to all but the most secure area at the CPA's Palace headquarters. She was discovered because a Lieutenant Colonel whom she had slept with had become suspicious about what she was asking of him, decided that she was too hot for him to handle and reported her. It turned out that she had been methodically gathering details of the background of all sorts of people, using every possible technique for the purpose. She made use of such information, including references to the background of my informant and of members of the CPA who had already left, to imply that she was a well-connected and authentic part of CPA's staff, which she definitely was not. My informant told me that it was clear that this Baghdad Mata Hari was some sort of spy and might have been of Afghan origin. When she wanted something, she dressed up attractively, in fine dresses, with make-up and high heels. When she dressed down, during normal working hours, she could become totally inconspicuous. But was she freelance, or working for someone else? If so, for whom?

Confronted with this enterprising breach of security, investigators had found nothing definitively incriminating beyond proof of the flagrant incompetence of their own procedures. Since they presumably did not want to expose this, the authorities had decided to let her go. She was taken to the gates of the Palace and left to make her way in the city. Who she worked for, and why, remained a mystery. Still chuckling with delight as he finished the story, my informant wondered wistfully what might have become of her.

At the end of October, the free and easygoing life of the Al Rashid Hotel disappeared. At about 6am on 26 October 2003, a Sunday, a series of rockets exploded in the eastern and western glass-and-concrete facades. A US Army colonel was killed and 15 others were wounded, including a young British civil servant who had made a considerable contribution to financial planning. A makeshift launcher rigged with 20 French- and Russian-made rockets was found in the north of the Green Zone – 11 of the rockets remained in it, having failed to take off. The general opinion at the time was that the target was Deputy Secretary of Defense Paul Wolfowitz, who was spending that night in the hotel. I was sent a series of photographs of the damage by a British colleague who had also been staying there. It seemed surprising that there had not been even more casualties.

Henceforward there was a much tighter security regime. The hotel's occupants were immediately moved into the Palace area to be accommodated in villas, dormitories, hutches and tents, or on floors in offices.

A few days later, in early November, I was in the Palace at about 7pm, visiting for a coordination meeting next day. There was a palpable sense of nervousness after the rocket attack, no doubt exacerbated by the resulting additional discomfort. But offices were humming with the customarily frenetic level of activity. Bremer's staff were dealing with messages from Washington – responses to the previous day's reports from Baghdad; more questions; reports of discussions around the president. Military staff in camouflaged fatigues were striding purposefully on nameless business. Worker-bee civilians were dreaming up more Orders, Regulations, Memoranda and Public Notices to launch upon the unsuspecting citizenry, whether or not they were able to understand English.

Jeremy Greenstock and I were talking earnestly together outside Bremer's office, in preparation for the next morning's meeting. For some reason, and unusually, we were both wearing suits, with red paper poppies in our buttonholes to mark the forthcoming anniversary of Armistice Day at the end of the First World War. To American eyes, we could not have looked more British.

Suddenly there were two explosions. A couple of rockets landed close to the Palace building. As sirens wailed, everyone was urged to descend to the relative security of the basement. I suppose Jeremy and I assumed that the fuss would soon be over, so we continued our discussion until Pat Kennedy, Bremer's Chief of Staff, felt it necessary to point out that we would be setting a poor example to others if we did not follow them to the depths. We did as we were told.

As we two elderly, be-suited gentlemen arrived in the basement, still deep in conversation, a loud American voice announced 'The British are coming!', recalling Paul Revere's fabled cry during the War of Independence. Peals of laughter broke the tension.

These rockets caused no casualties, but nerves were still taut the next morning. Assembled in the luxuriously restored Convention Centre for our coordination meeting, we had to submit to an introductory lecture on security procedures in case we were to be attacked again. If we came under fire a second time, we were told, we might be less lucky, so we should all lie on the floor and shelter under the brand-new desks in front of us.

I was sitting next to Graeme Lamb, the British Divisional Commander. 'We stay just as we are', he rasped to all the British in earshot, and to a good many besides.

No such attack took place, but the precautionary instructions brought back to my mind the famously unsuccessful coup attempt by Colonel Antonio Tejero, who, sporting a Guardia Civil shiny leather *tricornio* and a handlebar moustache, had brandished a pistol at the Spanish parliamentary assembly in the early 1980s. I had been dealing with Spain in the Foreign Office at that time and was always struck by the indignity of those who had taken cover and the contrast with those who remained seated, staring the comical figure out. Not quite the same as a possible rocket attack, it was true, but I could not imagine any of the six Divisional Commanders diving under their desks. Nor would the massive frames of several of them have found much cover there.

Chapter 5

Adapting to Ground Reality

I HAD REACHED the end of my first week in Iraq almost overwhelmed by the magnitude of the tasks facing the Coalition as a whole and, more pressing so far as I was concerned, facing me in particular. Conditions in the CPA's headquarters in the South, the former Electricity Accounts building, were intolerable and unsustainable.

The shortage of space and squalid living conditions were affecting operations. We had no room for the additional staff which I knew we needed, and the daily discomforts and privations risked affecting the quality of our work. Those astute enough to develop friendly links with the Royal Lancashire Regiment in their nearby camp sneaked off to have the occasional meal with them, to avoid the primitive and unvarying Tex-Mex food provided to us by KBR's eccentric kitchen staff. I relished my visits to Graeme Lamb's headquarters at the airport and did not hide the fact that I timed these to coincide with the Army mealtimes there.

But, most important, our combined offices and sleeping quarters were clearly unsafe. Although, in these early days, there were no instances of suicide bombs, we were still vulnerable to car bombs, rocket-propelled grenades, mortars, small-arms fire through our windows, siege and sapping. The building adjoined town houses and was flanked by roads on three sides, one of which was next to a canal. The only exit towards a military safe-haven if we were attacked was over a single bridge, which could easily be blocked by any assailants. We had to move.

When I arrived some nearby buildings had already been earmarked to serve as an alternative headquarters. The provincial offices of the Ministry of the Interior, which had been looted, were being refurbished by KBR. The site had the political and practical advantage of being in the town centre and therefore close to the Iraqis with whom we needed to conduct business. But in security terms it had most of the disadvantages of our existing site. One of the buildings, having been temporarily unoccupied, was now being methodically demolished, brick by brick, so that someone could re-use the construction materials or sell them on. The young boys who made up the demolition gang, some no older than eight years old, paused in their enterprising work to wave cheerfully to me as I inspected the site. Each day another few square yards disappeared. It would take armed force to stop this private initiative. No Iraqis would be prepared to intervene and, to my mind, it was inconceivable that the British Army should do so.

Opinion within KBR and CPA(South) was divided about what to do. KBR claimed to have spent $1 million already and wanted to continue. One of the several possible alternatives, to restore and occupy the Sheraton Hotel near the waterfront, was quickly ruled out when we found that it housed an unexploded 500-pound bomb.

My experience of terrorist threats in Pakistan had shown me that security considerations and the supposed risks to civilians are a more effective stimulus to government bureaucracies than almost any other argument. I remembered that my ambassador in Jordan in the mid-1980s caused an entirely new embassy to be designed, approved, built and occupied in the space of two years following a spate of kidnaps and an increased Palestinian terrorist threat. I had marvelled at such an achievement at the time and was even more admiring later as my familiarity, and exasperation, with public-sector project management increased. Knowing that I would not be exaggerating, I resolved to use the same technique for our situation in Basra, working with rather than against the grain of bureaucracy. It would be best if the idea seemed to come from elsewhere and then I could move in to support it, thereby increasing the spread of the pressure on the decision-makers. I formally called for separate and independent security reviews by the CPA in Baghdad and by the FCO in London, knowing that they could only agree on the need for us to move.

During August temperatures rose to the high 50s and, being close to the sea, the atmosphere was humid and dispiriting. The behaviour of the local Basrawis began to change and their attitude towards us shifted from one of neutral tolerance to suspicious hostility.

It was on one of these hot August days that the deputy head of Basra's city council, the Deputy Governor, came to call on me, since his boss was away. He was an irascible retired senior police officer, accustomed to preferential treatment, and when he came into my office he was angry. With scant regard for the initial courtesies, he launched into a tirade about the state of the offices which had been allocated to him and his colleagues on the Basra Council. It was a disgrace, he shouted, which undermined the Council's status and prestige and would therefore reduce its effectiveness. As someone who was familiar with Arab customs, he added, I should know that therefore the Coalition must be acting deliberately. Why, he complained, even the air conditioning did not work properly.

I sat quietly through this verbal attack, waited until Haytham had served us both glasses of sweet black tea, and put on a sorrowful expression. I was mortified, I said, to have to greet my distinguished visitor in such humble surroundings. Pointing to the display on the air conditioner in the wall of my office, which read 39°C, I explained that I understood the problem only too well. It was unfortunate that the intake of my machine was just next to the outlet of our electricity generator and that it was simply not up to the task. I therefore looked forward to the day when the Deputy Governor could have better premises and when I could greet him in a manner which was appropriate to his status. He promptly offered to give me one of his own air-conditioning machines since, he said, I was a guest in his country.

While it might have been possible to pacify individuals by means of careful personal appeals, the same was not true of the wider population. Crowds gathered outside our building in increasing numbers each day. From the time of ORHA's first arrival in Basra, different groups would turn up to lodge petitions or complaints, ranging from the trivial to the very serious. We had no way of knowing to what extent, if any, these representations were soundly based. And we had no swift way of making changes if they were: the rules had been laid down by Baghdad and officials there were far too busy drawing up regulations for other aspects of administration to concern themselves with fine tuning. In our eyes, Baghdad's attitude was hard-nosed and authoritarian: 'We've said what should be done, so get on and do it'. I came to realise they had no capacity to adopt any other approach.

But dogmatic responses cut no ice with aggrieved Iraqis. As the number of groups increased, so did their vehemence. By mid-July our Gurkha guards had to shut the metal gates, which we had previously kept open in the daytime as a sign of readiness to meet anyone who wanted to see us, against chanting groups of protesters. Initially, an intrepid British member of our staff, flanked by an interpreter, took delivery of pieces of paper setting out confused and varied demands, and promised to study them. This ploy soon proved inadequate; it had become clear that there was no follow-up.

We developed a new approach: our interpreter shouted through the bars of the gates that we would allow a small group of spokesmen inside the compound to discuss their grievance. Once the group had passed through a primitive metal detector, Robert Wilson, my political adviser who spoke fluent Arabic, heard them out and explained what we were trying to do. If this was insufficient to satisfy the visitors, which was the usual case, he promised that we would look into the problems and give a reply in due course. This was all we could do to persuade one group to leave us and allow us to proceed to the next in line.

We were not entirely unsuccessful in dealing with these petitions when the anomalies were clear and relatively easy to resolve. One such success was the reintroduction of previous salary differentials, to replace the flat rate applicable to all levels of workers and officials which had been laid down by the CPA in Baghdad. Once we had established what the difference in pay rates were, we could then take account of different grades of seniority and qualification.

The experience we gained and the accounts of our actions which we passed back to Baghdad might have been useful had the CPA staff there had the capacity to process the information and act upon it. But I concluded later that our approach and methods in the South were unique in Iraq, because of the differing relationship between the respective civilian and military arms of the Coalition effort and because the general security climate was more permissive. Although it was also relatively peaceful in the Kurdish north, in the three other regions there were initially very few other civilians on the ground. The US Army, who were not answerable to Bremer and the CPA under his leadership, had simply taken matters into their own hands, making use of the massive human and financial resources at their disposal. We did not want to do this in the South, both because we felt that these were civil issues which should properly be managed by civilians in the CPA and because the British Army did not want to impose further demands on their already stretched resources.

Nor could we have adopted the American approach, even if we wanted to: we did not have similar access to US-administered finance, and received virtually nothing for such purposes from the British Government. Yet we also wanted to try to conform to whatever practices were being followed nationwide, without being aware that no such common practice existed.

Despite our best efforts, however, our increasing discomfiture and evident inability to offer satisfaction soon infected the citizenry into further protest. Even our successes were turned to our disadvantage. As the various groups of protesters realised that representations could bring results, these results were interpreted as signs of our weakness and susceptibility to further pressure. Under Saddam, public protests would have been brought to an immediate halt by gunfire and slaughter. Since we stood as champions of democracy and human rights, it followed that we had to listen to grievances and do our best to rectify the many real ones. Our approach, of listening and, sometimes, agreeing to more generous terms, offered unlimited scope for opportunism.

One pressure group was particularly troublesome, with tragi-comic effects. Following previous practice, we had agreed to make payments to those who had been wounded or disabled during military service. Some of the disabilities had been sustained during the war against Iran in the 1980s; many stemmed from the first Gulf War in 1991. It was clearly right and equitable to continue with such arrangements and the process seemed straightforward enough. But it soon emerged that there was a sliding scale of payment according to the severity of the disability. The most tragic cases were those who had been blinded or who could no longer walk. They wanted and needed financial help just to survive. Other cases were more borderline and depended upon official certificates, issued under the former regime, which specified a category for payment.

Word soon got round that we were unable to check on the authenticity of such papers, or even to check upon the previous compensation scales. All sorts of claimants appeared with crudely forged documents and highly dubious arguments. The most blatant were groups of vigorous and fit young men demanding payment for the highest level of disability and emphasising their supposed rights by hurling large rocks at our windows. When our interpreters refused to entertain these claims, pointing out that such proficiency in stone-throwing was incompatible with the supposed level of injury, the mood became yet more inflamed. The temperature of the crowds rose in pace with the increasing summer heat.

Against this unpromising backdrop of a deteriorating mood on the streets, I set off back to the UK, as I had agreed with London beforehand, to report back to my masters and to tie up all the domestic loose ends at home.

*   *   *

My protection team's two vehicles sped me off on the southern motorway to Kuwait, stopping only to pick up fuel at a massive US

Army fuelling station on the other side of the border. The transaction was completed with the minimum of hassle; an exchange of a few words, delivered coolly and confidently, was all that was needed to obtain several hundred litres of diesel for our heavy and hungry armoured SUVs.

Before catching the morning plane to London, I spent the night in the luxury of the Kuwait Marriot hotel. The BBC World Service television informed me that its sister hotel, the Jakarta Marriot, had been blown up that day, presumably by Al Qaeda. This proved to be an omen of what was to come.

At the FCO's insistence, one of my loose ends was to visit St Thomas's Hospital near Westminster for a medical check, such as is customary for all middle-aged officers before a posting abroad. A similar check-up before my posting to Pakistan had revealed that I had inherited a mild form of haemophilia of which I had been completely unaware, although it explained why shaving cuts could be particularly annoying. St Thomas's solicitous staff made enquiries about the medical facilities available in Basra. They were not reassured by their findings and, although the condition is not particularly unusual, they became concerned about me returning to such an apparently violent place. But I reasoned that any service in Iraq inevitably involved risk and that a delay in the normal blood clotting processes would not add much to this. Submariners used to josh each other with the tag 'If you can't take a joke, you shouldn't have joined' – although, in their case, it was often accompanied by a wistful reference to the end of their contracted service: ROMFT, or Roll On My F***ing Time.

Conscious that I was determined to carry on with the job, even if ROMFT was in the back of my mind, the doctors provided me with a special medication kit and a supply of needles intended to clot the blood in the event of injury. It was all contained in an insulated plastic bag, to keep the medication cool. I was told to keep the whole lot in a fridge and to learn how to administer the potions myself since the accompanying instructions would be too complicated for non-specialists to follow in a hurry.

I went along with all this, without revealing that there was absolutely no prospect of finding a fridge in our Basra building or in any of our vehicles and that the ambient temperature had risen to more than 50°C. Soldiers on patrol in unarmoured Land Rovers had to face far worse hazards than me. I resolved to take my chances along with everyone else. The Foreign Office's famous 'duty of care' required that the hospital inform the Permanent Under-Secretary of the situation. Fortunately he did not intervene. The bag stayed at the bottom of a cupboard, to emerge six months later covered in sand.

Meanwhile, my civilian colleagues back in Basra were wrestling with the problem of how to head off any further escalation of violence, while at the same time enhancing the physical security of our premises. In the course of this, a crisis arose.

With the rising summer temperatures and the sudden influx of funds from increased salaries and reconstruction contracts, the local people had been buying up newly available electrical goods, especially air conditioners. The demand for electrical power and fuel for generators soared. Suddenly the supply failed to keep pace. Generators tripped and the diesel fuel distribution chain broke apart. Riots erupted outside our Electricity Accounts building. Instead of just stones and rocks, there was now gunfire.

For a while, it seemed as if our sanctuary would be under siege. The regular and Territorial Army personnel attached to our outfit drew their personal weapons and stood ready for action. I suspect that many of them recalled the tragedy of Majjar al Kabir just two months earlier and the deaths of the six Royal Military Police training team.

The attacks fizzled out, but not before a Gurkha guard, severely wounded, was dragged back into our building, where he died on the floor. This was the first fatality involving CPA(South) and greatly affected the morale of the usually cheerful and smiling Gurkha platoon. Within a day, however, the Army had stepped in to organise the fuel distribution network. Trucks full of fuel, supplemented by 25 million litres of petrol delivered by sea to the port of Az Zubayr, were soon being escorted to sub-stations all around the city. The violence subsided to a normal level as quickly as it had blown up.

Early in the following month, Foreign Secretary Jack Straw reported to the House of Commons that three separate attacks in southern Iraq in the month of August had caused the death of five British soldiers. A British mines-clearance expert had been murdered in the previous week.

The situation in Baghdad, however, was considerably worse, with dramatic and tragic consequences. On 7 August 2003 the bombing of the Jordanian Embassy claimed 17 lives. On 19 August, a truck bomb ploughed into the UN building on the Canal Road in eastern Baghdad. Among the 22 killed and 70 wounded was the UN Representative in Iraq, Sergio Vieira de Mello, who died before he could be extricated from the wreckage.

I cut short my intended stay in the UK and returned immediately to Basra to get down to work in earnest. These incidents changed everyone's attitudes and called for different approaches.

Soon after my return, Straw announced that more British troops would be deployed to the southern Iraq area of operations. DFID started to allocate new funds for reconstruction. Sir Jeremy Greenstock, one of Britain's most senior diplomats, who had played a crucial role in the UN before the start of the conflict, would arrive in mid-September to be Blair's personal representative in Iraq: not formally part of the CPA and not, as many assumed, to be Bremer's Deputy, but nonetheless in a key position to observe and to influence.

Straw reiterated the government's overall goal: to hand sovereignty to the Iraqi people as quickly as possible in conditions allowing them to build a secure and prosperous country. The Opposition foreign affairs spokesman, Michael Ancram, was supportive. 'What we did in the war was right' he said. But he was critical of 'a culpable failure of planning for post-war Iraq, for which the Government cannot this time escape blame'.

I had no interest in party political point-scoring. From my perspective, Ancram's criticism was an incontrovertible statement of fact. The evidence was before my eyes every day. But if discussion of the past came up, I would respond: 'We are where we are', and emphasise that we had to do the best in the situation in which we found ourselves.

While this was going on, the British Prime Minister was on three weeks' holiday in Cliff Richard's house in Barbados, having endured several politically and physically gruelling months beforehand. On his return at the end of August, Blair finally appointed a senior official, his recently appointed Diplomatic Adviser at Number 10 Downing Street, to coordinate the British effort in Iraq. The first manifestation of this was a generous tribute from the Diplomatic Adviser to David Richmond in Baghdad, Blair's envoy there pending Greenstock's arrival, and to myself for our reporting and programme proposals. But behind this expression of support was a clear implication that more was wanted.

At last, it seemed, the British approach in Iraq and the relationship with the USA would be coordinated; and steps would be taken to manage the increasing friction, very evident to us in the field, between British Government departments – the Foreign Office, the Development Ministry and the Ministry of Defence – and between them and the Army. But the test of effectiveness would be the delivery of results, for which we would have to wait and see.

* * *

I found on my return to Basra that plans to move out of our unsuitable premises had proceeded well. As I had expected, the security experts were unanimous that we could not stay where we were. Instead, we were to share the grounds of one of Saddam's palaces with the British Brigade a mile or two away, on the southern outskirts of the city, on the west bank of the Shatt al-Arab waterway. It was still close enough to key Iraqis to enable us to work with them; and it had the advantages of space and a high perimeter wall.

The estimated completion time after the formal decision of approval at the end of August was to be 75 days. The costs would all be met by the CPA centrally. Although the majority of my front-line staff were now British, the British Government were not expected to meet any of the core costs of the move apart from installing a long-overdue secure communications system.

I went to visit the site. Our two vehicles made their way through the town without incident and turned into the road towards the Palace's entrance. The Army had made a chicane with concrete blocks as a defence against car bombs. At the narrowest part was a group of Iraqis, who held long poles between which a white cloth banner stretched across our route. Seeing this, my protection team murmured to each other through their intercoms and our two cars drove resolutely on, their speed limited by the need to swerve around the blocks but nonetheless demonstrating no intention of stopping. The Iraqis, fortunately, stepped out of the way and waved us through, but the banner snagged on our car, and as we sped off it flew proudly from our roof aerial like a ship's paying-off pennant. Far from being a strident call for us all to leave, it was a plea for recognition of a local pressure group. I have it still among my souvenirs.

The area which surrounded the luxurious and over-decorated Palace building which housed the Brigade headquarters had been a public park before it had been appropriated for Saddam's summer use. It was a beautiful spot. Kingfishers darted into the waters of a placid and picturesque canal which flanked two of the sides. Their catches bore witness that the waters in this part of Basra were relatively unpolluted. Off-duty soldiers were fishing too, and groups of joggers made their way round the spacious grounds. Outside buildings now used as accommodation, soldiers' laundry was drying in the warm breeze.

The Brigade were less than happy at the prospect of a civilian cuckoo in this attractive nest. A major escorted me and my newly arrived and indispensable management officer around. He remarked pointedly that a wall would have to be built through this space to insulate the Army from the potential risks from the Iraqi visitors, who I insisted would need to visit us in our buildings.

As much as I sympathised with these additional privations for the Army, on top of the very real security threats to them, I could not help feeling irritated by an apparent obstructionism. Our own living conditions had been significantly worse than those in the Brigade headquarters for several months, although the officers who would have to deal with the consequences of our move may not have known this. And it was the Army, not us, who insisted that the CPA were their 'ticket out of here' and should therefore get on with the job. If this was their view, we felt, then they should have recognised their own interest in helping us to do so.

Not wanting to provoke a confrontation which might have soured relations for months, I deployed the chess tactic of Morton's Fork, a squeeze from two sides. The responsibility for implementing the contract on time would fall to KBR, who were employed by the CPA centrally rather than by me. I pointed out to Pat Kennedy, Bremer's constantly supportive Chief of Staff, that there seemed to be some 'glitches', the nature of which I was uncertain. It might be useful, I suggested, if someone could have a look into it.

Kennedy sent down his 'enforcer', a splendid US Marine Colonel called Dennis Sabal, together with KBR's overall manager in Iraq. Sabal introduced himself with a smart salute in my spartan office late one evening. Like my bodyguard Tom Fergusson, he revealed a hedgehog-like growth of hair on top of what had seemed, when wearing his uniform cap, to be a clean-shaven head.

'Sir', he announced, 'my job is to take cats off your back'.

That was just what I wanted to hear. This man's evident energy and determination was backed up by authority and resources: a winning combination.

Sabal returned to my office the following evening. He had had, he told me, some 'soldier to soldier' conversations with 'the Brits next door', meaning in the Brigade. The build time had now reduced from 75 to 45 days. We were now scheduled to make the move in mid-October, two-and-a-half months after my first arrival.

Our support from Baghdad was reinforced from London. General Mike Jackson, the head of the British Army, called in mid-September. I had encountered this legendary warrior before and had been subjected to the scrutiny of his penetrating eyes, barely visible under hooded lids. There was no point in not talking frankly: diplomat-speak would be inappropriate for the man and for the situation. He enquired neutrally how things were. I explained that I had noted that the Army headquarters judged that, despite the deteriorating security, their position was sustainable with their existing troop levels. In contrast, my organisation's position was not sustainable under the existing arrangements. If we were to travel to meet Iraqis and visit the other provinces, and since we had no self-defence capability of our own, our staff now needed to be escorted by military vehicles through the dangerous parts of the city. I recognised that this would take front line personnel away from their military duties and that this would not be welcome. But the Army still regarded us as their 'ticket out'. That anomaly needed resolution.

Jackson heard me out, commenting only with an inscrutable grunt. Having made my point, we moved on to other matters, but he seemed sympathetic and supportive.

So he proved. From then on, we had a steady and reliable system of escorts. They were inevitably never as much as we needed, so we had to cut back on our visits; but, by careful programming, which enabled several of our specialists to travel to their different destinations in one vehicle, we sustained a reasonable level of activity.

While I had occasional disagreements or differences of perceptions, I never experienced any lack of cooperation with the Army in the South again. I had acquired an invaluable ally in Denis Sabal, who time and again cleared the way when I encountered other blocks at the Baghdad end.

A month later I was grimly reminded of the debt we owed to the British Army for its support to us. An un-armoured Land Rover, just like the one that had taken me on a patrol, had been acting as escort for an armoured vehicle carrying some of our specialists. By this time our assailants in Basra were refining their deadly techniques. They had progressed beyond simply throwing bombs at vehicles as they passed. While they had not yet acquired the sophisticated devices which they were to use with such effect a year or two later, they were now able to set off their improvised explosive devices by using a remote trigger, operated either through a wire hidden along the roadside or by radio signal, usually from a mobile phone. In this way the terrorist could station himself at some distance, not arouse suspicion, and easily escape. Sometimes, however, there would be a time lag or, if the target vehicle was travelling fast, a vehicle on either side of it could receive most of the blast.

On this occasion it was not clear whether it was our conspicuous SUV which was the main target or the escorting vehicle. In any event, an explosion occurred in between the two, severely damaging the SUV but, thanks to the armour, only shaking up our experts. Some shrapnel, however, went through the Land Rover's thin skin and injured one of the escorting soldiers.

I visited the soldier concerned, with his Commanding Officer, in the tented Czech military hospital in Basra the next day. He was a big, tough young man from Newcastle and had been wounded in the back, the backside and the face. His cheerfulness and stoicism seemed almost a caricature of the plucky British Tommy. He was looking forward to some recuperation at the British military base in Cyprus and then to seeing his girlfriend again in England. He expected to be back out again before long. His injuries, he said, were part of the job.

It rapidly became clear that the decision to move took place not a moment too soon, and the prospect of the move helped prevent the dissolution of our entire operation. The destruction of the UN headquarters in Baghdad and the death of Sergio Vieira de Mello in August had altered perceptions about security, especially in capitals. The assassination, ten days later, of the leading cleric Ayatollah Muhammad Bakr al-Hakim and 94 others in the holy city of Najaf in the Centre South Region to the north of my patch, and the subsequent assassination of Governing Council member Aqila al Hashimi, deeply unsettled the Shia population.

The political consequences of these events for the South were hard to determine, partly because the southern Shia were far from monolithic and not necessarily aligned with those in Najaf. But there was nonetheless bound to be some backlash; and the growing insurgency movement would want to capitalise on the general concern. With such factors in mind, the UN decided to withdraw all its personnel from the country, including from the South, and several non-governmental humanitarian organisations followed suit.

In Baghdad the Americans had erred on the side of caution and had already turned the CPA headquarters into a fortress, as I had seen for myself. But the American dispositions involved a high operational price: they could not meet Iraqis in the CPA's Palace and very few CPA staff in Baghdad ever had any direct contact with Iraqis at all throughout their tours. With nothing else for many of them to do, they set about drawing up instructions and action plans which became increasingly divorced from reality. I was determined to avoid such a situation. We simply had to maintain our contacts with Iraqis; we could not rebuild their country ourselves, and they needed help which, we thought, only we could provide.

* * *

London had instructed me to send them at least one report every day until they had a better picture of the situation in the South. The military communications channels had been buzzing with activity. Signal traffic was supplemented by face-to-face video conferences, between the headquarters in Basra and Baghdad and between Baghdad and the UK. We had no similar facilities and, because of pressures on the ground and shortage of staff, civilian reports had been minimal. The military input was directed at the military Permanent Joint Headquarters at Northwood in Middlesex, not to the policy people in Whitehall. The picture which emerged from the Joint headquarters to the rest of Whitehall was a partial one. It seldom included much political assessment or prediction, and even less local colour. It certainly did little to satisfy the insatiable appetite of our politicians, who needed to show that they were at least as well informed as the media.

I have no doubt that the scope and frequency of my reports, generally drafted late at night, must have included errors or compressions which caused frissons at the military headquarters in Basra and in Britain. And, seeing the volume of my product, some of the Army may have assumed that I spent too much time crafting my despatches at the expense of more operational or organisational activity. But, just as the Army have their special professional skills, so my 30 years of practice had enabled me to match journalists' abilities to produce copy quickly.

The style and brevity of my reports were designed to catch Ministers' attention: it was they who were best placed to deliver the results I felt we needed: 'Snapshot in a Hot August'; 'What Needs to be Done'; 'Milestones and Challenges'; 'Knots Untied'; 'Bananas and Other Indicators'. Many amounted to repeated pleas for support and assistance: 'Resources'; 'Funding'; 'Staffing'; 'Security'. Others were straight reportage: 'Basra, the Venice of the Middle East'; 'The Political Scene in the South'; 'Southern Iraq Two Months On'; 'Health'; 'Law and Order'. Sadly, the titles were often remembered for longer than the content, since paper files had long since been abolished in the Foreign Office.

My final communication, incidentally, was a longer work – a Valedictory Despatch which, until recently banned, was traditionally sent by Heads of Mission on leaving their post. I was not inclined to have this published. But, since it was sent to London and to Bremer in Baghdad, I thought it right to read it out to my own staff in Basra. Perhaps it contained some home truths, because it elicited a sustained round of applause.

My daily news would arrive on desks before the Joint Headquarters' sometimes more sanitised product, causing Ministers or senior officials to ask questions which overstretched staffs could have done without.

Whatever the discomfort about methods, however, we civilians and the Army in Basra were entirely at one in our wish to convince London that the South was indeed different from other, more dangerous, parts of Iraq. The international press was almost exclusively based in Baghdad and the surrounding region. The situation described in increasingly sensational media reports should not be taken as applying throughout the country. London needed to be kept steady.

* * *

That this was necessary soon became clear. The FCO security people, alerted by the recent scares, showered us with advice and instructions. It was while we were exercising our emergency procedures late one evening that the Army warned us that a mass march had been organised a mile or so away and seemed to be heading in our direction. As part of our exercise, I was based in a makeshift control room in our Electricity Building, from where I immediately phoned London to let them know what was happening in real time. Someone had installed a television there with an aerial fixed outside the window. On hopping through the channels, I discovered that a stringer from Sky News television was relaying pictures of the march around the world and, most usefully, to ourselves too. So my telephoned reports to the depths of Whitehall perhaps conveyed the drama of a man really on the spot. After a couple of hours, however, the march halted and dispersed. But our procedures had been thoroughly tested and proved satisfactory.

The next morning, after a sleepless night, I received a peremptory telegraphic order to draw up emergency security instructions – which we had of course already done – and take disciplinary action against anyone who failed to conform. I reacted tetchily. I did not need to be instructed, I wrote for all Whitehall to read, about how to manage staff to deal with emergencies: I had been doing just that for the previous three years in Pakistan, when it had been necessary to evacuate High Commission staff on three occasions – a post-war record. I added that, much as I might like to conduct a public flogging of a miscreant before breakfast 'pour encourager les autres' – as Voltaire had observed about the exemplary execution of the unfortunate Admiral Byng – I had no disciplinary authority over any member of my staff, apart from the few British civil servants, short of asking their governments to have them return home. And anyway, I added petulantly, I needed each one of them and more. I received a couple of phone calls expressing mild disapproval about the tone of this despatch, but they were accompanied by understanding chuckles.

While that was the end of that exchange, a little while later I received a recommendation that our entire operation be transferred from our by now heavily reinforced Electricity Accounts building in the town centre to co-locate with the military headquarters at the airport, well out of town. This would have been the end of our operation: there were no facilities for us at the airport; we would not be able to meet Iraqis; and most of our international staff would almost certainly have been recalled by their parent governments.

Fortunately, Graeme Lamb and I independently came to the view that the prevailing security threat did not warrant such drastic measures. Graeme formally advised in this sense. I also had to scotch the instruction that additional armoured vehicles, which were due to arrive from the UK before long, should only be used by British personnel. If London did not understand or accept this, I wrote angrily, then I would formally advise Bremer – for it was he not the FCO who was my operational boss in Iraq – that London's instructions were contrary to my considered advice. I would also have to record my judgement that if I were to carry them out CPA(South) would cease to be viable.

My irritation stemmed not only from the substance of London's position, but also from the fact that they had clearly not considered its wider international implications for the objectives of the Coalition, of which the UK was a part but not the whole. This seemed to be another illustration of the lack of grip at a senior level.

I subsided once it was clear that my broadside had done its job. The pressure was eased, in the knowledge that we would soon be moving to our safer location next to the Brigade. But I was left uneasy. Why did I have to deploy such broadsides so frequently? What was the source of these instructions? Were they coordinated by Number 10 Downing Street? If so, why were we not consulted before decisions which had such wide implications were reached? Or were they the product of specialist sections within the bureaucracy? If so, why were they not monitored before despatch?

For all the idiosyncrasies of the military Joint Headquarters, I reflected, at least that system ensured close coordination and consultation; and there was never any doubt about who was in charge. There was no equivalent on the civilian side. No wonder the Army were so often exasperated with us. Where was our 'Commander's intent'? Where, or who, indeed, was 'the Commander'?

* * *

We moved into the new site on 15 October 2003, exactly on Denis Sabal's new schedule. I had lived in the old building since the end of July. Some of my colleagues had been there for an additional two months, when the conditions were even worse. It was security which had driven the move and which had ensured that it happened quickly, but it was the improved comfort which everyone appreciated the most.

The difference in living conditions seemed almost unbelievable. Instead of sleeping in crowded rooms or on floors, with unspeakable sanitary arrangements and virtually non-existent communications equipment, every staff member had their own cabin, or 'hooch' as they came to be known, with a proper bed, a cupboard, a shower and lavatory, and even an air-conditioning unit. Gone was the trailer in which we had been regaled with grits, chilli dogs and Jell-o. Instead there was a spacious food hall – with a notice which forbade firearms inside – with Indian and Pakistani chefs who on Sundays rustled up magnificent curries to the British, if not the American, taste. There was even a bar, which we ensured operated under sensible licensing rules, although I never enquired about the source of its supplies. A laundry service staffed by young Iraqi women operated on a two-day turn-round. All of this was a huge morale boost and greatly improved the atmosphere of our daily meetings, in every sense.

Within another couple of weeks FCO engineers had installed a secure communications system with sets of computers which enabled those with British security clearances to transmit and receive confidential messages very quickly to or from London or any diplomatic post in the world, including Baghdad.

Military cooperation extended to allowing us to use their well-equipped gym in one of the fantastical Palace buildings. We could jog around the internal perimeter instead of being confined to three floors of a small building. My protection staff joined the other fishermen trying their luck or skill in the Shatt al-Arab, although they never risked eating their catch. No longer would I be kept awake by the squeaking fan. Less stultified by sleep deprivation, I took to working out at the gym in the evening before supper whenever I could. The renewal of energy made it easier to continue working into the night, when I did my paperwork and reporting.

By this time, also, a young diplomat on his first foreign posting, James Roscoe, had arrived to act as my Private Secretary. I also acquired a Personal Assistant to manage my correspondence and programme. And an experienced Arabist who had just been our Ambassador to Damascus, Henry Hogger, arrived to coordinate CPA activities in Basra Province. Henry was to stand in for me when I was away, which ensured unbroken links with London, which my Italian colleague, Ambassador Mario Maiolini, despite his experience and skill, could not have provided. Both proved to be of inestimable value to me.

At last, two-and-a-half months after my arrival, I was starting to muster the staff and equipment which would enable me to do my job reasonably effectively. This support was as nothing compared with the general's staff, but it was something; and, of course, our respective tasks were different.

Everyone in CPA(South) was delighted at the move. KBR, who had done all the work, had performed splendidly. The grim prophesies about the impossibility of meeting such a tight construction deadline had proved unfounded. And we solved the problem of the potential waste of money and effort in refurbishing the Ministry of the Interior building, which had originally been earmarked for us. We presented it to the Governor of Basra for use as Council offices. His irascible deputy would no longer have cause for complaint that his workplace did not befit his status.

Wanting to avoid Baghdad's mistake of calling their headquarters 'The Palace', we named our new home 'Al Sarraji', adopting the name of the public park which had been on the site before it was expropriated by Saddam's henchmen.

In early November, therefore, the future looked promising. My bids for new staff were being processed; new personnel protection arrangements were in train; our relations with the Iraqis were developing well; and we were getting the hang of extracting resources from Baghdad. I felt that we were well on the way to being able to build up and sustain a solid civilian presence which would add value to the Army's splendid holding of the fort up to now. By the end of 2005, when we anticipated that the CPA would return full sovereignty to an Iraqi government, we might well hand over a better place than the one which we had entered.

Once we had moved, the pressure from the security people in London subsided, but we were constantly monitored. The justification, we were told, lay in the Parable of the Frog. According to this, a frog will jump to safety if dropped into a pan of hot water but will be insouciantly boiled if the water is gradually heated up. It seemed that we were the frogs and Basra the water; so, according to this reasoning, some outside cook was needed to keep an eye on the water temperature. I wondered who had conducted the experiments which lay behind this empirical theory.

Now that we were settled, however, I could take stock, review our objectives, and set a direction for the future. In the knowledge that nothing of any greater length would be properly digested, I drafted a four-page note setting out what it was we were trying to do, briefly covering our full range of activity. Its main thrust was that, while we should all make as great a contribution as we could, it was for the Iraqis themselves to reconstruct their own country. Our job was to help them do this. London agreed to the draft, with minimal comments from DFID and none from anyone else. I copied it to Baghdad for information, knowing that any attempt to secure formal approval would come to nothing. A copy of this note, which was given to all CPA staff in the South, is in Appendix 1 at the end of this book.

I had no inkling then that the entire basis of CPA's operations was about to change. My note was dated 12 November 2003. On 15 November, Bremer announced that the CPA was to be wound up at the end of the following June. This completely unexpected decision was to have a profound effect on our future work and on attitudes in our countries' capitals. Meanwhile, however, we had a job to do. We just had to get on with it.

PART TWO
FACTS ON THE GROUND

Chapter 6

Life in the Provinces:

Basra, Al Muthanna, Dhi Qar, Maysan

The reluctant obedience of distant provinces generally costs more than the territory is worth.

Thomas Babington Macaulay, *Historical Essays*.

I have been in Basra. People everywhere, and cars, thousands of them, each up the arse of the next.

Sahain, a Marsh Arab, quoted by Wilfred Thesiger.

I HAD BARELY arrived in the country, and Sheikh Rahim was railing at me: 'The Coalition has done nothing. George Bush and Tony Blair keep making promises. But what good has come of them over the last five months?' He paused. 'Why are you here?' he demanded. A portly colleague on the Amarah City Council joined in: 'We are tired of words. We are tired of promises. We want to see results'.

It was mid-morning in the summer of 2003, and the meeting room inside Amarah's pink-coloured Council building was crowded and hot. Tempers were frayed. Mohammed Baqr al-Hakim, a leading Shia religious figure, had been killed by a car bomb in the holy city of Najaf just five days earlier, and the Shia in Amarah were in mourning. Sheikh Rahim, as leader of Maysan Province's Council, spoke for all 21 of its members in expressing dissatisfaction and frustration with the consequences of a foreign occupation which they had not requested.

'I have come to learn', I replied. 'I want to find out what you need. I would like us to work together. If we are to succeed in this, we must know about the problems. I will make no promises that I cannot keep. But I do promise that I shall try to help you'.

I thought that I should also respond directly to the portly gentleman who was tired of words.

'If we are to help you, then we must talk together. And we should be ready to talk for a long time. If Sheikh Rahim's honourable colleague is tired, I will get him some medicine to keep him awake'. There was some laughter. Even the portly patient grinned. Some of the immediate anger subsided, allowing us to get down to more focussed discussion.

But Sheikh Rahim was very serious and persisted. He pointed out that it was the people of Maysan, not the Coalition forces, who had liberated their own Province, of which Amarah was the main city. They were proud to have done this without the need of anyone else's interference, before the Coalition forces had arrived. What they now wanted was material help to undo the damage caused by the confusion after the Coalition's invasion and by the previous long years of sanctions.

'Why do we have a British military camp just outside our city?' he demanded. 'We look after our own law and order. We do not expect foreigners to do this on their own behalf. They should go away. Now'.

As he spoke, a noisy demonstration started up outside the window of our meeting room. There was a pause in the discussion, to maximise the dramatic effect of this entirely contrived incident.

People rushed into the room, waving sheets of paper. Our personal protection team moved their hands. There was some shouting. We took delivery of the papers, the visitors left, calm was restored. Our guardians stood easy.

'You see', continued the Sheikh, 'the people are nearly starving'.

This would not do. Sheikh Rahim's last assertion was pure bluster. The Councillors did not know that just before my meeting with them I had taken a turn round the souk, as I had done previously in Nasiriyah in the next-door province. I had asked the shopkeepers how business was.

'Very good', they had replied. 'Many people have much money. Not like before'.

The Coalition had been spending a great deal on vastly overpriced contracts. Salaries of teachers and other government workers had been raised, even if the recipients were not working. Former Iraqi soldiers had been receiving stipends for several months.

As for the security situation, what the Sheikh did not mention was that Maysan Province shared a long border with Iran; that the Iraqi Shia there had fought with Iranians in the eight-year Iran–Iraq war; and that there was every reason to believe that the Iranians were out to cause mischief against the Coalition. It was essential for the Coalition to have a military presence on the ground.

'Did you like Saddam's government?' I asked rhetorically.

'It put me in prison for ten years'.

Ah. 'Then you know how much this region suffered under it. We too want you to have security. But we want you to work with us and not just on your own. Security can become the kingdom of one person, and not necessarily the most just person. Or do you want to go back to what you had before?'

'You should ask me a different question, since we are in the present, not in the past. Ask me if I am happy with you'.

'No. I will not ask you that now', I replied slowly. 'I want to ask you if we can work together for a while. Once we have done that, and you are better able to decide whether you are happy with me, then I can ask you your question'.

Perhaps the score in the debate was evens. I had kept calm, had tried to seem understanding and sympathetic, and had, I think, just about maintained the dignity of my position. I had repeatedly emphasised my genuine wish to help. Sheikh Rahim had faithfully conveyed his Council's concerns, had made no concessions towards collaboration with us occupiers, but had left a door open for future cooperation, having made clear that this would have to be to their advantage.

But it was inescapable that Sheikh Rahim's complaints were well founded. Law and order were disintegrating in Maysan – always the most difficult of the four southern provinces under the British-led civil and military management. The Marsh Arabs of the formerly great Al bu Muhammad tribe were feuding with others, as each saw opportunities to gain power and prestige. Iranians from across the nearby border and their many sympathisers were muddying the waters.

It was clear from the start that Maysan would be the most problematic of the southern provinces. That was why it was the British Army which maintained a Battle Group in a camp on the outskirts of town, as well as in Basra, while the more lightly equipped Italian and Dutch armed forces took the lead in the other two southern provinces.

* * *

Basra, my base, was very different from the wild tribal marshlands of Maysan Province. If Sahain's impression of overcrowding and a profusion of cars was right in the 1950s, when Wilfred Thesiger had befriended him and before the great migrations of population away from the Marshes and towards the cities, it was even more accurate in 2003.

Basra's cars were funded by the lavish expenditure on increased salaries and reconstruction contracts – largely Iraqi funds of which little had yet reached the outlying provinces – and were supplied by eager merchants with good connections in Kuwait. The standard of driving was terrifying. No one needed to consider taking a test or obtaining a licence, and there were no traffic cops. It was a free-for-all in which the local populace engaged with cheerful insouciance. The absence of road-sense was compensated by a general politeness and carefree disregard for mishaps.

But the majority in Basra had neither profitable jobs nor cars. With time on their hands, they passed their days standing around on the streets, strolling along the wide pavements on the waterfront, or sipping tea and discussing current events.

If the gods had tried to deter me on my first day in the country by sending a sandstorm, they must have dropped that particular tactic as I never encountered another. The climate and atmosphere, once away from the traffic, was benign and invigorating. Even the excessive heat was moderated by land and sea breezes. Ice-cream parlours were full. Bananas and slices of coconut were sold at every traffic jam, together with a selection of the several hundred different titles of newspapers which had sprung up around the country.

Six months later, despite the difficulties and the increased violence, the roads had become almost totally choked with cars and trucks. Traffic police were now to be seen at intersections, clad in smart uniforms run up by local tailors at the initiative of the occupiers' police trainers. They could do little but preside over a stagnant pool of vehicles and inhale exhaust fumes. But their hand signals and whistle drill were impeccable. Those who could not afford cars bought bicycles. Golden-coloured bike handlebars sold particularly well.

On my first tours of Basra, I constantly had in mind Bremer's assertion that Baghdad was the key to Iraq and that other demands would have to defer to that priority. But the more I saw, the more I felt that to neglect such an important centre would be to neglect to capitalise on hugely important assets and potential.

Basra had been a centre for maritime trade, culture and learning since the mists of time – probably since before its foundation by Caliph Omar bin Khattab in 637 CE. It was from here, so legend had it, that Sinbad the Sailor set off for his adventures. Later it became a battleground between Turks and Persians and then the front line in Saddam's eight-year war with Iran. Paradoxically, there were particular opportunities for the British. The Sunni Turks who had occupied this Shia region in the nineteenth century were never popular, especially because of their heavy taxation regime. The British occupation in 1918 was therefore not entirely unwelcome, the more so as it led to the development of the port area. Despite the unsuccessful revolt in 1920, the British were still remembered fondly.

In 2003, Basra competed with Mosul for the title of the second-largest city in Iraq. Its population of about 1.5 million, more than 5 per cent of the country's total, had grown by some 40 per cent in the previous 30 years. But in 2003 its nearby oilfields, its stock of industrial plant and its infrastructure put Basra in a different class. Its importance was clearly second only to Baghdad. Positioned next to the Shatt al-Arab and close to the Gulf states, it could once again become a national and international trading hub.

Dominated by water, the city had once been called the Venice of the Middle East, a title of which the Basrawis were immensely proud. But a lot would need to change before it could earn that accolade again. The city's six canals were black and stinking. Every form of garbage prevented the tide from sluicing them through twice a day, as had been the original design. The Shatt itself was so horribly polluted that even chemical purification would not make its water fit for drinking. Formerly, the Marshes at its northern end had acted as filters for the Tigris and Euphrates rivers after their passage along the length of the country and the surrounding water had been remarkably sweet. But Saddam's draining of the Marshes in the early 1990s as part of his persecution of the southern Shia had destroyed this role. As a result, Basra's water came from what was called the Sweet Water Canal, which runs from the Euphrates to a network in the city. However, the canal had been neglected. Its sides were constantly crumbling, leaking water and letting in pollution. The city's water distribution system depended on multiple purification plants and pumping stations. And these were in turn dependent on the availability of power and of fuel, which was both limited and unreliable.

The Basrawis were constantly faced with evidence of the city's former prosperity, before the depredations of the Iran–Iraq war, and hence with the magnitude of the task ahead. The main railway station, from which ran trains to Mosul even in September 2003, was flanked by a complex of cranes and gantries which had been idle since the 1970s. The Shatt water channel was obstructed by 240 wrecks – freighters sunk by Iranian forces – and mines and ordnance rendered it almost impossible to clear. It was so silted up that only shallow barges could proceed upstream. When I took a tour of the waterway in one of the Royal Navy's fast little patrol boats, I could see Saddam's former yacht as it lay capsized on the western bank, near the bombed and looted Sheraton Hotel.

A pontoon bridge blocked the channel downstream for all but the smallest craft. My armoured vehicle would clatter precariously over the slats which made up the roadway between the eastern and western sides of the Shatt. One of the British Sappers' first tasks on arrival had been to re-anchor the bridge with steel hawsers and concrete blocks to prevent the whole thing floating away downstream. By September, however, it was crammed with two-way traffic: buses could pass each other with no more than inches to spare. During the many traffic jams, occupants would merrily chat to each other through open windows until a surge of movement separated them again, and their talk was transferred from words to friendly gestures of fingers, hands and arms.

I had seen the poorest areas of Basra, called 'The Shia Flats' by the Army, when I had accompanied a military patrol and walked among the inhabitants. But only an aerial view could bring home the nature and extent of the more prosperous quarters of the city where the bosses of industries and businesses still lived. The impeccably laid out, well-constructed villas surrounded by seven-foot-high walls must also have housed Saddam's security henchmen, but they had now disappeared. On the right bank, next to the ruined Sheraton, was a wide boulevard which took on a pink glow when bathed by the setting sun. It must once have been a wonderful spot for taking tea and considering the joys and tribulations of life. Now, however, it was a constant reminder of death – the many deaths incurred by the southern Shias at the hands of Saddam and his people.

Along the waterside was a row of plinths. On these had stood a line of massive bronze statues of generals who, in Saddam's eyes, had distinguished themselves in the Iran–Iraq war. They all faced east, towards Iran, with outstretched arms, pointing threateningly. Most had been toppled when Basra was liberated, partly as a token of revenge by the Basrawis against their former oppressors, but also for the value of the scrap metal. When I first travelled along the road one statue remained standing: the effigy of a general who was regarded as relatively well-disposed and who was subsequently executed on Saddam's orders. But, following the fate of the original, it too disappeared.

Another of Basra's losses was also most apparent from the air. For centuries in the past, the city had been surrounded by palm trees, the dates from which were famous throughout the region. Nearly all of them had been felled during the war with Iran to allow, so I was told, a clear field of fire across the nearby front line at the Iranian border, and to eliminate potential shelter for the many Iraqi Shia who fought with the Iranians against Saddam. This destruction, at a stroke of an axe, extinguished a rich source of income, food and employment. And it magnified the changes to the region's micro-climate which had resulted from Saddam's draining of the Marshes further north. Basrawis would never forget how Saddam had decimated their people, polluted their water supplies, and reduced their food supplies and job opportunities.

If its power stations were working at full capacity, Basra would have a surplus of electricity, although that was never the intention since it was Basra's generation capacity which made up the power deficits further north. But the power transmission lines were constantly sabotaged and looted for their copper.

All it took was for a truck to pull up beside a pylon overnight and for one or two men to saw through part of the metal structure. After a while the pylon would topple, bringing others down with it, and the flow of power would trip. On that signal, men with trucks would scurry to the site, pull away the copper cables along the hundreds of miles of run, cut them into truck-size lengths, smelt them into ingots and sell the raw copper in Iran for high prices. This trade represented a mutually profitable alliance between terrorists, criminals and entrepreneurs. The citizens of Basra did not mind at all if there were problems over exporting power from their Province: all the more for them. It was impossible to police such tracts of land. Such simple actions successfully thwarted the efforts of Coalition and loyal Iraqi engineers to enhance Iraq's power production for years.

At a press conference on his first visit to Baghdad, Defense Secretary Donald Rumsfeld appeared to conclude from the extent of lighting at night that there was little problem over power supplies. But closer inspection would reveal that the citizens' first priority was to light the outside of their houses, to deter looters, while remaining in the dark inside. Blackouts stimulated immediate gunfire – not necessarily to hurt anyone, but just to let it be known that someone was at home and that burglars should beware. And, as in Baghdad, conditions in Basra were no indication of those in the outlying regions, where power was in chronically short supply.

The uncertain security situation was the main and constantly expressed concern of everyone we talked to. Straight criminality risked developing into organised crime. Saddam had ordered the release of all prisoners in jails at the start of the military campaign. Without the draconian controls of his security apparatus the former prisoners now had free rein. It was all made worse by hillbilly-style tribal feuding, in which neighbouring families pumped bullets into each other's houses, hitting non-combatants in the process. Car-jacking, involving the export of vehicles across the unpoliced border to Iran, extortion and kidnapping were rife. The real extent of lawlessness was hard to judge. But many, perhaps most, of the citizenry wanted the Army to go in and shoot a few criminals. They would tell us that if we insisted on due process of law then we should ensure that the offenders were hanged as a result.

* * *

Important as Basra might have been, however, it would have been unwise to regard it as the key to the South, just as Baghdad was never really the key to the rest of the country. Other cities, especially Amarah and Nasiriyah, and other provinces had their own characteristics and politics which could ill afford to be neglected.

Bremer too had come to the view that, even if Baghdad was to be the focus for resources, he needed to know what was going on elsewhere. A couple of months after his arrival in Iraq, and finding that the arrangement of four Regional Coordinators established by his predecessor was not proving to be of much value, he decided to set up an additional set of structures, based in each of the 18 Provinces, which would be answerable directly to him. Once established, they were to be Bremer's eyes and ears and coordinate the Coalition's civilian activity in their respective Provinces. Strangely, in his memoir *My Year in Iraq*, Bremer does not describe the motives behind this decision or even refer to it. It was not perhaps of strategic political significance, and its implementation was very far from being a success. But the decision had far-reaching practical implications and many consequences for the use, and wastage, of resources.

It was unfortunate that the CPA labelled these provincial branch offices 'Governorate teams'. This risked conveying the impression that the team leaders, formally entitled 'Governorate Coordinators', were some sort of colonial governors or successors to the appointees whom Saddam had installed in the bad old days. In practice, or at least in theory, one of the main functions of the provincial team leaders was to encourage the establishment and consolidation of Iraqi governors for each Province, ideally to be selected and appointed by more democratic means than was the case for either the Governorate Coordinators or Saddam's governors. In other words, they were meant to be facilitators to enable Iraqis to take the reins of power, not to do the driving themselves. Whatever might be the actual status of the CPA within the country, any notion that we foreigners saw ourselves as governors would reinforce the sense of occupation and undermine the concepts of liberation, cooperation and facilitation which we needed to reinforce if we were to gain Iraqi confidence.

In practice, however, parallels with colonial governorship were not far off the mark, even if that was not the intention.

The creation of this additional tier of Coalition authority came as an unwelcome surprise to the British Government, who wanted to preserve a more centralised management structure in the South, under my supervision as Regional Coordinator. This would enable advice and reporting from the four southern Provinces to be channelled upwards to Baghdad and London, with the addition of the wider perspective derived from the close association between my headquarters and the Army. Similarly, my set-up in Basra could feed resources and expertise into the Provinces according to a regional assessment of need. While Bremer's wish to have direct reporting and control, unfiltered and undiluted by the Regional Coordinators, was understandable, London doubted that the arrangements would be practicable, and feared that they would lead to a free-for-all between the 18 competing provincial teams.

Aware of these concerns, I took soundings in Baghdad.

A trusty source advised me not to meddle. The fact was, I was told, all the original Regional Coordinators, until my Danish predecessor appeared briefly on the scene, were former American military officers who had been selected by Bremer's predecessor, Jay Garner. Bremer did not trust them to serve his objectives: they were too close to the US Army, with whom Bremer had a famously prickly relationship. While I came from a different stable, I was still an unknown quantity for Bremer; and I was British, which might not be an attribute in his eyes. Furthermore, Bremer was allergic to any suggestion, from any quarter, that he should change a decision once he had made it. I would do best to leave well alone, keep my powder dry for more pressing needs and operate pragmatically.

I was content to accept this well-meant and plausible advice. I had no need to assert authority over the provincial teams: we would all find out soon enough to what extent our regional advice and assistance might be of value and, as long as we could all stay in close touch, I was confident that a satisfactory modus vivendi would emerge. I quickly agreed with the heads of the four provincial teams, as each was eventually appointed, that we should gather together every fortnight to compare notes and share our concerns. Basra's central location, and the size and security of our new headquarters, rather than any consideration of status, made it the obvious venue for these meetings.

The British Minister of State for International Development, Hilary Benn, was, however, worried about Bremer's arrangements for the Governorate teams. During his visit in mid-September, he told me he planned to challenge Bremer when he went up to Baghdad the following day. I was glad I was able to dissuade him: there were enough differences between the two occupying powers at that time on a whole range of issues. This one was not worth a fight. The main point was that, despite Bremer's concentration on Baghdad and constitutional issues, the Provinces could be the cause of failure. The presence of Coalition teams in each of the Provinces, irrespective of how they were managed, would help redress the balance.

I was constantly mindful that the people in the South, scarred by years of Ba'athist domination and oppression, objected to overly centralised control and wanted a greater say in their own affairs. They had a long tradition of distrusting rulers in Baghdad, and they had little respect for the Iraqi Governing Council, which they regarded as an American construct with no legitimacy. Unfortunately for all concerned, the Iraqi Governing Council's performance in practice did little to enhance either its authority or its credibility. Several of its members, having been exiles for years, were seldom in the country. And it was failing to control the ministries which the CPA wanted to run the country's administration. These failings and the Governing Council's perceived association with the Americans increased the Provinces' pressure for autonomy.

Such tendencies were to a great extent inevitable, since the lid had been lifted from Saddam Hussein's regime's oppression of any political processes. People could now speak out, assemble and form interest groups in a manner which would have been inconceivable previously.

Bremer was true to his word to me at our first meeting in early August. Before any of the provincial teams had been established, he set up joint meetings of the Regional Coordinators and the military commanders. The first of these, which Bremer introduced and then left, was totally chaotic. The four Regional Coordinators were sat in a line at a table facing a screen which showed a PowerPoint display. Behind us was a collection of Baghdad-based CPA officials and military officers. As soon as the display commenced, furious arguments broke out between the observers. We regional actors could not get a word in, could not see the unknown speakers behind us and were never once asked for an opinion. It did not have to be pointed out that such a fiasco should never be repeated.

The next such meeting, chaired by the head of the Governance Directorate, was better organised but barely more productive. Some of us highlighted the risks of neglecting the issue of local governance and made a plea to establish some broad parameters for a relationship between the CPA, the Iraqi Governing Council and provincial and local governments.

The idea was widely supported and the point was accepted by the Chair. But, no doubt because of the intolerable burden of work on a small staff, nothing came of it. Not until months later was there any advice about the establishment of councils or quasi-democratic local government bodies. Repeated demands from the Provinces that arrangements should be made to pay, and thus motivate, local government officials remained unfulfilled.

The 18 Provinces were therefore left to fend for themselves. The Coalition's contribution varied according to the particular conditions within each Province, the quality of the Coalition's team and its leaders, and the timing of its establishment. As a result, each Province ended up with different systems, differently arrived at.

* * *

In Basra Province, the largest and most important of the four southern Provinces, the outcome was relatively successful. With much help and stimulus from the Army, who worked closely with us, an Interim Committee was created under the leadership of retired Judge Wa'el Abd al-Latif. This became in effect the new Basra Provincial Council. Judge Wa'el, like many other judges, had not been a member of the Ba'ath party and, partly for that reason, the CPA in Baghdad arranged matters that he should be a member of the Iraqi Governing Council as well as leader of the Interim Committee. Using his status and natural authority, he busied himself in establishing a range of central working committees and 20 local councils.

We gave the judge a pot of money to encourage these local bodies to embark on a campaign to clean up the city, to start quickly and be highly visible. The idea was to create jobs for local youths who might otherwise cause trouble, to demonstrate to other citizens that organisation and stability were being restored, and to stimulate community leaders to take on responsibility for themselves.

I had another objective in mind as well. The rubbish left out on the streets and the piles of old and flammable tyres which I saw on my first tours of the city reminded me of the streets of Quetta in Pakistan at the start of the Afghanistan campaign a couple of years earlier. In October 2001, plane-loads of foreign journalists flocked to that wild-western desert town in misguided anticipation that Osama bin Laden was about to be arrested. Local militants, rising to the occasion and always ready to put on a spectacle, obligingly set light to similar piles of rubbish and created photo-opportunities for visiting journalists hungry for spectacular stories. Some of the protestors, who had been marching peacefully, had acquired brief moments of fame by hurling stones directly at television cameras.

To the intense irritation of the journalist stringers who lived and worked in Pakistan, the photogenic 'blow-ins', framed by the fire and smoke of burning tyres, had themselves become part of the story, had duly broadcast overblown accounts of violent rioting and had prophesied the imminent downfall of the Pakistani regime. Such assessments had affected opinion and policy thousands of miles away as governments concluded that the situation was worse than the reality. It was essential to avoid any repeat of such sensationalistic commentary in Basra: the situation was precarious enough as it was without being exaggerated further.

With the arrival of Henry Hogger, an experienced ambassador in the British Diplomatic Service, as the head of the Basra provincial team at the end of September, we could now seriously strengthen the relationship between CPA(South) and the Basra Council, which was assuming increasing political and practical importance. After a period of keeping his distance, Judge Wa'el and others in the Council started to work closely and constructively with us. Henry encouraged the judge to bring representative groups into the Council and skilfully steered their efforts by providing more funding for promising activities, such as the promotion of women's groups, which might otherwise have been a low priority. Our efforts were reinforced by a series of 'gifts': a refurbished Council building; mobile phones and new cars for Council members; and material support for the city's police force. CPA representatives were welcome at all Council meetings and were invariably invited to attend its press conferences.

Progress at the local level assumed a slower pace. Basra Province alone originally had more than a hundred neighbourhood committees, who were responsible for day-to-day administrative affairs such as sanitation, refuse collection and street cleaning. This arrangement had worked after a fashion, but allowed for only a minimum of input from local people in decisions which affected them. The CPA and the Basra Provincial Council therefore sought to establish a third tier of local governance, between the Provincial Council and the village level. As each middle-tier committee was formed, it was supplied with funding, although the members of the committees remained unpaid. If it spent its funding well, the pot was replenished. If the funds seemed to be squandered, then consultations followed. The local Iraqis concerned quickly got the hang of the process and proved ready to work with it.

The main weakness of the 'Basra model', for all its practical effectiveness, was that the members of the Provincial Council had essentially been selected by the Governor, albeit through a consultative process, just as the Governor had been selected by the CPA. This did not of course correspond to Western concepts of democracy, but it was not far removed from the better models of consultative rule which existed in other parts of the Arab and Islamic world.

By early November, we were receiving increasing feedback that our collective efforts seemed to be working. Governor Wa'el was responding more and more positively to our presence and contributions. But I was more heartened by what I heard from Sayyid Ali Abd al-Hakim, who was perhaps the most respected cleric in Basra, based in a historic mosque in the north of the city and actively engaged with the emerging social order. He was the local representative of Grand Ayatollah Ali al-Sistani, who was based in the holy city of Najaf, further north and outside the area for which I had responsibility.

During the first holy month of Ramadan after the fall of Saddam, which fell that year in October and November, I received an invitation to break the fast at sunset at the house of a retired Iraqi doctor who had studied and practised medicine for many years in the UK. In Ramadan, Muslims take neither food nor water between sunrise and sunset. When the sun has set, the fast is broken by an Iftar meal, which is customarily an occasion for families to join and celebrate the holy month together.

This invitation was by way of return hospitality for an Iftar party which I had given at the CPA site a week earlier. Hakim and I were named as the principal guests, although I made a point of deferring to the cleric. The meal was copious, delicious and a thoroughly agreeable occasion. Politics were not discussed and were indeed conspicuous by their absence. But after the meal, consumed in silence, when we had settled in armchairs and had praised the hospitality of our host, I enquired of Hakim what he thought of Ramadan this year.

He answered warmly and positively. It was excellent, he said. 'First, Saddam is gone. Second, we can meet together like this and not be arrested'. There were about 20 of us present, which would have been a suspiciously large assembly previously. 'Third', and Hakim pointed to our host's elaborately large and bright chandeliers in the middle of the room, 'the lights are on'. He paused. 'And fourth, we are eating bananas!'

By that time, the generators supplying Basra's electricity had been patched together and outages had become rare. And bananas, a previously prohibitively expensive luxury, were on sale cheaply at every traffic intersection.

Hakim became more expansive and went on to recount a story in a book about the previous occupation of Iraq by the British in the 1920s, which most commentators do not regard as the most enlightened period of colonial history. The Iraqi author writing at that time had maintained that the British had brought many good things to Iraq. So much so, said Hakim with a wave of his wrist, that the author believed that every troubled country should have a period of British occupation.

Of course the flattery was blatant and I did not for a moment believe that it represented Hakim's opinion. But it was also gratuitous; he had no need to be so courteous. Hakim had a personal representative on the Basra Council, as one of the three Deputy Governors, responsible for local government. He would therefore have been well informed about what was happening in the city and about our own actions. He seemed, like the Governor, to be offering us encouragement to continue to make progress over reconstruction and security.

* * *

Sayyid Ali al-Musawi, whom I had met in his mosque in my first few days in Iraq, and clerics like him played an important role in providing social leadership without engaging in politics. But others were more concerned with acquiring political power. With the passage of time a number of religious parties became key players. The best organised and funded of those in Basra was the Supreme Council for the Islamic Revolution in Iraq (SCIRI), which had been one of the leading Iraqi opposition parties in exile, with its leadership in Iran. SCIRI had an official representative in the city, Salah al-Battat, who in practice acted as leader of several other Islamic and nationalist parties which included Christian representatives. Though somewhat cool towards the Coalition in the early days, he proved to be a good and moderate politician as time went on. He demonstrated a sense of responsibility and leadership when he toured Basra's hospitals distributing gifts to casualties after Basra's first car bomb. SCIRI was widely and no doubt correctly believed to have been under Iranian influence. But it did not have deep roots among the people, many of whom considered it to be tainted by the Iranian connections it had formed in the exile years.

In late 2003, the Badr movement, which had its origins as the military wing of SCIRI but which had struggled against the Ba'athists inside Iraq, was also developing into a political movement and was commanding increasing support. Unlike SCIRI, however, it was not particularly associated with Iranian influence. And SCIRI had other competition, including that from three varieties of the Da'wah movement – the Hizb al-Da'wah, Tanzim al-Iraq and the Harakat al-Da'wah – which had stronger roots among the people than SCIRI.

Amid this mixed bag of political and religious forces were two religious groups which rejected the processes, encouraged by the CPA, which had led to the appointment of a provincial council in Basra. The Fudala, under the leadership of the fiery rabble-rouser Abu Salam, had proved able to summon up demonstrations with crowds of thousands. And supporters of Najaf-based Moqtada al-Sadr were also gaining ground. Both groups acknowledged, to a greater or lesser degree, the spiritual leadership of Ayatollah Muhammad al-Ya'qubi in Najaf. These groups were to become conspicuously more powerful over the next couple of years. But during the short period of optimism in the autumn of 2003, even the Fudala admitted to us that they accepted the fact of the existence of the Basra Council and worked within the framework which it represented. This reflected a public weariness with large futile demonstrations and a growing awareness that many of the Shia clashes with the Coalition were being manipulated by Sunni Ba'athists. This applied only to the early days before a new indigenous insurgency had developed. Later on, Fudala became a constant and painful thorn in the Coalition's side.

Of the 38 parties which had set themselves up in Basra, some 22 were secular rather than religious. They were highly diverse in their objectives and relevance. Some were little more than a front for family or tribal interests, competing with tribal unions and organisations. Apart from the Communist Party, virtually none had any recognisable political programme. The Royal Democratic Alliance, harking back to the days when the British put King Feisal on the throne in the aftermath of the First World War, improbably pestered us to bring about the restoration of the monarchy under a Jordanian Hashemite. It sought to attract support by promising jobs in the security forces, although it was in no position to deliver.

The political parties, religious and secular, were by no means the only focuses of power and influence in the South. Historically, Iraq had been a tribal society. Wilfred Thesiger's famous accounts of the Marsh Arabs evoke an age which had all but disappeared, and not just because Saddam had drained the wondrous Marshes. The role of tribes had changed significantly over the previous turbulent and war-torn decades and as a result of increasing urbanisation, especially in Basra Province. In the other three Provinces in the South – Maysan, Dhi Qar and the largely desert Al Muthanna – tribes remained quite important, although in different ways. But in the urban populations they inspired as much opposition as respect. This was partly because they were perceived as obstacles to change and progress, and partly because many were closely associated with Saddam's regime, or received salaries for cooperating in containing opposition that developed after the 1991 uprising in the South. In this way, Saddam had created a new class of tribal leaders, often dismissively referred to as the '1990s sheikhs'.

During the first few weeks after my arrival in Iraq, I received a succession of approaches from impressively robed tribal leaders. They arrived sometimes singly and sometimes in groups, and invariably claimed to command widespread support, being the natural and traditional leaders of, they said, large numbers of followers. They also made clear that their supporters were armed and that they would be ready to assist the CPA if we were to reciprocate by giving them certain privileges. The implied threat was not subtle.

To each, after I had declared that I had been honoured to receive them, I responded with no greater commitment than that I would carefully consider what they had told me. I also observed that I had met others who had spoken in similar terms. This always elicited an angry denunciation that the others were Ba'athists.

Who were we to believe? Despite Robert Wilson's unique knowledge of some of the tribes and of the leaders who had been in exile, our inability accurately to assess the realities of the complex tribal factors inevitably hindered our efforts to promote democratic processes. And the interplay between tribal dynamics and other competitors for power was often incompatible with such efforts.

*   *   *

None of the other three southern Provinces included a city of national significance like Basra. But each had its own importance, for better or for worse, and each had distinct characteristics of its own.

The westernmost Province, Al Muthanna, was largely desert and lightly populated. It possessed only one significant town, Al Samawah, which had the misfortune of being a major road intersection, and the focal point for the US supply convoys from the ports and Kuwait in the South to Baghdad and further north. Trucks thundered through it in both directions, day and night. The roads were constantly under repair, and movement by its stoical inhabitants became almost impossible. Immediately after its occupation in 2003, the Americans appointed an acting governor, whose status and personality was such that he probably commanded a good level of local consent. But his brother, whom the Americans had also appointed to take charge of day-to-day administration, proved inept and corrupt. This led to a breakdown in relations between the provincial administration and both the Coalition and the Samawah town council.

The South's first CPA provincial team leader, following Bremer's decision the previous month, arrived on 25 August and was assigned to Al Muthanna. As a test case for the new arrangements, it was not promising. The new arrival was an American who had recently joined the Foreign Service, having previously been a party political worker in one of the US states. His tour length was to be only three months. He fell under Baghdad's chain of command, reporting and responsible directly to Bremer. But Baghdad was able to provide him with no vehicle, driver, protection or communications; and he had no prior knowledge of the region or of developing countries. Remonstrations to Andy Bearpark elicited the resigned, honest, but ultimately unhelpful response that as Operations Director he realised more than anyone else the resource implications of Bremer's decision to establish the provincial teams. But he was unable to conjure support materiel out of nowhere. Its provision would take time and we would have to be patient. If those concerned found this unacceptable, they were free to leave.

The provincial teams' managerial chain of command envisaged no role for the regional teams or for the military. But we had an interest in establishing such presences on the ground. In practice, therefore, the Dutch Battle Group provided some personal protection to the team in Samawah. But competing priorities led to a fractious relationship locally which infected the CPA's dealings with local Iraqis and threatened wider interests. When, after three months, the first incumbent was replaced by a US State Department official with more experience of the developing world and of government, there was more infrastructural support for him and he was better able to fulfil his primary tasks.

As a result, it was the sterling efforts of Jim Saliero, the new CPA provincial team leader in Samawah, which caused Al Muthanna to be the first Province in Iraq which selected its Provincial Council through a secret ballot, with minimal corruption or, so far as we could tell, manipulation.

Following that experience, we and Baghdad tried to replicate Jim's methods in other Provinces, but without success. Particular local problems complicated attempts to introduce relatively simple procedures. The fact was that Al Muthanna was, and remained, the most peaceful and stable Province in the southern part of Iraq, which facilitated Coalition efforts there. Samawah's strategic importance as part of the US supply line ensured that any dissent would be instantly snuffed out.

It was for such reasons that the Japanese Government selected Al Muthanna Province for the deployment in 2004 of some 600 members of their Ground Self-Defence Force, to help with reconstruction.

* * *

The Province of Dhi Qar, to the north-west of Basra, established its Council soon after Al Muthanna. Initially the appointment of a provincial council was delayed by the ambition of a sheikh of one of the al-Nasiriyah tribes to secure the governorship for himself, when his public support was in doubt. Robert Wilson knew the Sheikh well during his exile in London, and he and I had long discussions with the Sheikh as he pressed us for our support. But Robert was wise enough not to let his long acquaintanceship cloud his judgement, and we were careful not to appear partial as the local forces played themselves out. Our caution was well founded as it soon became clear that the Sheikh's claims were mirages.

When it was eventually established, the Dhi Qar Council spent much of its time in procedural wrangling and, in the absence of firm and respected local Iraqi leadership, it proved incapable of producing tangible results. When confronted with potentially controversial issues, the Council members tended to turn to the local CPA representative, the British civil servant John Bourne, who had arrived in September, to take the decisions. John tried hard to resist this since, were he to succumb in the interests of rapid results, the Councillors would be left free to criticise the outcome without assuming any responsibility for it.

I saw this for myself at the end of October when the Council was discussing whether to expand its membership to include representatives of some recently formed political parties. It was still a long way from discussing reconstruction or management issues. Despite the presence of television cameras, the proceedings continued fruitlessly for several hours and degenerated into exchanges of insults. While such behaviour is far from unknown in 'The Mother of Parliaments' in Westminster, these early attempts to introduce democratic notions to a country which had never experienced them vividly brought home to me the difficulties which the CPA was facing nationally.

At about 10.15 in the morning of 12 November, a truck bomb was driven into the building housing Italian paramilitary police and army personnel in Nasiriyah. Twelve Carabinieri, five soldiers, two civilians and a number of Iraqis were killed. Italian newspapers described the tragedy as Italy's worst military disaster since the Second World War. While Berlusconi's government stood firm in its support for the Coalition, it was clear that the Italian body politic and public opinion would not tolerate the humanitarian cost of more casualties. Until then, Nasiriyah and Dhi Qar Province in general had been peaceful. From that moment on the Italian military contingent had to operate in a much more risk-averse manner. The psychological impact on all of us, and especially on the normally ebullient Italian members of my team, was very great, but none of them wanted to return home. I sent letters of condolence and we observed a period of silence during my weekly meeting of all our staff.

* * *

It was Maysan, to the east and bordering Iran, which was the most problematic of the southern Provinces, as it had been for Saddam Hussein and as my early encounter with Sheikh Rahim had demonstrated. Here tribal traditions and rivalries were very strong, complicated by well-entrenched criminality, including oil smuggling and a history of violent blood feuds.

Sheikh Abdul Karim al-Muhammadawi, called Abu Hatem, who claimed to have spear-headed Maysan's self-liberation, had opposed Saddam for years. He made a great impression on Bremer, who referred to him as 'The Lord of the Marshes' and appointed him a member of the Iraq Governing Council. Although this was a sensible appointment, Abu Hatem shamelessly leveraged his position to advance his personal status and authority in the region, which accentuated existing tribal rivalries.

I accompanied Bremer in September on a visit to a village called Chubaish, in the heart of the Marshes. The visual impact of helicopters with still-whirring rotors, parked beside a cathedral-like traditional *mudhif* or reed hut, could not have been more dramatic. Smiling and excited small children crowded around us. The cavalcade of international television cameramen whom Bremer had brought with him tripped over themselves for shots of the tall and elegant 'legendary warrior,' in his gold-trimmed flowing black robe, as he acknowledged the obeisance of his local tribes people.

For Bremer and the rest of us in the CPA, who took care to be conspicuously associated with all this, the objective was to demonstrate the mutually supportive relationship between the CPA and Abu Hatem's heartland. But Abu Hatem had a different, somewhat wider, agenda. He wanted CPA resources, but for political purposes which were not identical to ours. He was at pains to show us the poverty of the region, the devastating social consequences of the draining of the Marshes, the shortage of housing and the limited employment opportunities. CPA funding and wholesale regeneration, he suggested, would help alleviate all these problems; and he personally would monitor the expenditure to ensure that it was well spent.

I had my doubts about the priority to be attached to this relatively thinly populated region and indeed to Abu Hatem himself. But he was a key figure in the Governing Council whose political significance in the south of the country ensured that Baghdad tried hard to keep him sweet.

In many respects, the relationship between the local CPA staff in the Provinces and our regional base in Basra was similar to our own relationship with the CPA headquarters in Baghdad. The strong 'alpha' personalities of the intrepid volunteers who filled the Team Leader positions were constantly pressing us in Basra for financial and material resources, staff, technical advice, greater physical protection and instant approval of their project proposals. Conscious that their authority derived directly from Bremer, and unlike me they had formal letters of appointment to prove it, they initially directed their efforts towards Baghdad. The need for patience was to be Baghdad's repeated but inevitable refrain for months afterwards. Of course the Provinces did not find that acceptable and constantly pushed for more, and immediate, action.

Meanwhile, I and my larger and more diverse staff in Basra were making very similar representations to Baghdad. The provincial teams, who were too numerous for Baghdad to manage, found that their appeals produced no results at all from the main headquarters. So they turned their energy in our direction. We tended to be more successful with Baghdad because we had more bureaucratic firepower. But our results also fell well short of our needs. Just as we complained about Baghdad's deficiencies, so the Provinces complained about ours.

All these complaints were well founded. The bottom line was that, despite these inadequacies and frustrations, none of the provincial teams wanted to quit. Nor did I want them to. Instead, it fell to us and to the Army to make the best fist of whatever was available.

It was to manage these tensions that my fortnightly meetings with the provincial team leaders became essential. Over the weeks, and as the provincial teams settled into a more realistic, or fatalistic, appreciation of the collective shortcomings of our new-born bureaucracy, our discussions became more focussed and productive.

For a period of a few months, before the security climate started seriously to decline after the offensive at Fallujah in April 2004, the CPA and the military made some genuine progress in establishing workable arrangements for provincial government.

Maysan Province offered some telling examples of what was to come. The US State Department had decided to supply an Arabic-speaking diplomat, Molly Phee, to head up the CPA team there. But Molly was not able to arrive until November and her young British Deputy, Rory Stewart, literally held the fort in Amarah city until her arrival.

As I had seen for myself, the provincial council under Sheikh Rahim's leadership, known as the Supervisory Committee, was riven with internal strife and generally uncooperative with the CPA. Rory therefore established a parallel committee of technocrats, called the Regeneration Committee, which represented all the technical ministries. These officials were not accustomed to meeting collectively: they had taken direction from Baghdad rather than engage in consultation. But once sat together, with the CPA as participating observers and stimulated by the prospect of CPA funding, they proved to be both business-like and ready to accept decisions about prioritisation without insisting on the primacy of their particular interests. Many were well-trained engineers who readily grasped the importance of earmarking funding for, for instance, the repair of collapsed water channels before improvements to a power distribution line.

Rory's committee of technocrats, which got on with real activity while the Supervisory Committee squabbled, was a unique arrangement in the South and probably elsewhere in Iraq. And it was an astute one. Despite the reservations of Bremer's Governance Directorate in Baghdad that the Maysan Supervisory Committee had not been elected and was proving troublesome, it was inconceivable for the CPA to attempt to dissolve it. By presenting the new committee as purely technical, and by implying that it would be beneath the dignity of the proud Councillors to regard it as a threat to their authority, it proved possible to circumvent the procedural wrangles of the sort that were dogging progress in Nasiriyah. A more direct, confrontational approach would have greatly increased the already high level of violence directed at the Coalition presence in the Province. Neither the Supervisory Committee nor the technocratic Regeneration Committee could be said to be truly democratic by Western standards since they were not elected. But both, in their separate ways, were truly representative of the citizenry. And, just as in any democracy, they had their weaknesses: the representatives of the centres of power found it impossible to agree among themselves; the technocrats had little or no political clout. A flare-up of inter-tribal violence in mid-October illustrated the risks and was a taste of worse to come.

The leadership in Amarah was boiling with rivalries. Factions linked to next-door Iran were at odds within themselves and with other tribes in the region who were themselves competing for power and influence. The colonel of the British Battle Group, stationed outside the city, and the head of the CPA's provincial team had both recently changed over. At the instigation of the wily

Lord of the Marshes, members of an anti-Saddam militia, the Fauj, had been co-opted into the local police force, and an illiterate but effective former Fauji, Abu Rashid – a relative of Abu Hatem – had been appointed Chief of Police. Kidnappings of pro-Iranian clerics and another tribal leader followed. The other tribes were infuriated by these developments, which they unhesitatingly ascribed to the new police chief, and he was assassinated.

Maysan suddenly seemed to be on the brink of tribal war. Rory Stewart and my police adviser Stephen White negotiated with all concerned, appointed an interim police chief and, with the essential underpinning provided by the colonel of the Battle Group, a fragile order was restored.

Still in his late twenties, Rory Stewart had already packed a great deal of activity and experience into his life. After service in the Army and with the Foreign Office in Kosovo, he had taken a solitary stroll across post-Taliban Afghanistan in mid-winter. Familiar with Islamic culture and with post-conflict challenges, he was a rare combination of energy, steadiness and imaginative good sense. At Rory's suggestion, I visited Amarah a couple of days after Abu Rashid's assassination, on 29 October, when the atmosphere was still very tense.

Although it was a Friday, the holy day of the week, the city's Supervisory Committee sent a delegation to call on us at the makeshift CPA building near the Council offices, next to a picturesque bend in the Tigris. Faced with multiple accusations as to who was responsible for the murder, Rory and I had no way of knowing the truth. We brainstormed about how best to handle our visitors, three Sheikhs who were opponents of Abu Hatem. We met them in Rory's cramped office, offered them tea and locally made biscuits, and sat down to listen to what they had to tell us.

We heard a litany of complaint: about the CPA; about the Army; about the Americans and the British; about the late Abu Rashid; and about Abu Hatem. We responded to the first part of the list as best we could. But the real interest and concern of the trio of sheikhs was about the jostling between the various factions for shares of the influence and benefits which were up for grabs. It boiled down to tribal power play.

'Tell us', we asked, 'since we are new to your country, how did you resolve such differences in the past?'

'We did not have them. We were united against Saddam. If there was any trouble, Saddam's people killed those responsible – and many others also'.

'Forgive us, because we are not familiar with your customs. But was it not the case in former times that tribal leaders, sheikhs such as your good selves, would sit down together to discuss their differences according to tribal custom? In the case of death, then blood money might be paid in compensation?'

'That is true' our visitors replied.

'Then why do you not do this now? Why do you come to us?'

'Because you are the Sheikh of sheikhs. It is you who must call a meeting. Only then will the tribal leaders agree to sit together'.

Rory and I had anticipated such a request, although not the honorific. It did not stem from any urge to flatter us; no one in Amarah had ever hesitated to criticise, and often insult, the foreign occupiers. The fact was that we had armed force behind us, in the form of the Army presence a couple of miles distant. We knew that the sheikhs were refusing to acknowledge that any single one of them had the right to preside at a tribal gathering. And we had guessed, and hoped, that an external agent backed by a capability to use force, such as ourselves, might unblock the deadlock.

But it was essential that our involvement in any political process to resolve this serious dispute had to be by invitation and by consensus. Otherwise our only locus would be our ability to use force without any popular support, which would simply not be effective.

Pretending to be surprised by the idea which had been put to us, we promised to reflect upon it. We observed that, to be effective, any such meeting would have to include Abu Hatem. Our visitors agreed. We said that we would speak to him accordingly. After many concluding politenesses, we accompanied them to the gate of our small compound.

Rory had already arranged that we should see Abu Hatem soon after this meeting. He swept into the office in his traditional black and gold robe a bit later than the appointed time. We sought to impress on him that, whatever he may have thought of the failings of the other tribal leaders and the indignities which he and his tribe had to face, his senior position conferred upon him a higher duty to the nation as a whole. We were this time genuinely surprised that, after some seemingly inevitable bluster, he quite quickly accepted the procedure which we had discussed with his opponents. A tribal meeting would be convened on the Sunday, two days later.

I had to return to Basra that evening. It was readily agreed that Seyyid Rory, an Englishman who met his visitors in a bespoke suit and cufflinked shirt and looked younger than his years, would preside as representative of the Sheikh of sheikhs over an assembly of hardened tribal leaders with centuries of rivalries and blood feuds behind them.

It did not surprise me when, on the Sunday evening, Rory telephoned me to report that, despite further machinations by Abu Hatem, he had succeeded in forging a truce.

With hindsight, it seems likely that Abu Hatem had anticipated the outcome before our meeting with him and had always been ready to go along with our proposal. At that time, no-one really wanted such a tense situation to escalate further. Perhaps our actions were no more that a convenient catalyst – but we could never be sure to what extent they may have been determinant or essential.

Later, however, no amount of diplomatic subtleties could halt the steady erosion of security and trust. As violence in the city and attacks on the Coalition increased, the provincial team in their desperately insecure offices in the centre of the town had to draw back into the shelter of the Battle Group's camp. And the Battle Group became engaged in what the British Army then described as their fiercest fighting since the Korean War.

Chapter 7

Bugs and Bodyguards

AS OUR MEASURES to deal with physical security settled into a steady routine, so we focussed more on other aspects of security. We were conscious that our environment included former members of Saddam's intelligence agencies. They must have been adept at the techniques of espionage; and they might have an interest in knowing what we were up to. The US and British Governments were concerned, as they always are, that official information should not get into the wrong hands. The wide-ranging Freedom of Information Act, introduced in Britain in 2000 and the bane of bureaucrats' lives ever since, was not going to apply to our opponents in Iraq.

But in 2003 those best placed to spy on the British in Basra were neither the supporters of Saddam nor others who objected to our presence. They were our allies and fellow 'occupying power', the Americans.

I had been allocated an empty office on an outside corner of the Electricity Accounts office. On the table was a single telephone which I discovered was connected to the city's switchboard, and was therefore intermittently available for local calls to or from subscribers who were fortunate enough to have lines which still worked. It could not connect to anywhere beyond Basra.

Occasionally I received calls which turned out to be from customers of the Electricity Company enquiring about when they might expect some supply (I could not help them). If anyone wanted to tap this phone, I would not have minded at all: I simply did not use it.

In the absence of any office supplies provided by the Foreign Office or anyone else, beyond some basic stationery which my predecessor had bought downtown, I asked my team for help. I was quickly and generously supplied with an American laptop. An American technician came in to install it. Having done so, he made a rapid and almost incomprehensible announcement reminiscent of the emergency instructions delivered by aircraft cabin crew suffering from too many long-haul flights. These were official US supplies, he said. The computer network passed through official US communications systems. I would therefore be liable to prosecution if I were to use the laptop for any improper purpose.

The technician looked at me through his thick spectacle lenses as he warned gravely that there were ways of detecting any such misuse. I nodded appropriately and thanked him for his generosity in lending me the machine and for his time. As he left, he brightened up. He had had to say all that, he explained, because what was really meant was that the machine should not be used to surf porno websites. But of course, he said, I would obviously not want to do that. I wondered how he knew.

The more interesting implication, however, was that every communication I made on that laptop would pass electronically through a central hub based in the USA. Since modern technology easily allows this, every note I recorded on the word processor was capable of being read remotely by someone for whom it was not intended.

Unconcerned about this possibility, I happily set up free subscriptions to Yahoo and Hotmail for myself and sent off my first despatches to London. I also wanted to keep the British Office in Baghdad informed of my reports, but the Baghdad communications systems were incompatible with mine. So I asked London to download my Yahoo emails, all of which passed through the Washington hub, and retransmit them around Whitehall and on to Baghdad. This tedious process inevitably involved glitches and delay – computer crashes at my end were frequent and generally meant the loss of work in progress; and someone at the London end had to get round to the arrangements. Ironically, therefore, it would have been easier for Washington, had they wanted to do so, to read a private message from me to Jeremy Greenstock in Baghdad than it was for Jeremy.

I found out later that these technical difficulties had other consequences. About six months after my return, the FCO decided to conduct a 'lessons learned' exercise. Someone accordingly drew up a lengthy questionnaire, reminiscent of market research into competing brands of soap powder, which was sent to all FCO staff who had been out in the field. I and other colleagues had been surprised that no one in the FCO or elsewhere had thought it desirable to de-brief us methodically as soon as we had got back. Although it had been gratifying to receive personal praise and thanks from the Prime Minister and the Foreign Secretary, my mission had ultimately been a failure. It seemed to me that I was more concerned about this than were the policy-makers. No one had followed up the copious suggestions about lessons to be learned which I had already put forward in my reporting from on the spot. So my reaction to the questionnaire was peevish.

I responded to a nervous young man at the other end of the phone that, while I was ready and keen to encourage the learning of lessons, I would rather not fill in a standard questionnaire. I would instead prefer to debate the suggestions which I had already made. Perhaps, I suggested acidly, someone would care to dig out my telegrams and, having read them, we could start again.

A week or two later I received an email which did nothing to appease my dismay. The nature of the storage system in the FCO communications system had not allowed my reports to be retrieved. I had been aware for some time that the replacement of paper records in the FCO archive system by frequently modified electronic arrangements had caused difficulties, but I had no idea that the result was this bad. I mentioned the problem to one of the

FCO Research Analysts, who consult the archives more than most. Equally surprised, he promised to investigate. He told me later that the outcome of his enquiries had been reported to the Permanent Under-Secretary, Michael Jay. It turned out that it was not impossible to retrieve records from the system but, unless you knew the details of a specific paper, such as date, subject or some other identifier, the search process was laborious and time-consuming. For immediate operational purposes, therefore, it was all but impractical. As for my Hotmail and Yahoo reports, which I had sent in the early days before I was eventually given a more appropriate communications system, they had never entered the FCO electronic system and were lost and gone forever.

Among the many Iraqi staff who worked with us, some of them may have had other employers as well, whose interests were not as benign as our American Coalition partners. But the possibility of being spied upon by some of our own Iraqi employees never worried me. While there was a fair level of violence mainly due to criminality, there was little organised insurgency in the latter part of 2003 and therefore only a relatively small threat from organised espionage locally. To my mind, it would be a positive advantage if as many Iraqis as possible had a good knowledge of what we were trying to do, since it might lead them to understand and appreciate our efforts to help their country. They may have been aghast at our collective ineptitude and lack of readiness to undertake the responsibilities which we had assumed, but at least they would have realised that we were sincere, were trying to make the best of what we had and were doing everything possible to improve our capabilities.

This possibly cavalier approach was not shared by the US and British Governments. Their concerns about the security of information led to a bureaucratic Catch 22. Because our offices in the former Electricity Accounts building were insecure, secure communications equipment, which was itself highly sensitive, could not be installed. But I was constantly pressed for reports by London and by Baghdad; they wanted as much as they could get, and more. Since secure equipment could not be installed, we had to continue to use insecure means.

Eventually, mobile phone networks were established, initially with Kuwait and then more widely. But mobile phones brought other disadvantages. In the early days, before I had any Foreign Office support staff such as the Private Secretary and Personal Assistant who arrived later, there was no way of lining up a phone conversation in advance. Busy officials in Whitehall tended to give me a ring at the end of their day, to catch up and relay their current concerns and interests. After full programmes of meetings and other stresses, they often forgot about the difference in time zones and caught me, very tired, trying to snatch a late evening snack at the hut which served as our dining room.

To my subsequent shame, I generally responded waspishly, as if these were cold calls trying to sell me time-share holidays. I could not hear them properly; I was often in the middle of some other conversation; I might also be trying to relax; and, fundamentally, I could not give a damn about the problems of those at the other end. While they wanted information from me in order to satisfy some enquiry from some more senior official, all I was interested in from them was a positive response to the various requests which I had made. I wanted their active support, not to be bled by them. The calls started to fall away.

In the interim, a secure phone system kindly supplied by the British Army allowed me to communicate with the British Divisional headquarters at Basra Airport, some 20 miles away. I was profoundly jealous of the satellite phones which DFID had supplied to the small number of officers whom they had contracted and it constantly grated on me that the FCO had no similar capability. I suppose that I could have commandeered a set. But I was mindful of the need to maintain harmony and not throw my weight about within my own team, even if I had no hesitation about doing so outside it.

*   *   *

If security of information proved an impossible objective, physical security had the benefit of much greater resources. My personal protection team was very different from the overweight

Pakistani policeman who had nominally protected me in Islamabad. The latter's primary concern was not my safety, but to keep a tag on my activities and on whom I met so that he could report to his real masters, the notorious Inter-Services Intelligence Department. In contrast, the team of American ex-Marines assigned to me could not have been more professional and motivated. After our initial meeting on the drive from Kuwait, I came to know them well.

At first my protection team seemed not to know what to make of me. They seemed surprised that I constantly sought to engage them in conversation. It emerged that they had little experience of life outside a military environment. Any visits outside the USA before this posting were as part of previous military assignments, surrounded by their peers. If they were taken aback by what they encountered in the CPA, they were of course not alone and could be forgiven for it. The organisation, if it can be called that, was a far cry from the professionalism, discipline and expertise expected from the US Marine Corps, of which they were rightly proud. I doubted also that my protection team had ever dealt with a Brit before, and certainly not as a 'principal' whose life it was their duty to protect. Much of the banter which subsequently developed between us concerned the differences between our two languages – theirs, military American and full of clannish jargon, slang and acronyms; mine, received English pronunciation with lapses into bureaucratic qualification and impenetrability.

So far as I was concerned, however, we were all in this together. If I was under threat, then so were they; and I was the cause of the threat to them. So I was determined that we should get to know each other, especially if this led them to regard my protection as having some merit in a greater scheme of things. I could not take their respect for granted, as might have been possible had I been a high-ranking US military officer who had achieved his position within a system which they understood and valued. As was my objective with the Iraqis, anyone working in the CPA had to earn respect as a result of their own actions.

The first test came when I announced my intention to visit the main towns in the three other Provinces outside Basra. I needed quickly to acquire a feel for my patch and assess what progress was being made in establishing the CPA provincial teams there; and London and Baghdad were hungry for reporting. Nasiriyah, the principal town of Dhi Qar Province some 80 miles north west of Basra, was the closest. A good programme was arranged, to the extent that any arrangements were possible in the chaos and uncertainty which prevailed in the country. My protection team, forewarned, prepared their armoury of weapons in readiness for their first excursion outside our compound. I could hear the clunks and clicks of firearms being checked through the door of their room, opposite mine.

We started early, as the sun rose, driving on the fine wide highway which Saddam had had constructed for his military purposes. The roads were practically empty, with only an occasional pickup truck, and farm vehicles as we passed villages. Beside the road were the corpses of tanks and other burned out military vehicles, too rusty to have been the consequence of the conflict a few months earlier: they were the detritus of the war with Iran. In between naps, I saw children wave at us as we sped past. Once through Nasiriyah's outskirts, we reached the makeshift headquarters of the CPA provincial team. Still awaiting a civilian boss, they were a mixed bunch of military and civilians, muddling through as best they could. We picked up an interpreter and made our way to an appointment in the town.

As we passed a market, I asked my driver to stop. I had visited towns and cities in many different countries as part of my trade. A visit to Faizabad in Badakhshan Province in northern Afghanistan shortly before 9/11 had impressed upon me the influence of neighbouring Turkmenistan because of the range of goods on sale. Much could be learned, or intuited, from the souks. The state of economic activity could be assessed from the selection of products on sale, their price and source of origin. The well-being of the population could be judged by the appearance of the shopkeepers and their customers. Did they look healthy? Were they cheery or gloomy? How were they dressed? The quality of local government could be seen from the state of the streets and infrastructure.

For these reasons I wanted and, I judged, needed to visit Nasiriyah's market, and made my wish plain. But first I needed the concurrence of my bodyguards since, without it, I would be exposing them to a danger against their advice. I asked Pat, the team leader, explaining my objectives and making clear that these did not include tourism. Would he be prepared for me to walk around so that I could see the place for myself? He looked at the entrance of the market area: a single covered alley with shop stalls crowded with people. The only ways out were at the end, which we could not see, or back by the way we came. Pat looked down at his feet, glumly. Then he looked up and, after a pause, replied 'Yessir' and asked me to wait inside the armoured car while he discussed a plan with his team.

So we started down the souk. Two of the team walked about five paces in front, on either side of the alley, with large automatic weapons held at the high port, pistols strapped conspicuously on the thigh, their khaki jackets bulging. Two others were behind, walking crab-wise and looking to the front and rear. I went in the middle with Robert Wilson, my political guru, Ed Botterill, my Army Private Secretary, and a couple of others who had joined me on the expedition, including an Iraqi interpreter. Tom Fergusson, responsible for my close protection, towered above me, never more than three inches away. It was not quite a Greek phalanx such as Alexander might have used when he had passed through the same region, but it must have looked like it. Our two drivers, also heavily armed, remained behind with the vehicles, ready to move quickly if necessary.

The souk contained a bustling crowd of men, women and children, of all ages: shoppers, strollers, hawkers, stall-holders. Some were dressed Western style in jeans and sloganned T-shirts or short-sleeved shirts with colourful patterns. Many of the older men wore flowing robes with a keffiyeh over the head. Women generally wore the hijab, the traditional headscarf, but none had her face entirely hidden and I saw no burkas which covered the form from head to toe. Some of the women were on their own, some in small groups, some with children. This was not like the market areas of Peshawar in north-west Pakistan, where women were not to be seen on the streets. Nor was there any sign of the tasteless tourist tat which characterises so many picturesque souks in the Middle East and South Asia. The place was busy doing business. I reminded myself that, for all its deprivation, Iraq was classified in development jargon as a middle-income country. It had, or used to have, the valuable assets of oil and water – and hence agriculture – and a high level of education among its people.

As we made our way down the passage, the advance guard were spotted first and elicited a horrified reaction from the crowd. I wondered what passed through the minds of these people who had suffered so much at the hands of Saddam's security and intelligence police. Armed swoops upon citizens in the souks must have been commonplace enough in the old days. They must have hoped that things had changed now that Saddam had gone. Men and women froze at the sight of these armed foreigners and then looked around to see where they were coming from. That was my cue. Looking quite unthreatening with my pepper and salt balding head, spectacles, baggy trousers and a by-now grubby, open-necked shirt, I put on a big smile, stuck out my hand at a man nearest to me and said: 'Assalaamu aleikum, Peace be upon you'. The transformation was as instantaneous as the first reaction.

'Wa aleikum assalaam. Kaif al Haal. Peace to you. How are you?' My smile was reciprocated.

'Hamdulillah', I replied.

I felt like a politician working the crowd and realised that that was indeed what I was. I was no longer a semi-detached observer, as I had been on previous diplomatic postings, an official of a foreign government with comforting privileges and protection and no responsibilities towards the people in my host countries. Now I was this region's senior civilian representative of two occupying powers which, had usurped the law of the land and its previous systems of governance and finance.

I carried on, moving from one shop stall to another. I asked the same questions of everyone I met, trying to put them neutrally.

'How's business?' 'Is it better than it was?' 'What do you feel now that Saddam has gone?' And, most important, 'What do you want to happen now?'

I was surprised by what I saw and by the answers I received. Being painfully aware that we were so ill-prepared to fulfil the wide range of responsibilities which we had assumed, and conscious of the awesome challenges which had already revealed themselves, I had assumed that the local populations would have had a similar view. I expected a litany of complaints reflecting disappointment and even despair. In the late summer of 2003, that is not what I heard.

Business, I was told unanimously, was booming. And I could see this for myself. All sorts of goods were available: foodstuffs, pots and pans of Chinese origin, porcelain sinks from Iran, locally made pungent perfumes which were pressed upon us to sample, washing machines and refrigerators. Colourful fruit and vegetable stalls were loaded with melons, grapes, aubergines, peppers, beans and greenery, all produced in the fertile areas between the two great rivers. Money changers had piles of dollar notes and Saddam's dinars on portable trolleys, like old-fashioned ice-cream stalls.

The reason for this brisk trading was the recent, sudden transfusion of hard currency, the result of the very high initial American expenditure. Military commanders had quantities of cash at their disposal, which they used for labour-intensive small projects. And the newly formed CPA under Bremer's energetic direction was spending as much as it could and as rapidly as possible. These dollars were used particularly for labour, but also on vastly increased salaries for teachers and the stipends of former army personnel. Hence the money changers.

Iraqis, after so many years of privation, had lost any tradition of saving. They wanted to spend; and there was plenty to buy. The borders were fully open, to traders as well as to others less desirable, and goods of every description were flooding in. If they were available, and if the shoppers had the money, then they would be bought; past experience suggested that they might not be available for long.

Nasiriyah, being predominantly Shia and close to the Marshes, had been heavily oppressed by Saddam and his intelligence services. The people were glad to see him go. As to the future, the predominant impression was of optimism and very high expectations. The Americans were wealthy and had put a man on the moon. They would make everything better, and quickly. Of course there were problems now, particularly for the many people who were now out of work because their previous jobs had disappeared. If a man was out of work, his whole family suffered. It was apparent to all that those who worked for the Americans, and their dependents, were doing all right. My own impression was that their good fortune needed to be spread more widely, quickly.

The mood was encapsulated for me by an elderly gentleman dressed in smart traditional robes who I noticed had been watching me from a few yards away. I turned towards him and he approached, unconcerned by my protection team. Others moved aside and treated him with respect. We exchanged greetings and he took my proffered hand, grasping it tightly in both of his as we talked. I introduced myself as a member of the Coalition who came from Britain and who wished to help.

'You are very welcome', he said, 'this time'. He paused. 'Last time we fought you'.

There was no doubting that this polite welcome was conditional. I interpreted it as meaning that it could not be taken for granted for any length of time. It was not long before the mood changed, as I found out when I made my next visit.

Nonetheless, I was elated by this expedition. I had met many people and learned a great deal. Yes, there were problems now and many more around the corner. But it could have been worse. It was just this sort of experience, like my subsequent walk round the souk in Amarah, which had allowed me to take issue with Sheikh Rahim, the leader of Amarah's Council, when he had blustered to me that the people were starving. I could see for myself that this was simply not the case.

I was not, however, surprised when, the morning after our expedition to Nasiriyah, the leader of my protection team put his head round my office door and asked if he could see me, with his second in command. I immediately agreed and we all sank into the over-soft foam armchairs. I asked Haytham for some glasses of tea and I readied myself for a clearing of the air.

Pat and his colleague had prepared themselves and put their position calmly and sensibly. They realised, said Pat, that I needed to take soundings of ordinary people's opinions and that this meant meeting as many Iraqis as possible. But, while they had agreed to the walk in the souk the previous day, they had not realised what it would be like in practice. The market street had been narrow and crowded. They had not been able to reconnoitre it beforehand. Had there been an incident, any use of weaponry would have had dreadful consequences. The sheer volume of people made it impossible to leave quickly. There was no difficulty, said Pat, about having Iraqis come to meet me in our headquarters in the Electricity Accounts building, because they could be checked out for hidden weapons using discreet electronic means. In public places, however, such precautions were impossible.

But what made it most difficult for Pat and his team was that they had clear instructions about the manner in which they should carry out their duties. Their bosses in the NCIS back home in the USA had required them to be conspicuous and aggressive, with a view to deterring and warding off any potential assailant. They had indeed been conspicuous in the souk, but my objectives on that occasion ruled out any aggression intended to keep others at their distance. Instead, they said, I was actually encouraging people to come and talk to me. They therefore felt it necessary to talk it all over with me to see what should be done.

I heard Pat out without interruption. I regarded him as a very experienced, true professional, and he had made his points courteously and sympathetically. Equally, however, although we were both new to Iraq, he had no experience at all of developing countries, or of Islamic customs. Furthermore, my protection team's terms of reference, to be conspicuous and aggressive, came as a complete surprise to me. I had not been consulted about them beforehand or even told that I was to be provided with any special protection from any source; no one in London had any idea about such modalities at that stage. Nor had I thought to raise the question. But I was clear that I simply could not do my necessary work with any such threatening accompaniment. And, from what I had already seen and heard of the situation, I did not believe such precautions to be necessary. A balance always has to be drawn between security and the ability to do one's job: too much of one negates the other. Since we were operating within a crisis, the effects of which could only be reduced by making a rapid political and physical impact on the ground, the balance had to be in favour of the job. This was not a matter of finding a middle way.

I was one of the very few members of the Coalition team in the South with any prior experience of developing countries and of the Islamic world, and I carried responsibilities for reporting, for judgements and for policy-making. I had to be able to exercise my political antennae. That meant moving about and seeing things for myself. I could not accept a cocooned regime of personal protection. Less heroically, however, I reckoned that Arab traditions of courtesy and hospitality would come into play. As an obvious civilian who carried no weapons and who made no threats, there was no reason for any aggression against me or my party unless our opponents had staked the place out beforehand. There was another more practical factor as well. An approach such as the NCIS headquarters had in mind would in practice have increased the risk for all of us. No amount of 'aggressive, high profile' activity could wish away the traffic jams of Basra, in which we frequently found ourselves stuck. Rather, it would simply cause offence to anyone we encountered. Foreigners' bullying tactics would invite resentment and reprisal.

I did not put my position quite so starkly but explained the background to my thinking in the knowledge that what I said would be reported back to the USA, 7000 miles away. Far from being conspicuous and aggressive, I explained, I needed my protection to be discreet and conciliatory. The requirement was openness and friendliness, with smiles and greetings. It would therefore be best if Pat's team could dress in such a way that their weaponry was covered, with no sunglasses over the eyes, and with conventional civilian clothes rather than paramilitary khakis. Similarly, it would be good if we could drive around town at only a moderate speed. Aggressive arm signals with weapons showing outside windows and screech turns simply drew attention to ourselves. High-speed driving just made us arrive at the next traffic jam more quickly. It would, however, be essential, I emphasised, that the team itself should be content with any such arrangements. Their lives would be on the line, perhaps more so than mine since, being unarmed, I presented no direct threat to anyone. I would therefore be grateful if they would consult their senior officers and establish whether such changes of procedure would be agreeable to all concerned. It would be good if their views could be made known within a day or two. Meanwhile, I would not go into another souk until I heard back from them.

Within 24 hours, Pat gave me NCIS's positive response. They had agreed. I imagined someone wearily saying: 'Oh well, he's the boss. And he's not one of ours. So what the hell'.

Pat added that, having seen for themselves that the place was not exactly a war zone, his team were entirely content with the procedure which I had outlined. This judgement must in practice have weighed heavily with the NCIS headquarters, and I was glad that Pat and his team were such sensible and experienced professionals, able to respond to unfamiliar situations. I detected no sign of doubt among them.

Pat's team loosened up a great deal after this and even explained to me that their previously monosyllabic responses to my attempts at conversation had been because their procedures absolutely forbade any talk with a principal; anyway, in their experience, principals never wanted to talk to them. Perhaps that was a sound procedure, since personal remoteness between the protectors and the protected may help reduce the psychological impact of a misadventure. But perhaps other principals had not had to travel for many hours over featureless desert where every occurrence was an occasion of interest and discussion. Silence and formality would have greatly reduced the fun and chuckles.

After his three-month tour of duty had ended and knowing me to be a dog lover, Tom sent me an email. He had acquired a bulldog puppy and wanted my permission to call it 'Sir Hilary'. An attached photograph revealed a tiny, wrinkly beast which sat comfortably inside Tom Fergusson's massive hand. Was that how I was regarded? Potentially aggressive, but essentially harmless?

Chapter 8

A Tower of Babel?

The Challenges and Delights of Multinational Operations

'Go to, let us go down, and there confound their language, that they may not understand one another's speech.

So the Lord scattered them abroad from thence upon the face of all the earth: and they left off to build the city'.

Genesis 11: 7-8.

THE ZIGGURAT AT UR, near the city of Nasiriyah in Dhi Qar Province, was once believed to have been a stairway for the gods to descend to earth, a Tower of Babel such as is described in Genesis. This narrative reports that those who constructed it were thrown into confusion by a divine intervention which caused them to speak in different tongues.

When I arrived in Basra I found that the front line CPA team there was made up of 11 different nationalities. By the time I left, when the organisation had moved to a much larger site and we had gathered recruits from wherever we could find them, the number of nationalities associated with us, including our support staff, had risen to 22.

Although numerous, we were much smaller than the CPA population in the Green Zone in Baghdad. But we were far more diverse since Baghdad was overwhelmingly dominated by Americans, of whom there were very few in Basra. I had no wish for any additional confusion arising out of our different languages and customs; we had enough of our own already. So we had to ensure that our diversity did not cause friction. We were sufficiently compact that we could get to know each other and, if all went well, bond as a single team. This would require tolerance and patience within an environment which was highly stressed. Some attempt to create corporate activities might help, provided they were not too patently artificial.

As an antidote to stress, however, there were always sufficient absurdities arising to inject humour into even the tensest situation. Since tears were out of the question, laughter was the only alternative. And, despite our diversity, we had in common a powerful bonding agent: the urge to attract Baghdad's attention and resources. If ever we felt out of sorts, we could indulge ourselves by blaming Baghdad or others whom we presumed could not possibly understand what we were trying to do. This tempting tendency needed to be kept within limits, but could be very useful in the short term. And it was easily assuaged on those occasions when a head of section arrived off a plane from Baghdad with a suitcase full of dollars.

English was inevitably the working language in Basra, although native English speakers were seldom if ever in the majority. The highly effective Japanese civilian contingent were required by their government to pull out in August after the increased tension following the bombing of the UN headquarters in Baghdad. The dozen or so Japanese were a tight-knit community who lived together in a single, largish room in the Electricity Accounts building. The primitive food which was initially available to us, comprising grits for breakfast, burgers or hot dogs for main courses and alarmingly coloured Jell-o for a sugar rush, was understandably not to Japanese taste. On passing the closed door of their dormitory, we could savour the aroma of assumedly succulent Far Eastern dishes. Within this same room, the group brainstormed their way through the challenges which fell to their lot to pursue. The single English-speaker who led the team customarily presented the evening debriefing to my predecessor. His contribution on the first evening of my arrival was unfortunately incomprehensible. But it soon became clear to me that the work which they were undertaking was of immense value.

It was the Japanese who first established links with those managers of the power generation and distribution authorities who remained after the de-Ba'athification process. Their plans of the power networks, which they drew up as a result of these contacts, proved invaluable to their successors in the CPA and to the Army Engineers who initiated our joint Emergency Infrastructure Plan. One of the main power generation plants at Hartha, on the outskirts of Basra, had originally been designed and built by the Japanese. When it caught fire in early September as a result of decades of insufficient maintenance, the Japanese groundwork helped accelerate its repair.

Having seen the results of such concentrated Japanese effort, I was delighted when I received a visit in mid-September from the Special Adviser to Prime Minister Koizumi, Yukio Okamoto. He was accompanied by Katsuhiko Oku from the Japanese Foreign Ministry. Oku and I had become good friends five years earlier when we had both spent months negotiating the conclusions of the Asia–Europe Heads of Government meeting which took place in London in 1998.

Okamoto told me that he had greatly regretted the decision the previous month to withdraw the Japanese team just because the security situation had deteriorated. He now had $1.5 billion to spend on development projects. Bremer had been told that this would be available to be used throughout Iraq. But having toured the country and seen that the US Army dominated the civilian activities in the other regions, and for other reasons, Okamoto said that he would prefer to have a good proportion of these funds spent in the South.

I was naturally delighted to hear this. I knew that we could put such funding to good use and that we could identify projects which would suit Japanese priorities. The refurbishment and re-stocking of all the hospitals would be a good start. I was also pleased because, since Okamoto had done his homework, his offer suggested that he had been impressed by our operation in the South. I knew also that Bremer was seeking a massive new injection of funds from Congress. But if the Japanese were to concentrate their resources in our area, we could help ensure that it fitted into our strategic priorities rather than as part of a wider Baghdad-based strategy within which we sometimes sat oddly.

Okamoto was not a young man but was entirely sanguine at finding himself billeted in a sleeping bag on a tiled floor with no mattress: our building was full to capacity and there was no other space.

Okamoto and Oku visited us several times, discussing the overall situation with me and then getting down to details with our sectoral specialists. The main Japanese interests lay in health and water supply, both of which sectors were in desperate need of large injections of funds. We also encouraged them to show some rapid and visible results in the short term, such as the supply of special trucks which used high-pressure water to unblock drains and which could easily be delivered through nearby Kuwait.

Okamoto followed up their visits quickly. In mid-October, I learned that the Japanese Government had decided to put $1 billion into a Trust Fund for Iraq which was to be considered at a Donors' Conference in Madrid later that month. But, conscious that the Trust Fund might not deliver rapid action, they wanted to devote $500 million to projects in the South, making use of British technical inputs and military support.

Of course I jumped at this attractive prospect and worked up the details. When Bremer, following up the original Japanese approach to him, called for proposals from each of the four Regions, he may have been surprised the bid from the South hit his desk very rapidly; and that it covered the entire total of $1.5 billion.

On 29 November 2003, Katsuhiko Oku was shot dead in the Tikrit region of Iraq, Saddam Hussein's heartland, when his car stopped for a break in its journey. He was aged 45. The news came as a personal blow to me. He was a remarkable man. A flawless English speaker, he had gained a Blue in rugby when at Oxford University, the first Japanese national to gain such a distinction. As well as being a good friend, he was a vigorous man of action who had been fearless in travelling the country in search of reconstruction and development projects. He had showed confidence in us and I knew that he was a man to deliver results.

The news also shook Japan, where he was widely mourned and rightly revered as a hero. The Japanese Government promoted him to the rank of Ambassador posthumously. With his departure, the Japanese aid effort tailed off until the arrival of a contingent of the Japanese National Defence Force in Al Muthanna Province. Despite their difficulties, the Japanese stuck to their preference for operating in the British area of operations.

For some time, until the British Government succeeded in recruiting more experts, the Danes had more civilians in Basra than any other single country. The role of the Danish police officers under Kai Vitrupp's leadership is described in Chapter 10. Danish Foreign Ministry officials visited us frequently – more so in the early days than British officials. One of them confided in me that their computations had arrived at the conclusion that 'little Denmark' was providing a greater contribution in proportion to GNP even than the UK, one of the two designated 'occupying powers'. I saw no reason to doubt this.

My predecessor, Ambassador Olsen, had appointed as his Chief of Staff another Dane who was seconded from Maersk shipping company and whose knowledge of shipping and ports was invaluable, since the South contained all of Iraq's once-copious port facilities. I continued with this arrangement until I decided that it would be expedient to appoint an American, Colonel Peter Duklis, into the Chief of Staff position, to maximise leverage with the Americans in Baghdad.

The Danish contribution to agriculture, in the form of Ole Stockholm Jepson, proved to be beyond price. His lean, deeply lined face with a grey goatee beard bore witness to decades of experience in agriculture in the developing world, while his personality and intellect remained sprightly and inventive. Here was another example of someone whose unique expertise could have been put to wider use had the CPA's management structures allowed for it. Certainly, the CPA's chief of what was left of Baghdad's Agriculture Ministry, Trevor Flugge, a domineering Australian with close links to the Australian Wheat Board, was no match for Ole's firm but gentle confidence in his field.

All the Danish volunteers attached to us at Basra seemed to share a humorous steadiness. At the end of a hot and often frustrating day's work, I often found that I unconsciously gravitated towards a group of Danes sitting around a makeshift table on cheap plastic chairs. As they puffed on small aromatic cigars or less aromatic pipes with cans of Carlsberg beside them, they mused on our situation with philosophical chuckles. It was on such an occasion that I discreetly enquired of Ole's age, hoping I would not be the oldest in CPA(South). He turned out to be six months younger than me.

If my mobile phone broke the relative peace of such an occasion with some frenetic request from London for 'metrics', I tended to bring up to date Nelson's technique of looking at signals with his blind eye: I claimed that the telephone signal was too weak to be audible.

The Italian contingent presented no problems about audibility. Their presence, like the Danes', also reflected their Government's, and particularly Berlusconi's, political commitment to the Coalition. A distinguished former diplomat, Mario Maiolini, who had been Italian Ambassador to Saudi Arabia among other places, had arrived just before me. Although very senior in rank, he never betrayed any discomfort at my appointment and was always morally supportive and a wise source of advice. His connections with the ministries in Rome proved invaluable in recruiting other Italian Government officials to join us in Basra.

Our original home, the Electricity Accounts building, had quickly become too small for our needs, especially when we had been supplemented by platoons of private security contractors. But when we moved location in mid-October, I was delighted to discover that Mario had managed to fly in a large group of newcomers, eager to get started, at the precise moment that we could accommodate them at our new location in the compound of one of Saddam's palaces.

One of the first to arrive had been delivered to the wrong building by mistake, just as our final batch of people were leaving for the new place. Barbara Contini, larger than life, with a devastating smile and knowing no one, grabbed me by the arm and asked how she should get to the new office. I told her to jump into my car as, like the captain of a sinking ship, I was the last to leave for the comparative luxury of our new camp.

Barbara had long experience with non-governmental organisations and had been in Iraq for some time. She was a natural second in command to Ambassador Maiolini and, although not a government official like most of the other Italians, seemed to slip into the role by tacit consent all round. But that evening, after we had had time to unpack and as the sun was setting, I was astonished to discover Barbara leading an ebullient team of merry Italians back into the compound having taken them on a shopping trip around town. It was only when I enquired whether they were aware that such jaunts had been strictly forbidden on security grounds for the previous two months that Barbara realised that the man whose arm she had grabbed that morning was 'the Boss' of the place.

Later on, in early 2004, Barbara was transferred to lead the CPA provincial team in Dhi Qar Province. I had earlier visited the Italian Battle Group there and was interested to see that cartons containing Italian wine were freely on hand to accompany their meals. A British officer with me observed that such an arrangement would never have been practicable with our troops.

The Italians did not, like the Japanese and the Danes, supply a coherent team specialising in a particular sector such as electricity or policing. Instead, they were generally quite senior officials from several sectors of government and included a surgeon and specialists in local government, trade and industry, and so on. With some guidance from those who had been longer in Basra, they quickly put their expertise to good use.

The original version of *The Italian Job*, with Michael Caine, was filmed largely in Turin. A group of us were watching it after lunch on Christmas Day when we heard a piercing scream. A diminutive Italian lady, whose changing hair colour had surprised us every ten days, had recognised both her office and her apartment block as Caine's troupe of Minis sped round the city. The film was punctuated by nostalgic cries of 'There it is again! There it is!'

Perhaps because we wanted to escape from that reminder of reality, or perhaps because we felt besieged, we went on to watch Zulu. Much better. That evening, almost as surreal, Robert Wilson regaled us with a fanfare played on a bicycle pump.

* * *

As our numbers swelled, the largest national components of the front-line specialists came from Britain, Denmark, Italy and, to a lesser extent, the USA. But there were others from Australia, Norway, the Czech Republic, the Irish Republic, Serbia and Germany. Some of these reflected their respective governments' wish to contribute tangibly to the Coalition's activities. Others were recruited from the UK in response to my early call for technical reinforcement. All were volunteers. Despite the varied mother tongues and cultures, the shared challenge pulled us all together. Although many, hardly surprisingly, had never had such an experience before, they almost without exception found a specialist niche somewhere and managed to make a contribution. In only one or two cases were contracts not renewed or was it suggested that they did not come back from leave.

My lasting regret was that we did not have more such specialists at the outset. When it became clear to me, very early on, that I would get no extra personnel from Baghdad or the USA, who were having enough difficulties finding civilians for their own sectors, I took the precaution of formally clearing my lines with the Director of Operations in Baghdad, Andy Bearpark. At the end of September, during one of the Regional Coordinators' meetings in Baghdad, he concurred that we no longer needed to be guided by Baghdad's Joint Manning Document, which had been drawn up in very different circumstances a couple of months before. This agreement ensured that the USA would continue to supply and fund all the 'Life Support' infrastructure which might be necessary – a task which KBR proved only too happy to fulfil since, as I discovered subsequently, they operated on a 'costs plus' basis and therefore could be certain of yet greater profit. As a result I felt free to try to recruit talent from wherever I could. My hopes that the British Government would be a sufficient source were sadly disappointed, but I pressed visiting Ministers from other countries too.

While I was careful to make a note of Baghdad's agreement to my plan at the time, I regretted that I did not get it in writing: not that any such practice was practicable in such an infant bureaucracy. By January, Baghdad was swarming with accountants from Washington, attracted by the buzz of stories about financial short-cuts and worse. Some of these flew down to Basra and, having no responsibility for the success of the Coalition's endeavours, were horrified to discover that our complement greatly exceeded the irrelevant original Joint Manning Document, which no one had ever got round to amending. I thought it best to ignore this fuss. This was easily done because, after the decision to wind up the CPA prematurely by the end of June, attention in Baghdad shifted towards this prospect. As far as we were concerned, however, our team of specialists could still do a lot before they all had to be sent home.

The number of nationalities was greatly increased by our support personnel, including numerous ex-soldiers from several private security companies. The Gurkha platoon, who guarded the gates and perimeter fencing, were replaced in October by Fijians. It transpired that many of the Gurkhas, despite the impression conveyed by the private contracting company who deployed them, had not previously served in Gurkha regiments of the British Army, but included ordinary Nepalis who were clearly elderly, unfit and more accustomed to the relatively care-free tasks of guarding embassies. The Fijians, in contrast, seemed to have been recruited from their international rugby team. It was doubtful that many Iraqis were aware of the well-founded legends of the dangers of the Gurkha kukri. But they could see for themselves that they would do well not to tangle with a giant Fijian.

The KBR support personnel included many colourful Americans, familiar with hard living and attracted by the high levels of pay on offer. Collectively, they could supply almost anything, provided only that it originated from the USA and could be transported by lorries in convoy from Kuwait. When I asked why we never enjoyed any Iraqi foodstuff, such as the fruit which was available in every market, I was told that this was a decision of senior management: it might be poisoned. As a result, the fine-looking, glossy red apples which decorated our self-service food counters were left untouched. After months of cold storage on their journey from Oregon or somewhere, they tasted of cotton wool.

In the first few months the British sometimes muttered about the unvaried diet of burgers, hot dogs and Jell-o. Sensitive to our needs, KBR recruited a British chef. Soon after his arrival, on discovering an unaccustomed substance on offer, Americans and British were asking each other whether this novelty was a speciality of the other's country; but it was the new chef's version of Cottage Pie. Several decades earlier he had been a cook in the British Army, well before the Army's long-overdue catering reforms.

Health and nutrition surged forward with the arrival of cooks and kitchen staff from the Indian sub-continent – India, Pakistan and Bangladesh. What is known as Indian food in Britain is often prepared by cooks originating from the town of Sylhet in Bangladesh, which has produced lines of cooks for generations. They even extended to Iraq. After I had initiated some conversations in Hindi, my plates were overfilled and my diminished waistline started to return to normal.

'Kya haal hain, Sahib? Saab thiik hai?' 'How are you, Sahib? Is everything all right?' greeted me each time I entered the mess hall.

The Dutch Army formed an important part of Graeme Lamb's MND(SE). I visited their camp outside the dusty desert city of

Samawah, in the western Province of Al Muthanna. I was impressed by their commanding officer from the Dutch Marine corps and by the state of readiness of his units. Like some other military contingents, however, the Dutch operated under some constraints resulting from national political considerations, called 'national caveats'. These amounted to a total restriction on any involvement in quasi-political processes in Iraq: for the Dutch, political activity was to be left to the Iraqis, no matter how the other Coalition partners saw their role.

This gave rise to a rather sharp encounter between me and a Dutch Cabinet Minister who visited the Basra military headquarters in mid-September. As requested, I had made a lengthy journey to brief the Dutch press and, separately, the Minister about our activities in the civilian domain, which did not include any Dutch civilians. In return I was given a school-masterly lecture about Dutch political attitudes, at the end of which I was instructed to make clear to the Iraqis in Basra that the Netherlands would not become involved in governance matters.

I responded tartly that I could personally assure the Minister that the Iraqis 'would not give a damn' about Dutch sensitivities; they just wanted to see progress on the ground. But if the Minister wished us to publicise the limitations of Dutch engagement in assisting Iraq, we would of course be ready to oblige him. The Minister switched to conciliatory mode and the instruction was dropped.

In early November the Prime Minister of New Zealand, Helen Clark, dropped in to my office by helicopter, having visited her country's military contingent further east. Although it was a bright sunny day, the helicopter trip had evidently chilled her and she kept a parka on throughout our discussion. We then flew together to the air-conditioned Army headquarters which chilled her yet more, so she curled up for warmth during a lengthy PowerPoint military briefing. Apart from the political processes in Iraq, with which she drew somewhat tenuous comparisons with tiny East Timor, the Prime Minister expressed an interest in involvement in agricultural projects. I encouraged this enthusiastically, and I was later glad to help publicise the New Zealand Army's role in installing a water purification plant on the outskirts of Basra. I still treasure photographs of cheery New Zealand soldiers and delighted Iraqis watching me as I downed a glass of the first product, while trying to hide my apprehension in case the purification had been less than effective.

Chapter 9

Civvies and Soldiers:

A 'Ticket out'?

Every man thinks meanly of himself for not having been a soldier ... .
James Boswell, *Life of Johnson* .

HAVING FOUGHT IN the post-9/11 campaign in Afghanistan and in combat operations in Iraq in March and April 2003, the British Army were fully stretched. These duties had followed on from others in Sierra Leone, in Kosovo and in Bosnia. By the summer of 2003, many of the officers serving in Iraq looked upon the civilians, whom they thought should take over from them, as their 'ticket out'. The receding prospect of this became a cause of irritation and resentment.

The differences between the civilian and military arms of government in terms of human and financial resources and command and management structures are obvious to all. That there are also social, cultural, customary and hierarchical distinctions becomes more apparent when the two institutions encounter each other. The differences between respective approaches can be quite subtle and may be clouded by prejudice and preconceptions on all sides. At best, mutual recognition of different skill sets and abilities leads to profound respect, and fosters constructive cooperation which is more effective than the sum of their parts. At worst, misunderstanding or animosity can give rise to hostility, isolationism and obstructionism.

There are also, of course, deep cultural and historical differences between each arm of the services and within them. The Royal Navy has its stock of stories about the Army and the Royal Air Force and vice versa. These poke gentle or not-so-gentle fun at the others, or show them in a poor light. There is rivalry between 'big ships' and 'small ships', between fighter and transport wings, between the cavalry and the guards.

Such characteristics are common to any large and disparate organisation. But the differences are more accentuated in the case of the armed forces as a result of their rich traditions and the development of particular narratives intended to develop the martial spirit. Within individual fighting units, comradeship in combat is literally vital; it is therefore fostered by special means, which include the creation of distinctions from other units. It would be invidious for me, an outsider, to analyse these intra-service differences. But, as a most basic illustration, one can observe from the wide variety of ceremonial and formal evening wear that the concept of Army uniform, as a mode of dress, is a complete misnomer. Military customs sometimes spread into civilian life: a sharp eye may often be able to identify the provenance of certain officers even when in mufti.

If these differences and the subtle distinctions that accompany them are noticeable within the British armed forces, they are even more significant between the US and the British Armies. In his article *Changing the Army for Counterinsurgency Operations*, which caught the attention of the US publication *The Military Review* in 2005, Brigadier Nigel Aylwin-Foster has thoughtfully described how the differences between the American and British cultures and resource bases have their reflections in operations, in planning and in relationships within their respective hierarchies.

The differences of approach within the British civilian administration are much less marked than those within military organisations. They generally merely reflect the different roles and corporate objectives of the department to which an official is affiliated, rather than the vivid perspectives of history and achievements of the regiment or military arm.

There is nonetheless a different ethos and manner of working between the three British Civil Service Departments of State which are actively engaged in foreign affairs: DFID, the FCO, and the Ministry of Defence (MOD).

Each of these three ministries was deeply involved, either directly or indirectly, in southern Iraq. In addition, the Cabinet Office, under the operational direction at official level of the Prime Minister's Diplomatic Adviser, had a role in coordinating the efforts of the government as a whole, including of these three executive ministries, and in ensuring that there were sufficient means to fulfil the task. Other departments were involved in this process, to a greater or lesser extent, including the intelligence agencies, the Departments of Health and of Trade and Industry, the Law Officers, the Home Office and so on.

When officials from these ministries were deployed on the ground in Iraq, the cultural and practical baggage associated with the parent departments generally dissolved in the face of the new common challenge of living and operating in the highly peculiar new environment. As is often the case within small communities when under stress, a solidarity and strong sense of comradeship emerged spontaneously, undiluted by the fact that most individuals had never met each other before. Less positively, this solidarity in adversity was accentuated in practice by a shared disappointment at the perceived failure of parent departments to respond and adapt to such an unusual situation and to deliver what those on the ground considered was needed.

The FCO had no significant deployable capital to spend on equipment beyond some small project funding. Its main resources are the 5900 specialist personnel posted in several hundred different diplomatic posts in most countries of the world and in the UK headquarters offices. Its aim, 'To work for UK interests in a safe, just and prosperous world', is immensely wide-ranging. Because of the steep rise in global travel and the pressures for immigration, it is increasingly engaged in consular and visa activities and other aspects of service delivery. However, its particular comparative advantage lies in political analysis, languages, policy advice and the exercise of influence.

Few diplomatic staff have experience of project management, and certainly not on the scale which was involved in the stabilisation and reconstruction of Iraq. The FCO presents few opportunities to exercise management, still less proactive leadership, of sizeable bodies of personnel. The head of even the largest diplomatic missions has overall authority over little more than a hundred British Crown Servants and budgets of a few millions of pounds. The FCO Diplomatic Vote, or budget, at the time of the invasion of Iraq was £869 million, and spending was set to be constant in real terms over the previous year.

In the same year British public expenditure on development, administered by DFID, amounted to £4.9 billion. The trend has been steeply rising: one to two years later the figure grew to £6.6 billion. These resources are focussed on the poorest developing countries in the context of a core objective of the elimination of poverty. In contrast with the FCO, DFID does not seek to use its resources to exercise political influence in support of wider British interests. Its primary task is development cooperation, which is generally very different from state-building or reconstruction, although they are not incompatible with each other. However, it also has some capability in crisis management and the provision of humanitarian aid.

In executing its practical functions, DFID employs large numbers of consultants and contracted staff. These are experts in their field, but seldom have the skills necessary to wield influence and secure results within the wider British political and governmental machine. This role falls to senior officials from DFID's permanent staff of civil servants, who are informed by a significant network of overseas offices.

With an annual budget of some £30 billion, the MOD's human, capital and financial resources, in the form of its officials and the armed services, are far greater than those of the other two departments. Its key values – to defend the UK and its interests and strengthen international peace and stability – are not as wide as those of the FCO. But they are closer and more complementary to the FCO's broad aim to 'work for British interests' than to DFID's strategic aim of halving world poverty by 2015.

Within the MOD, civilian officials work closely with the Army; and at some levels staff are interchangeable. But there is an inherent potential tension between those who see their role as fulfilling 'The Commander's Intent', which is essentially a fixed concept at any one time, and those who have a role in advising political figures, the ultimate Commanders, what their Intent should be. When, as was the case in many aspects of post-conflict operations in Iraq, the Intent from the body politic is by no means clear, then tensions can be strong.

Relations between these three Departments of State reflect the differences and complementarities between their skills, objectives and resources. And relations can be affected, for better or for worse, by the nature of the leadership and example shown by their presiding Ministers, each of whom is of Cabinet rank.

Relations between DFID on the one hand and the FCO and MOD on the other were particularly strained when Clare Short was Development Secretary, to the extent that Short and the late Robin Cook at the FCO were barely on speaking terms. Successive Conservative administrations had adopted a practice of subsuming development issues within the overall structure of the FCO: a Minister of State running the Overseas Development Administration was answerable to the Foreign Secretary, who had Cabinet rank. Successive Labour administrations, both before and after the 18 years of Conservative government between 1979 and 1997, separated the two roles. The exhilaration on the part of the new DFID on their release from the FCO's shackles in 1997 was palpable.

The civilian administrators within the respective departments are usually able to work pragmatically through the tensions, but sometimes they cannot. Ultimately, since a Cabinet Minister has considerable autonomy to direct and deploy the resources of his or her Department, it was and is not unknown for Departments to work at cross purposes unless actively managed by the Prime Minister or, at official level, by the Cabinet Office.

Such differences, of practice, attitude and approach, directly affected the aftermath of the military campaign in Iraq. True to their traditions and their stated objectives, the MOD and the Army started to prepare for the possibility of conflict, on a contingency basis, at a fairly early stage, since British and American political leaders were discussing and making public announcements about just such a possibility. But, although well ahead of the other ministries, even the military planning included omissions and confusion.

The original expectation was that the British Army would be deployed as part of the thrust into Iraq from the north, through Turkey. But Turkey's refusal to become a party to a northern operation required a new role for the British at short notice. British forces were therefore switched to join the main American offensive into Iraq from Kuwait, in the South. These changes inevitably caused military planners to concentrate more on combat rather than on post-conflict operations. And, taking the lead from the US expectation that the main post-conflict challenge would be humanitarian relief, it was this aspect, rather than the administration of a failed state, which was the area of main attention.

The FCO were even less engaged in post-conflict planning. They were apparently no better aware than anyone else of the likely consequences of the removal of Saddam's control of the state. In addition, however, the FCO was not adequately resourced to conduct major planning exercises. The section within the FCO's Middle East Directorate which dealt with Iraq, and which had the lead responsibility for such a task, was also responsible for briefing and providing day-to-day tactical advice to Ministers. And in the lead up to the conflict, Ministers were deeply engaged in active negotiations – in the UN, within the European Union, bilaterally, especially with the Americans, and in Cabinet. Officials' service to Ministers took priority. In 2003, the most senior official with specific responsibilities for Iraq, above the level of head of FCO Department, also had to pursue important other responsibilities concurrently. No single senior official was designated to oversee and manage the consequences of unfolding events in their entirety until the late summer of 2003, when the task was specifically devolved to the Prime Minister's Foreign Policy Adviser, who had recently been appointed.

There may also have been a tendency within the FCO to believe, or hope, that since the American administration had been contemplating the possibility of action against Saddam for some years, they would themselves have made adequate preparations for dealing with the consequences of their actions: US resources were infinitely greater than the UK's. There was also certainly an expectation that the UN would take on a major operational role after any conflict, which proved unfounded. The FCO did, however, try to keep in touch with military thinking by attending the regular, high-level MOD meetings which discussed such matters.

DFID leadership took a different approach. Far from being over-stretched or focussed on some other target, Clare Short was publicly and vehemently opposed to the UK engaging in a conflict in Iraq at all. Although still a member of the Cabinet, she believed that the Government's energies should be directed at ensuring that it did not take place. She wished to resist any implication that the British Government might have accepted the possibility that it would.

As was well known to officials and journalists at the time, consistent with such a rejection of any inevitability of conflict, DFID undertook little or no planning for possible post-conflict humanitarian or reconstruction work. And yet it would be DFID which would be expected to take a lead within the UK on the civilian aspects of development, humanitarian aid and disaster relief. Short finally resigned from the Cabinet in May 2003, five weeks after the fall of Baghdad to Coalition forces. After she had been replaced by Baroness Amos and subsequently Hilary Benn, DFID's role changed: they started to focus on the problem and to become actively constructive. But the loss of time and of initiative was irretrievable. DFID's reputation with other Departments, and especially the military, whose contempt was seldom disguised, was severely damaged.

This loss was compounded by the fact that, despite the UK's position as one of the two 'occupying powers' in Iraq, the British Government had not expected to assume a leading role in the civilian domain on similar lines to that assumed by the Army, namely to oversee the Coalition's effort in the four southern Provinces. That role had originally fallen to my Danish predecessor, Ambassador Ole Olsen, and only became a British lead upon his departure in July 2003, when I was appointed to replace him.

With such an unpromising background, it was hardly surprising that by the mid-summer of 2003 the civil-military differences in southern Iraq had become both visible and audible. On the military side, a roulement had occurred within MND(SE). The major component of this international military force, the 1st (UK) Armoured Division, had fought in the main combat. At the end of its tour of duty it was replaced by the 3rd (UK) Division, with a new General Officer commanding and military staff.

The battle over, it was reasonable for soldiers to consider that the primary post-conflict role should fall to civilians, who were supposed to be the experts in politics, governance and reconstruction. But the civilian side of the CPA in the South was barely visible to the Army or to Baghdad. Although by July some staff had arrived, they had to spend much of their energy in establishing themselves and simply surviving. The biggest single national components, with some 13 staff each, were Danes and Italians, who initially outnumbered the small number of British civilians. They had none of the support, quartermaster's staffs and equipment which came with army units. For some time they relied on the Army even for their food and lived on a diet of Meals Ready to Eat (MRE) – high-calorie, expedition ration packs – with unwelcome consequences for their digestions. Nonetheless, many had quickly infiltrated the regional offices – the Directorates – of Baghdad ministries and had started to find their way round and develop valuable contracts with Iraqi counterparts.

Little of this substantive activity was visible to the military. At the senior level there was scant inter-communication, perhaps because the leadership of CPA(South) expected to deal primarily with Baghdad. There were problems here too: Bremer's able and helpful Chief of Staff told me, when I called on first arrival, that he had found it difficult to talk to the civilians in the South because 'I could not cut through their anger'.

Without meaningful guidance or assistance from Baghdad, the CPA(South) branch office was living hand to mouth, with neither a plan nor direction. Unlike the military arrangements, in which a general's staff will have worked together as a team for months or even years, and individuals within it may know each other well either personally or by reputation, the CPA was an entirely new bureaucracy in which the small number of staff had never met before and had no idea of each other's competences or roles.

After the initial dissemination of some broad objectives for the CPA as a whole, Bremer issued a '60 Day Vision' document, which was intended to guide activities over the months of August and September. By that time, however, the then head of CPA(South) had gone. Matters were made worse by the fact that the first batch of civilians had been recruited only for a three-month period, causing them to leave from July onwards; and no arrangements had been made for replacements.

The consequences of this awful oversight over succession planning were brought home to me in my first week. I received an excellent briefing from an energetic young man seconded from Her Majesty's Customs and Excise Department, who had done splendid work in encouraging his Iraqi counterparts to do something to control smuggling by sea. Two weeks later he too had gone, never to be replaced by his home Department and no one with whom to share his hard-won knowledge.

The new British military Division discovered on their arrival that not only was the civilian capacity inadequate, but that the security situation was increasingly precarious. That there was a linkage between reconstruction and other aspects of civilian activity – hearts and minds – and the maintenance of a secure environment was never in question. But which is the chicken and which the egg? To what extent was inadequate civilian activity contributing to the rising level of threat?

These questions were legitimate, as was the resentment caused by the shortcomings of the civilian capacity. Many of the officers who had just arrived had been preparing for their impending tour in the UK beforehand and had been involved in the MOD's planning processes. They had therefore been following developments with increasing gloom and had witnessed the service chiefs' growing frustration that the concerns which they were expressing were not being heeded. Now they were having to face the consequences on the ground.

Without an operational plan or the resources to fulfil one, the civilian arm had little to contribute to military strategic or tactical planning. The Army therefore had no option but to try to deal with the challenges themselves, so as to reduce the damaging security side-effects. Since they also had a remit to support the civilian operations, they decided to stiffen that effort by seconding military personnel to the civilian office. This was probably not a very popular assignment, but it had the advantage of increasing the flow of information to the military headquarters about what the civilians were getting up to. In essence, if the CPA, the designated instrument, were not up to the job, then the Army would take it on themselves. The collective military experience of civil–military operations in Northern Ireland and the Balkans, among other theatres, instilled in them a justifiable confidence that they could have a shot at it. Anyway, there was no choice.

These steps were consistent with the fundamental characteristics of a military response to a vital challenge. Failure is not an option. If failure looks possible, irrespective of what went before, then every possible step will be taken to forestall it. The aggressive instinct used in battle will be used outside it as well, whether or not it is welcome to others. They will if necessary speak in plain terms.

It was as well for British and Coalition interests in southern Iraq that the Army did indeed step in to fill the vacuum. The sudden insertion of military officers into the CPA offices entailed stepping on toes, literally and figuratively. But something had to be done.

There were downsides. In some cases, the 'can do' attitude was accompanied by a mindset which contrasted the military refusal to contemplate failure with a presumption that civilians were ready to accept it: an assumption that civilian administrators had succumbed to the defeatist view that 'because we failed to plan, then we are bound to fail'. Some middle- to senior-ranking military officers, who could see the deficiencies, nonetheless took the view that it was the Army who had fought the war and delivered victory, and it was for civilians to deal with the 'peace'. Hence the concept that we were to be their 'ticket out'.

This approach was as unrealistic as it was unfair. In the anarchy and confusion which became apparent as soon as Saddam fell, there was no question of any civilian reconstruction effort being able to take place without a very significant military presence to provide a secure environment. The political turmoil which was bound to follow the removal of a long-standing, centrally directed dictatorship was bound also to threaten stability. Even if the civilian teams had been adequately resourced, they could never have constituted the military's ticket home: both parts had essential roles to play.

And it was less than fair to blame the civilians on the ground for failing to get their act together. With or without a coherent plan, there was no way in which the numbers of personnel involved could have taken on the physical tasks such as were, fortunately and as is described in Chapter 12, taken on by the Army's Engineer Branch. Sometimes the Army seemed to forget the enormous differences of scale which existed between the deployable resources available to the military and the civilian arms of Coalition policy, and to blame the shortcomings on a failure of will, determination or backbone. It took some time for the scars of these early months to start to heal.

My appointment at the end of July 2003 represented a significant increase of political attention in London to the civilian function in Basra. This reflected London's acceptance of their new responsibilities which arose as a result of British representatives being in charge of both the military and civilian arms of the Coalition effort in the South. But it also raised expectations on the part of those military officers who, lacking experience of civilian affairs, mistakenly believed that civilian institutions can react with a speed and scale of deployment which are comparable with those of the military.

The commanding general of the 3rd Division, Graeme Lamb, shared my view that it was essential, if we were to work together effectively, to understand and take account of each other's views and capabilities. We had first met over a lavish meal in my house in Islamabad soon after 9/11, when Graeme was actively engaged in the Afghanistan operation and, in the absence of any British Embassy in Kabul, I had proxy responsibilities for the diplomatic aspects of it. We had therefore had an opportunity to take the measure of each other already. I had great respect for this 'soldiers' soldier': for his experience and energy, and for the keenness of his mind. And I greatly enjoyed his colourful vocabulary and turn of phrase. We resolved immediately to see each other frequently and to share our concerns and assessments frankly.

For my part, and in everyone's interests, I needed to explain to the Army where our responsibilities lay, what were our strengths and what were our limitations. There was generally little difficulty about the last, which were glaringly obvious, although it was a relief if we were not reminded of them too often. But our strengths could complement weaknesses or gaps in military capabilities. If we were to succeed in this, however, there first had to be a shared, even if tacit, recognition that such weaknesses or gaps existed. This was not always easy when confronted by the confidence, whose value is beyond price, and the can-do attitude of highly trained and motivated soldiers.

I had a first attempt at public relations on these lines at one of Graeme Lamb's weekly meetings with his Divisional, Brigade and Regimental staff officers, a large group comprising many different nationalities. I travelled to the military headquarters outside Basra city for the purpose, with just my trusty security detail for company. I was astonished by the weight of numbers of the General's team, and at the range of activity and planning which they represented. Putting aside mentally the contrast between the intellectual, human and technical resources at the General's disposal and my own team of seven managers who covered the entire range of administration and civilian operations, I learned enormously from their concise and detailed briefings such as staff officers are accustomed to convey up the line.

I had suggested to Graeme that I make us of this opportunity to introduce myself to his staff. The final spot on the show was therefore reserved for me. Knowing the background, I had not expected an ecstatic reception for the first CPA civilian to offer a briefing to the military. I announced myself as someone who had seen naval service and who in several posts had served in some hot spots, climatically and politically. I described my immediate objectives and my impressions of Bremer's intent in the light of my meeting with him. I made no promises, but emphasised the Prime Minister's personal assurances and my own determination to deliver as best I could.

I did not experience any of that subliminal nourishment from a supportive audience which can so enhance the performance of an actor or speech-maker. I had once been in the audience at a matinee performance at the Glasgow Empire Theatre when I was based in nearby Helensburgh. The atmosphere was sadly similar. I was heard out in silence, which continued after I had finished. Graeme Lamb asked if there were any questions.

A low growl emerged from the Brigade Commander: 'When'.

It did not seem to be a question.

'I beg your pardon?'

'Yes, but *when* are you going to deliver?'

I experienced what a politician must feel after some abject setback which his position does not allow him to acknowledge. Not normally at a loss for words, I found that I was only able to mutter something about 'patience'. It was not perhaps the best choice.

My subsequent consolation was that military complaints were not directed exclusively to the civilians in Basra. All parties were able to unite in complaining about the lack of understanding and support at the London end. I accompanied a senior visitor from Whitehall to a briefing from the same Brigade Commander in his headquarters near my own. At the end of the ensuing discussion, the soldier took me aside and asked if I thought that his message, which was critical, had been registered. I answered consolingly. The response was a sceptical grunt: 'He struck me as more on Transmit than Receive'.

When the Prime Minister returned from his summer holiday in September, he evidently noticed that all was not well with relations between the three ministries engaged in the Iraq operation. His appointment of his Diplomatic Adviser to coordinate day-to-day policy at last presented a target for everyone to aim at.

British Ministers had been visiting Basra periodically. But my own first encounter with a ministerial-level visitor there was with Hilary Benn in mid-September. Still a Minister of State and under Baroness Amos's leadership in DFID, Benn was not to replace Amos for another month. Accompanied by DFID's Permanent Under-Secretary – the Department's most senior official – and other DFID staff, he had also visited Baghdad. His experience there had done little to reassure him by the time he visited my headquarters in town and the Army's outside it. I was especially glad of the opportunity to put across our concerns at the political level. And I admired the fact that Benn had persisted with his plans for a visit when a committee in London had ruled that it was at that time unsafe to travel to the region.

I was delighted by how the visit went. Benn showed a keen and expert interest in what we were doing and in the political and social environment in which we were operating. He met many Iraqis and had talks with representatives of the media, which was expanding exponentially. Important issues which had been blocked in London were unblocked as soon as we were able to explain the reasoning face to face. Benn agreed that project funding procedures should be simplified and speeded up so that the CPA would no longer be treated as if it were a foreign recipient government; and my earlier requests for more specialist staff, which had been bedevilled by some requirement for multiple tendering and fixed periods of notice, would be expedited. He turned to his Permanent Under-Secretary for confirmation that it was all feasible and received a positive nod. This then allowed us to start our carefully planned Emergency Infrastructure Programme at once. I was due to meet a group of sheikhs a few days later and would be able tell of this important new development.

Benn told me that he was an avid reader of my reports and urged me to keep them coming; he liked their frank style, their

1. My room in the Electricity Accounts building. The fan and air-conditioning unit were too noisy to use at night, despite the boiling temperatures. August 2003.

2. Petitions outside the Electricity Accounts building, before the security situation deteriorated. August 2003.

3. James Roscoe attaching a stick to our flag pole to make the flag appear to be at half mast, following an assassination, September 2003. This photo was later taken out of context and reproduced on the cover of the Foreign Office's in-house magazine, with the heading 'Winning the Peace'.

4. Negotiating with a sheikh in Nasiriyah. Like many people who presented themselves to us, he proved to be much less influential than he had claimed. September 2003.

5. Bremer visiting the village of Chubaish with Abu Hatem, 'The Lord of the Marshes' (to his right), to demonstrate cooperation between the CPA and the Marsh Arabs. September 2003.

6. Travelling to one of my monthly meetings with Bremer in Baghdad, with James Roscoe my Private Secretary, and Tom Fergusson my ex-US Marine bodyguard, in the General's plane. By this stage, I had persuaded Tom to abandon his professional practice of silence. October 2003.

7. Seeing for myself. Accompanying a British Army foot patrol in downtown Basra. December 2003.

8. Being briefed by the Royal Navy about the river patrol on the Shatt al-Arab. December 2003.

9. Bremer giving a cheerful peroration, after the decision to wind up the Coalition Provisional Authority (CPA). December 2003.

10. Examining the winter tomato crop, with Ole Jepson on the right, December 2003. Tomatoes are a staple ingredient of the Iraqi diet, and this crop had to supply the whole country. It would have failed if we had not found some plastic sheeting to protect it.

11. A *mudhif*, a traditional reed house used as a meeting place, where I met a Marsh Arab tribal chief. December 2003.

12. The 'hooches'. Our new premises were an improvement on past living conditions, though, as we discovered on the night that Saddam was captured when celebratory gunfire hailed down all over Basra, they were not bulletproof. December 2003.

13. A publicity shot: distributing winter uniforms for the Iraqi police. Fed up with delays from the Coalition's privately contracted uniform provider, KBR, we had got a local tailor to run some up. December 2003.

14. Christmas Day in our new building in Al Sarraji, a former palace. Haytham, my assistant is on my right. After lunch we hunkered down to watch Zulu: the sense of being under siege fitted our mood rather well.

15. Introducing the Prime Minister to the CPA(South) team in Basra. January 2004.

16. My second personal protection team – American former police officers. January 2004.

directness and their brevity. I was glad that they were reaching their targets. I also resolved to make no stylistic exception for my report of this visit, successful though it was. My telegram carefully listed the decisions reached and added the warning that, since we would now act upon them, they had better be fulfilled. The final paragraph recorded that General Lamb, also pleased with the outcome, had instructed his staff in Benn's presence to 'take the pins out of the DFID doll'. This visit was therefore good for civil–military relations, which immediately took a more positive turn.

Official reaction from London was more mixed. I received a plaintive request from a senior DFID official to ease up on my implied and direct criticisms about perceived shortcomings. I should understand, I was told, that officials were doing their best and were already working excessively long hours: complaints and criticism undermined their morale, upon which their effectiveness depended.

I did indeed understand the point. I knew that officials were overstretched, and I fully recognised the importance of maintaining morale, not least because I had made mistakes by pushing some of my own staff too hard in my previous posting in Pakistan in the difficult days after 9/11. But I was unrepentant. It was unfortunate if staff in London were overworked and underappreciated, but the solution to that did not lie in bouquets from Basra. It lay with Ministers and senior officials to provide adequate numbers of personnel and appropriate management structures to respond to what the Prime Minister had told me personally was a challenge of prime national importance.

It was soon after this visit that both Jeremy Greenstock, from Baghdad, and I, from Basra, launched independent salvos of dismay that, despite the courage shown by Benn, it had been decided to postpone a visit from a key senior official in Number 10 Downing Street. A committee which had been set up in the mists of time to monitor the risks to royal and ministerial visits in more normal circumstances had been apprised of a continuing high threat and had ruled against. None of us in the country could understand why Whitehall should regard it as acceptable that we should live in and move around the country, but unacceptable for

London-based officials to pay us a visit. Our frustration was all the greater because of our certainty that British performance could only increase with a better understanding of the realities on the ground. It was scant consolation to learn that, as a result of this unfortunate misjudgement, the authorisation procedures were adapted to take better account of the prevailing realities.

Such hesitations and changes of plan offered a dreadful example to civilian volunteers in the field, and elicited such disdain from the Army that it bedevilled relations between the Army and senior officials in London for some time.

Over the autumn and winter months Basra was host to an eclectic succession of visitors. Graeme Lamb and I ensured that we had at least one joint session with them in addition to more specialised programmes tailored to their particular interests.

When General Sanchez, the Coalition's most senior military officer in Iraq, came down from Baghdad, I was able to supplement his military briefing with some commentary about political developments. The briefing over, we joined in a traditional Arabic lunch seated on the floor, to which had been invited all the principal tribal leaders. Among the guests tucking into the boiled lamb, fish and rice was Sheikh Rahim from Al Amarah. It was he who had given me such a hard time at his Council meeting just ten days earlier, as is described in Chapter 6. But on this occasion he greeted me as a long-lost friend and brother. The distinction between official and social contacts could not have been made more clear.

Similarly, when the Defence Secretary, Geoff Hoon, came to visit the Army, his programme included meetings with my team in the city and with some of the key political figures there. If the security situation or shortage of time did not allow the visitors to travel to the city from the military headquarters, I would go there in my armoured convoy.

In this way, in addition to our regular one-to-one meetings, Graeme and I were able to keep close track of each other's thinking and of developments in our respective fields. This was essential if we were to avoid the constant risk of misunderstanding. But I was always deeply jealous of the highly professional and practised military briefing techniques as specialist officers stepped forward to explain carefully prepared PowerPoint slides and then take questions, keeping the General in reserve to provide an overview. With no similar resources, my own briefings to visiting Ministers were limited to a one-man show, with the challenge of maintaining the attention of often deeply fatigued travellers by the use of words alone.

A visit by the Prime Minister in early January 2004 was, from my perspective, one of the least successful. While I was taking a few days' break over the New Year, I got a phone call from Henry Hogger in Basra that all was not going well with the planning. I had been told by Number 10 that Blair intended to concentrate on the civilian effort in the South. But the visit's organiser, who came from the Labour Party headquarters rather than the Civil Service, was insisting that it should focus on the military and that we were going to be cut out. I rushed back to Basra to get it all back on track.

Straight off the plane, I had an intemperate discussion with the minder from Number 10/Labour Party. I was told that the plane-load of press reporters and photographers who were accompanying Blair would want stories and photographs about soldiers, not about foreign civilians. With a great effort I remained unruffled, while I was subjected to a string of four-letter words by the woman concerned, witnessed by my multinational heads of section, who were astonished by the display. Having dealt with such people on other recent prime ministerial visits, I was less surprised than my colleagues. I knew that they did not necessarily represent Blair's personal wishes, but were doing their misguided best to fulfil their own ideas of priorities.

The upshot was that Blair would meet my multinational team for half an hour. In practice, he proved content to do whatever was asked of him and made a hit with my team by agreeing to be photographed with nearly all of them. His minder had also conceded that he should also meet the Governor of Basra, Wa'el Abd al-Latif. When I managed to usher Blair to the arranged meeting point, against a photogenic backdrop of the Shatt al-Arab waterway, I discovered that all the visiting journalists had been herded into their bus so as to be ready for the next appointment when Blair arrived there. Nor were any Iraqi journalists allowed to be present, for security reasons. As a result, apart from my own reporting telegram, there was no record of the Governor's considerable praise for the Coalition's contribution to reconstruction and security. Such opportunities to publicise the support of a key Iraqi personality did not arise often. It was they whom we were trying to help and, if we were to succeed, we needed to show that we were making progress.

In a gracious personal letter after his visit, the Prime Minister said that he wished he could have stayed longer. Having been told at the outset that that had been his intention, I was deeply disappointed that that objective had been thwarted by a party-political spin doctor.

By the time of Blair's visit, the civilian and military teams in the South had settled down into a functional and cooperative working relationship. We civilians would never be able to do as much as either we or the Army wanted, but we came to understand what each of us could and could not do and to recognise that we were all doing our best according to our lights. This constructive state of affairs continued with the change of commanding general early in the New Year.

However, neither we nor the military ever managed to craft a harmonious relationship with civilian departments at home. From our perspective, there was insufficient grip, leadership and knowledge of the conditions in which we were operating, and not enough understanding of what was needed. There was never any doubt that all concerned were busy: we saw the outcome of their labours. But too few senior officials came to see the situation for themselves, and too infrequently. Preoccupation at senior level with the admittedly important constitutional aspects of central governance was at the expense of the delivery of essential resources on the ground. Diffuse lines of responsibility between ministries left unfilled gaps. Traditional procedures were followed when fast-tracks were needed. If we shouted sufficiently loud to attract high-level attention, we would get results; but the steam dissipated when that attention moved on.

The problem, I was convinced, lay in the absence of a management structure in London which was appropriate for dealing with such exceptional challenges. It was not sufficient simply to adapt existing, peace-time management arrangements, which were designed for entirely different purposes. The Army have demonstrated their ability to learn lessons from their past experience and have well-established mechanisms to implement change accordingly.

Civil Service Departments have also been subject to incessant change; and officials have drawn up copious lessons from past practice. But it is not clear that the lessons have in fact been taken to heart, and still less that they have been implemented. Until they are, and so long as Britain continues to deploy civil and military resources in pursuit of the stabilisation of fragile states, civil–military relations seem set to remain scratchy.

PART THREE
EFFORTS AND FAILURES

Chapter 10
Plans are Nothing

Plans are nothing. Planning is everything.

General Dwight D. Eisenhower.

No plan survives first contact.

Traditional military adage.

DESPITE APPEARANCES, PLANS had been laid before the Coalition's invasion of Iraq. One of the fullest of these ran to 13 volumes; but it wasn't used. Not only was it not used, it was rejected. And one of its architects was thrown out of Baghdad once the US Defense Secretary learned that he was part of the post-conflict management team there.

Planning had started in the US State Department in October 2001, less than a month after the attacks on 11 September, under the direction of a former State Department official, Thomas S. Warrick. The operation was called The Future of Iraq Project. Its papers were released under the US Freedom of Information Act and in September 2006 they were published by the National Security Archive, an independent, non-governmental research institute at The George Washington University, together with some supporting documents.

The full Future of Iraq study runs to 1200 pages. They amount to the documentary outcome of 33 meetings of 17 working groups. The subjects range widely: public health and humanitarian needs; transparency and anti-corruption; oil and energy; defence policy and institutions; transitional justice; democratic principles and procedures; local government; civil society capacity building; education; free media; water, agriculture and environment; and economy and infrastructure.

The report would have been better had it been even longer. It is not light reading; nor were the deliberations completed. But, with all the wisdom of hindsight, it is fascinating to dip into it and to consider the National Security Archive's commentary. There had been some leaks to the press previously. On the basis of these and rumours which drew on inside knowledge, the conventional wisdom in 2003-4 was that, while the State Department had indeed addressed the question of the post-conflict challenges in Iraq, the outcome had been of little practical value.

The other popular view within the CPA in Baghdad at that time was that, whatever the merits or demerits of the Future of Iraq Project, it had not found favour with the Pentagon or with Secretary Rumsfeld in particular. Therefore, when President George W. Bush signed Directive 24 on 20 January 2003, which conferred responsibility for post-war planning to the Department of Defense, the Project's report was in effect binned. Although the Pentagon half-heartedly denied that it had ignored the report, it was well known that Tom Warrick, the architect of the Project, had been summarily removed from any involvement in General Jay Garner's original ORHA operation. It has emerged subsequently, notably in Tom Ricks's book *Fiasco*, that Garner was told to get rid of Warrick by Rumsfeld personally, seemingly at the behest of Vice-President Cheney.

Whatever the fate of the planners or the qualities of the planning process, it was strange to me and to many of us on the ground that the knowledge and expertise which must have been built up during the many meetings of sectoral experts should have been jettisoned.

It is clear, however, that the Project did not itself amount to a plan of the sort which could have been executed as it stood. Specialist sectors received widely varying attention. The enormously important issue of education was the subject of only one meeting, recorded in six pages. Local government was covered in more detail: 44 pages, including PowerPoint slides and supporting evidence. Agriculture, probably the country's greatest single source of employment, was dealt with in less than eight pages, mainly concerned with increasing cereal production – the result of just two sessions of a working group on water, agriculture and environment. Transitional justice merited over 200 pages.

One could have some sympathy with those who, in a desperate hurry to start the invasion and mistakenly expecting that state institutions would hold together, might have flicked impatiently through such a tome and decided that it was of no practical use. Inconveniently it would need a lot more time if it were to be of value, and time was simply not available. So perhaps it seemed more sensible just to get on with it and hope for the best. But hope is not a plan.

Corelli Barnett, a noted British historian, has pointed out that detailed planning for the aftermath of the Second World War, including the appointment of specific ministerially-led committees and of senior officials, had commenced in 1941: four years before the plans could start to be realised.

By contrast, the State Department's planning for the Second Gulf War started in October 2001, at about the same time as the start of military planning and about a year and a half before the end of the combat operations in April 2003, whereupon it was rejected.

The US Department of Defense also considered the wider aspects of Iraqi nation-building through its Office of Special Plans, formed in August 2002. Coordination of these various strands only started when the Department of Defense assumed control, just two months before a plan needed to be implemented.

All these plans, and the initial creation of ORHA, suffered from the fatal flaw that they were based on assumptions which were to prove faulty. In practice, it was only when Bremer arrived on the ground in Iraq, in May 2003, and started to create and direct a new civilian bureaucracy, that real planning could commence.

Two of Bremer's first acts – de-Ba'athification and the dissolution of the Iraqi Army, promulgated within a fortnight of his arrival – were his most controversial and are now generally regarded as very serious mistakes. Several of those who may have been directly or indirectly involved in the decision-making process in Washington and Baghdad have given differing accounts of their genesis. But for those facing the consequences – Iraqis and Coalition military and civilian personnel – the background to the decisions was immaterial. Even the Future of Iraq Project, for all its faults, envisaged a measured approach to both issues. Considering the consequences of the removal of senior members of the Ba'ath Party, the report could hardly have been more percipient:

> Nevertheless, a temporary problem may still arise. The civilian agencies are governed by political appointees loyal to the regime rather than by these professionals, and as the structure of the state disintegrates, senior officials ... and others responsible for issuing orders and running the engine of state, can be expected not to report to work. The chain of command in the government departments and agencies will be broken, creating temporary but serious administrative paralysis. Cities and towns will be left without a civil administration, leading to disruption of law and order, the food distribution systems and emergency health care. Because of the high likelihood of a political vacuum and the possible administrative vacuum in the period immediately preceding and following the fall of the regime, other strategies must be devised to fill these needs quickly.

This proved to be an accurate but understated description of what happened in southern Iraq, as is described elsewhere. And it was written before, rather than after, the events it describes.

The 400,000 strong Iraqi Army, dissolved by CPA Order 2 on 23 May 2003, ended up on the streets, unemployed and discontent. The Future of Iraq Project envisaged that its senior officers should be sacked and the Republican Guard and Special Republican Guard, Saddam's storm troopers, should be disbanded. But the rest of the Army should be gradually reduced in size and turned to other profitable tasks, such as helping to rebuild Iraq's agriculture sector.

The impact of these ideas was reduced by the fact that what amounted to records of a small number of meetings of 'experts' did not add up to thought-through recommendations accompanied by ideas for their practical implementation. In early May, however, it was a very high political priority in Iraq and in Washington to demonstrate who was in charge. Bremer, his close advisers and Washington were faced with a vast range of issues which called for very rapid decisions. Unfortunately, on de-Ba'athification and the dissolution of the Army, their call was wrong.

These important decisions had been taken some two months before my arrival. Had I had the advantage of reading the Future of Iraq Project report while I was in the country, I might have been less surprised by what faced me. On the other hand, all of us quickly reached the same conclusions for ourselves: it seemed obvious that, if one removed the top four tiers of management of almost every institution in the country, which was the consequence of the de-Ba'athification order, CPA Order 1, paralysis would ensue – with the risk that this would be quickly followed by anarchy.

But on my arrival I was not aware of any of the prior planning. I received no briefing or papers about it, either from the FCO or from Baghdad. Alastair Campbell reveals in his book *The Blair Years* that a senior British general had warned a year before the invasion of Iraq that post-conflict had to be part of the conflict preparation. Despite this sound advice, so far as I was concerned there may as well have never been any prior planning. We were already facing the serious consequences of the failures of foresight.

In the short period of notice before I arrived in Basra, I was given some oral briefing and a pile of recent reports from British diplomats in Baghdad. The fact that there was virtually nothing from the small diplomatic team in Basra reflected the difficulty of communicating, as I was to find out so clearly for myself on arrival. But some long telephone conversations with Janet Rogan, who was holding the fort between my predecessor's departure and my arrival, revealed a significant gap between perceptions in London and the reality.

It was natural that I should be dismayed by such a state of affairs. The USA and the UK had responsibilities for the direct governance of a country of some 26 million people. The Regional Coordination team in the South had delegated responsibility for four of the country's 18 Provinces, which covered a quarter of Iraq's land mass and a population of 4.5 million.

It was only later that I came to realise that, if I had a problem, Bremer had a much greater one. My task was to do my best to manage the region according to Bremer's plans. Bremer had the awful task of formulating the plan itself.

The first expression of any such plan emerged at the end of July 2003, close to the time of my arrival in Iraq. It was called 'Achieving the Vision' and was broken down in 90-day phases, with a particular focus on the 60 days from 1 August. The 'Vision' itself was for:

> ... an Iraq that is stable, united, prosperous, at peace with its neighbors and able to take its rightful place as a responsible member of the region and the international community. This Iraq must be free of weapons of mass destruction and terrorists.
>
> The ultimate goal is a unified and stable, democratic Iraq that: provides effective and representative government for the Iraqi people; is underpinned by new and protected freedoms for all Iraqis and a growing market economy; is able to defend itself but no longer poses a threat to its neighbors or international security.

I forced myself to sit down and try to read the Vision's electronic manifestation. It was well produced, and I reflected that whoever had prepared it was a dab hand with computers. If the 'Vision' amounted to a goal, the 'Plan' which accompanied it sought to make progress towards five objectives: security; governance; essential services; the economy; and strategic communications.

The trouble was that it did not amount to an operational plan of action, only a list of subsidiary objectives under each of these headings. There were no indications about how in practice they would be achieved: no details of funding, of personnel involved, of support systems or of timing. It was particularly notable that the ultimate objective, of handing full sovereignty back to the Iraqi people, had no timing attached to it at all.

I read it all wearily, with a deepening sense of gloom. I reflected that a list of objectives was a start, although it seemed to me, as a newcomer, to have appeared a bit late in the day. But how often had I read mission statements and departmental, section and personal objectives in the past? And how often had they truly contributed to the betterment of anyone who read them? The difference on this occasion was that the issues involved were truly ones of life and death.

The fact was that the CPA's Vision Statement, a copy of the introduction of which is in Appendix Two, was of no practical value to me at all. How on earth were we, detached from Baghdad in more ways than our distance of several hundred miles, expected to contribute to these worthy objectives? I took refuge in the hope that we would soon receive more detailed operational guidance.

A follow-up emerged in October. With the friendly title 'Welcome to the Coalition Provisional Authority', it took the form of ever-popular PowerPoint slides. Strangely, it started with the CPA's bizarre history which comprised the creation, deployment and abolition of ORHA in less than five months: nothing, surely, to draw attention to. The goal, strategy and plan were all expressed in different terms from the first document, which no doubt reflected the development of thinking, but which conveyed an impression of confusion.

What caught my eye, however, was the slide about the mission of KBR, the American contractors who were to provide us with life support – our food, accommodation and services. Our Regional Office in the South was to receive life support for up to 100 personnel. And yet at this time we were on the point of moving premises and plans were well afoot to collect many more people than that. In fact, our security personnel probably exceeded that number already. Nor was there any mention of support for the CPA's provincial teams which Bremer had conceived three months earlier. I decided to ignore that slide and wondered what credence to give to the rest of the document. What followed over the next few weeks demonstrated that I was not alone in feeling that the planning process might have been a step or two removed from reality.

In the afternoon of 4 November, I travelled to Baghdad for one of the periodic meetings of the four Regional Coordinators and six Divisional Commanders. That morning I had visited the Basra Technical College and witnessed the signing of a high-value contract to renovate it; and I had taken delivery of 40 shiny new police cars, which were parked outside the food hall until we had a chance to hand them over to a delighted local police force.

The evening before I had been interviewed by a young journalist employed by a major British newspaper which should have known better. Out to make his name, he tried every trick to induce me to criticise our American Coalition partners and to endorse the imprudent claims by some British Cabinet Ministers that progress in the South showed that the British were doing the job better than the Americans. I did not find it hard to resist these transparent efforts to extract a scoop: I believed that the two situations did not bear comparison and that such hubristic claims risked jeopardising the American support on which we were entirely dependent.

I was therefore in a bullish mood on my way up to Baghdad, buoyed up with hope for the future. The meeting was exceptionally crowded as a good number of the provincial team leaders were now in place and each invitee brought others of their teams with them. Before it started, small groups coalesced around the coffee and doughnuts which were freely available outside the hall. Everyone was busy: networking, lobbying, fixing, complaining or pleading, depending on their interests and characters. We were then ushered into allocated seats behind individual desks, each with its own microphone, in a large modern auditorium in the heart of the Green Zone. It must have had its own power supply because the air-conditioned temperature was icy. It all seemed far removed from the realities outside the 'bubble', in Iraq proper.

The meeting had an inauspicious prelude. A PowerPoint show entitled 'Overview of Planning Milestones' was accompanied by a commentary by a young man from CPA's Office of Policy Planning and Analysis. Wearing jeans and a checked shirt, he walked round the space inside the stockade of desks and described the main points, gesticulating and making direct eye contact in traditional management consultancy style. He was over-exuberant, used too many adjectives and, as far as the generals were concerned, was a scruffily dressed civilian who went on for far too long. He lost his audience within a couple of minutes but, unfortunately for him, did not notice.

Generals Petraeus and Odierno engaged in one of their mutually supportive routines which had so devastated me on another occasion when I had presumed to doubt the effectiveness of the planned introduction of a new currency. But this time they were explosive rather than mildly ironic as they had been with me. Why had they not heard of any of this before? Why had they not been consulted? All the Divisional Commanders had sizeable planning staffs of their own who had been engaged in similar exercises and who could have offered advice from the field. Was such expertise and effort to be both wasted and ignored?

Under the cover of this preliminary barrage, some of the Regional and Governorate Coordinators joined in, having used the time meanwhile to have a look at a document which had been circulated during the unfortunate introductory speech.

The CPA's working draft plan, which had been refined by a small group of advisers in October, offered two possible options. Both were predicated on the nature of the political process to be followed: progress over the economy or reconstruction was apparently secondary to the consequential timescales and was adjusted to fit into the time available. The first option, based on the concept of 'partial elections', was that a new Iraqi government should take power in March 2005, when the CPA would dissolve. The other, which envisaged 'direct elections', saw the changeover taking place in October 2005. The plan as a whole was described as a 'consultative document' on which participants' views were invited. This was the first time for most of us present that an end-date for the CPA's operations had been specified, and even this was variable within a seven-month period.

Each of the main areas of activity, which had been identified in Bremer's original Vision document as the priority objectives, was described in parallel bar charts. Red triangles under a running dateline marked particular events. But, on examination, there was no coherence to the whole: they were simply lists of jobs which someone thought had to be done, with no account taken of the impact of one on the other.

From my parochial perspective in the South, I was little concerned about the feasibility of the constitutional processes. Such was the stuff of Baghdad, London and Washington who, unfortunately, seemed preoccupied by it to the exclusion of the more practical matters which were my main worries.

Of greater interest to me were the headings labelled 'Economy' and 'Essential Services'. Under these were descriptions of the privatisation of the state-owned enterprises, and the abolition of subsidised rations and of subsidised prices. In July and September 2004, the State Enterprises, having been set up to be 'stand alone' the previous February, would have to set about laying off staff. Each of these two steps would be preceded and followed by increases in the prices of energy, electricity and of diesel fuel. The social and security-related consequences of such actions were obvious to all present, except presumably to those who had drafted the paper.

I was not alone in drawing attention to these and other anomalies. I was particularly exercised about the plans for early privatisation of state industries and the withdrawal of food subsidies, albeit by replacing the goods with financial payments. I pointed out that neither of the offending practices was incompatible with democracy, as could be attested by India, known as the world's biggest democracy, and that they were common to many developing countries. The abolition of state ownership and food subsidies might be consistent with best theoretical economic practice, but it would add to the pressures on the population at a time when we were all trying to encourage stability.

I also remarked on the conspicuous absence in the plan of any action time lines for strategic communications. There were no red triangles and no text, and yet this was one of the five key objectives in Bremer's Vision statement and had been a major weakness throughout the CPA's life up to then.

Baghdad was concerned about the presentational effect of the disparities in the various selection processes of the provincial governors. Under the heading 'Local Governance' therefore, the plan envisaged that the governors should be reselected by the following February. Meanwhile, the provincial police chiefs should each be selected by the Ministry of the Interior, not as a result of a consultative process within the Provinces themselves: this was intended to strengthen central control and enhance uniform practice. Such ideas starkly highlighted the disconnect between the Green Zone's theoreticians and those with experience on the ground. I suggested that if the effective Governor of Basra Province, Judge Wa'el Abd al-Latif, who was also a member of the Iraq Governing Council, were to be told that he had to offer himself for reselection, it was very likely that he would resign forthwith and present us with a dangerous vacuum until a replacement had been found and successfully elected.

As for selection of police chiefs by Baghdad, the very idea would be anathema in the South – and speakers from elsewhere confirmed the point. The Provinces would demand autonomy about such sensitive and powerful appointments. The South hated the very idea of control from Baghdad. And, as the murder of the Police Chief in Maysan Province had demonstrated, it would be essential to take account of local tribal power structures, of which Baghdad knew nothing. Such an arrangement would be an invitation for the Ministry of the Interior to engage in wholesale corruption without the constraint of local checks and balances.

The Generals launched another salvo. It was employment, they said, which was the key to stability and security. The CPA should be doing more to create jobs, not doing away with them. Had they been able to get a word in, the drafters of this 'consultative document' might have pointed to the action line for security affairs, which ran in parallel with the lines for economy and essential services. This suggested that by 1 June, New Iraqi Army recruits would arrive at Iraqi bases to begin unit training and that the problematic militias would have been integrated into the Army one month before that, thereby generating employment and reducing the threat. These aspirations, too, were patently far-removed from reality, as was soon to become clear for all to see and as the Divisional Commanders already knew. But the fury of the reaction from the floor precluded any further detailed debate.

Faced with such an unprecedented barrage of criticism – 'mutiny' had the military been under Bremer's command – the CPA senior management counter-attacked. It fell to Andy Bearpark, the Operations Director, to respond about essential services. It was a pity, he gently observed, that the local military commanders were so exercised about the plan, bearing in mind that it had been drawn up in consultation with the Joint Task Force Commanders, CJTF-7. It was hardly the fault of the CPA if the military did not disseminate information between themselves.

Bremer's Director for Private Sector Development, Tom Foley, explained that thinking on privatisation had developed further since the plan had been drawn up and it would no longer proceed at the pace originally envisaged. This tactical withdrawal appeared to suggest that, despite its tardy appearance, the plan had already been modified.

Bremer himself, caught up in other business, had missed most of the discussion and had not heard the reaction from the assembled committee. When he arrived towards the end of the meeting and was told by the cautious chairman that the plan had received some criticism, he delivered the coup de grace by revealing that, whatever we might think of it, it had already been presented in Washington. There was no question of reassessing it, he declared brusquely; it would proceed.

I imagine that my own reaction could not have been dissimilar from others. What was the purpose of purporting to discuss a plan with those who, like us, worked in the field, if we had no opportunity to feed in our views? And what could be the value of any plan which did not take account of views from the field? We had no confidence that advice solely from CPA headquarters and CJTF-7 would be a sufficient basis to plan for the future of such a complex country.

This experience represented the nadir of my experience in Iraq. It was at this point that I decided that CPA's endeavours were bound to fail. The plans for governance, although not my direct area of specialisation, seemed to me and my advisers to be too complex to be workable. And I had absolutely no doubt that the practical plans took insufficient account of realities on the ground. I had not at this stage come to the conclusion that, because the CPA was not working, the country as a whole was doomed to fail. Rather, I hoped that this stormy meeting and subsequent activity might lead to positive changes. I was convinced that something would have to give. And if it did, there might still be hope.

What we did not know at that time was that, when Bremer had visited Washington in late October for consultations, his plan had been questioned there. The criticisms about practicalities by a collection of angry individuals in Baghdad paled into insignificance compared with the challenges in Washington to the plan's fundamental principles. At the same time as Bremer was dismissing local criticisms, he was preparing new ideas for Rice and Bush.

*   *   *

Less than a week later I was back in Baghdad again. The security situation had not yet deteriorated to the extent that I could not get to the airport outside Basra and hitch a lift on one of the regular British C130 flights there. The weather was humid, dank and gusty, and as we took off the pilot warned that we might have to turn back because of sandstorms. But we landed with the usual corkscrew motion intended to flummox any incoming missiles, and I arrived in time to attend the US Marine Corps Birthday Ball, to celebrate their 228th Anniversary.

It was the 1st Marine Division which, on 10 April, had captured Saddam's former Palace that now housed the CPA headquarters. On the following day a Marine Corps air–ground force had occupied Tikrit, Saddam's birthplace and the centre of his al-Bu Nasir tribe. That unit's name, Task Force Tripoli, resonated with the first lines of the Marine Hymn:

> From the Halls of Montezuma
> To the shores of Tripoli;
> We fight our country's battles
> In the air, on land, and sea ....

There is a hallowed ritual associated with such anniversaries. A huge gathering assembled in the ceremonial hall of Saddam's Palace. Two of the tables had just one place setting. One of them, draped in black, commemorated fallen 'brothers', as the Marines referred to their comrades in arms. The second, draped in white, was in honour of prisoners of war and those missing in action.

A bugler sounded 'Attention' and a band played the 'Adjutant's Call', before the Presiding Marine, Major General Gallinetti, and the Guest of Honour, Lieutenant General Sanchez, who commanded CJTF-7, marched into the hall. The Colour Guard marched on the Colours. A cake was escorted by the oldest and youngest Marines present; messages were read and speeches were delivered.

My invaluable contact in Pat Kennedy's office, Colonel Dennis Sabal, who, in his words, had taken 'the cats off my back' over our move of premises a few weeks earlier, offered a toast to the Marines; a tough Sergeant Major toasted fallen comrades. I discovered that evening that Sabal held two Master's degrees and the Secretary of State's Medal for Heroism: a useful man to have on one's side.

Perorations by the two principal guests struck slightly jarring notes. Sanchez warned darkly that the military mission in Iraq could not fail since, if it were to do so, the Marines' next assignment would be in the streets of the USA. Bremer, never one to indulge in false modesty, informed the assembly that he had celebrated more Marine Corps Birthdays than anyone else present, having apparently participated every year since 1983.

The occasion was uplifting and moving. I proudly wore my Royal Naval submariner's tie and felt honoured to have been invited. But I was even more interested in the other guest at the small table which I shared with Andy Bearpark.

Ambassador Bob Blackwill had been appointed three months earlier to the National Security Council (NSC) as Deputy National Security Adviser for Strategic Planning and Presidential Envoy to Iraq. He was visiting Baghdad for a few days and was, in effect, National Security Adviser Condoleezza Rice's eyes and ears on the ground. I had never met him before but we knew each other well by proxy; he had been US Ambassador in India when I was High Commissioner in Pakistan during the troubled years of 2001–2, when a war between India and Pakistan, both armed with nuclear weapons, had seemed entirely possible. With my approval, my British counterpart in India used to show Blackwill copies of my reports of developments in Pakistan, and I had heard that he had found them useful. That would be a sufficient basis to have a serious exchange of views about our present situation.

Blackwill had a fierce reputation within the US Foreign Service and was one of those people who could operate at full steam with only a few hours sleep each night – an asset which I have always envied but have never been able to achieve myself. He softened me up with lavish praise for the British Diplomatic Service, which he described as the best in the world, and could not have been more affable. He had heard, he said, that we were doing great things in the South.

The courtesies over, Blackwill adopted a technique which I had experienced from another American diplomatic heavy-hitter, one of his predecessors in New Delhi. He grabbed me by the upper arm and proceeded to interrogate me, not letting go, despite the tantalising Maine lobster tails on the plate in front of me, until I had responded to his satisfaction. What was the situation in the South? How were we handling it? What did we need? Were we getting enough support?

Since I prided myself on an ability rapidly to detect obfuscation and evasiveness by others, I assumed that Blackwill's skills in that regard were yet more highly developed. So I spoke frankly. I stressed that the situation in the South was not nearly as hazardous as in the central region, where there was a Sunni majority. But it was clear that the CPA would not be able to set the country on its feet by its own efforts alone. It was essential to develop Iraqi capacity, which had been emasculated by the disbanding of the Army and de-Ba'athification. To do this we needed expertise and a good sense of the art of the possible. Experience of developing countries was of greater value than either force or political theory. Major reconstruction programmes were of little immediate value;

we needed a multiplicity of small-scale projects which produced rapid and visible benefits.

Blackwill heard me out, interjecting supplementary questions. When I had finished, he declared that he completely agreed with my analysis. And to my great surprise he added: 'And so does the President'.

I did not take such flattering assurances entirely at face value. But, like others, I had heard rumours of growing tensions between Bremer and the National Security Council after the White House had announced the formation of the Iraq Stabilization Group there in early October. Press reports had suggested that this group, headed by Rice, would take charge of key policy decisions and limit Bremer's role. Rumsfeld, who was formally Bremer's boss, had told the press that he had not been consulted. Bremer meanwhile had made no secret of his distaste for what he frequently described as the 'Eight Thousand Mile Screwdriver', referring to micro-management by various sources in Washington, of which Secretary Rumsfeld must undoubtedly have been one. Until then Bremer had been regarded as the Viceroy, benefiting from strong personal backing by the President himself. It was even being rumoured that he would succeed Colin Powell as Secretary of State. Blackwill's remarks seemed to corroborate the stories that efforts were being made to clip his wings: the President was evidently receiving advice which was seriously at odds with what I knew of Bremer's thinking.

As the evening's festivities were drawing to a close, Blackwill and I agreed to meet over breakfast next morning to continue our discussion. That night, Graeme Lamb and I stayed in Maude House, a subsidiary palace which housed the senior British General in Baghdad – Sanchez's deputy. After a welcome tot of whisky, our host announced that Graeme would sleep on a camp bed in his room while I would have a proper bed in the spare room. I felt a bit uncomfortable about being accorded such precedence. I soon discovered that the gesture was not entirely charitable. The spare room was divided into two by a plywood partition from floor to ceiling. This acted as both a sounding board and an amplifier for the already loud snores of the Royal Air Force officer who was billeted on the other side. I held my peace as I was greeted by knowing grins over coffee next morning.

I made my way to Jeremy Greenstock's office, which was next to Bremer's, for my breakfast rendezvous with Blackwill. I was astounded to find out that both he and Bremer had taken off back to Washington that very night.

Bremer's autobiography reveals that, while the generals were tearing into his plan at our coordination meeting, he had been sounding out Shia leaders about the political aspects of it. That explained why he had not been present to hear the criticism personally. On the evening of the Marine Corps Birthday Ball, Condoleezza Rice had told Bremer on the telephone that his developing ideas on the constitutional process, his proposed seven steps to full sovereignty, were too complicated to discuss on the secure video. He should therefore get himself back to Washington to brief the NSC principals and then the President by the next morning, Washington time.

On learning of this sudden departure, which Bremer has now confirmed was as much of a surprise to him as to the rest of us, we naturally suspected that all was not well. The outcome turned out to be an even greater surprise. Meanwhile, however, I needed to head back to Basra.

* * *

No sooner had I returned, on 12 November, than I started to receive reports of the attack that morning by a large truck bomb on the headquarters of the Italian Carabinieri in Nasiriyah. Some 19 Italians – soldiers, para-military and civilians – and about a dozen Iraqis had been killed. Many others were wounded. Within an hour of the attack I started to receive electronic photographs of the scene which showed massive damage to the building. This was the most serious attack on Coalition forces in the South since the end of the main military conflict seven months earlier and was a devastatingly sad blow to all of us, especially to our Italian colleagues.

Tragic though it was, an attack such as this was not unexpected. I had constantly warned at my meetings with all of the

CPA(South) team every Friday evening that something of this sort might happen and that we should prepare ourselves psychologically for it. Such advice may have been unnecessary, because everyone could see for themselves how the security situation was starting to deteriorate and must have reasoned that the troubles further north were quite likely to seep southwards. Perhaps for this reason, and despite the grief, everyone continued with their tasks; no one asked to leave. John Bourne, the provincial team leader in Nasiriyah, took his team temporarily to the shelter of the Italian Battle Group outside the city, but courageously carried on with his work of meeting and seeking to influence Iraqis at all levels.

The next day I made a tour of the defences at our Basra base with our ex-military Head of Security and Pete Duklis, my American Chief of Staff. Later that afternoon, the British Brigade Commander informed me of an intelligence report that the group which had attacked the Italians planned to conduct operations against our offices and the CPA office in Al Samawah over the next couple of days. The Brigadier and I decided in concert that we should shut our gates and suspend all contacts until the threat seemed to have passed. We locked down.

That night, and with our Basra operation still shut down, I was faced with a decision which, I was told, was so pressing that only I could make it. Pete Duklis asked if I would please decide whether or not, in view of the security threat, the 'honey-sucker truck' should be allowed into our compound.

'What are the arguments?' I asked crisply.

'The intelligence people have picked up a threat to us from the same team responsible for the attack on the Italians. If we let the truck in, it could be carrying a bomb, like the one in Nasiriyah. If we don't, we could be overrun by sewage'.

The tanks were full to capacity and there was nowhere for any surplus to go except over the top. No contest. The choice was between an uncertain threat and a certain health hazard. The truck came in and we were not blown up.

These events coincided with a visit by the FCO and DFID heads of personnel and the head of the FCO's Medical and Welfare

Department. Because of the lockdown they had to be dramatically airlifted out of our compound to enable them to catch a plane back to the UK. I was glad that they had seen such a situation for themselves and gratified that they compared the spirit of the team in Basra favourably with that which prevailed in the Palace in Baghdad, which they had visited earlier. But I was apprehensive about the consequences for our operations in Nasiriyah and the other Provinces, which were far more exposed than we were in Basra.

* * *

It was while these events were unfolding, and just days after the tragic attack on the Italians, that the US Government decided to wind up the CPA. On 15 November, just five days after Bremer's team had presented us with a plan which envisaged the dissolution of the CPA in October 2005 or, at the earliest, the preceding March, Bremer informed his Directors that the date would be brought forward to the end of June 2004.

When the news was passed on to us, I realised that it would change everything. Instead of pressing ahead with more staff and resources, building on the progress which the Governor in Basra had publicly acknowledged was now showing valuable results, we would have to start running down, planning for a dignified exit, while preventing the erosion of our achievements and work in hand. I knew at once that the mindset of everyone – CPA civilians, the military and our Iraqi colleagues – would be affected and that the adrenalin behind our efforts would inevitably sap away.

It seemed to be no coincidence that, as a result, the increasingly controversial CPA would have been well and truly buried by the time of the Presidential elections in November 2004. Nonetheless, I recognised that the wider political picture within Iraq, and not just within the USA, had rendered such a decision almost inevitable. It had become clear for all to see that, despite the best face being put on events by our governments, the CPA was unable to fulfil its declared function: it could not run the country and would never be able to do so. The only option was to return full sovereignty back to the Iraqis and to offer to help the Iraqi authorities try to get the country back on its feet themselves.

But that cool calculation did little to mitigate our disappointment in the South. We had not been caught up in the macro-political machinations in Baghdad, but had been almost obsessively focussed on the mechanics and local politics involved in reconstruction and economic and institutional reform.

We tried to carry on as best we could with our original objectives for getting the country back on its feet; but it was becoming abundantly clear that Baghdad's, Washington's and London's main concerns were about winding down rather than keeping up the pressure until the end.

It was just at this time, mid-November, that I headed off for a break in the UK. This provided an opportunity to take soundings of the mood within the British administration after this momentous decision.

My impressions were not encouraging. My first call was in the Ministry of Defence. Senior officers had started to think about a 'Plan B' in the event of a failure of the whole Iraq endeavour – a concept which would have horrified Bremer and the US Marine Corps, who would never allow themselves to acknowledge any such possibility. The idea was to preserve so far as possible the UK's reputation for having made progress in the South. I asked if other parts of Whitehall were focussing in any detail on what needed to be done there and was told that the South was not seen as a problem but a success, corresponding closely to the Prime Minister's wish that it should be seen as a model. This greatly dismayed me, since it did not seem like that to me. I thought that I had been sending back honest and frank reports. Perhaps my readers had compared them favourably with others from elsewhere.

I was also dismayed by my calls in DFID. As I had feared, they seemed little concerned with fulfilling my copious demands for more resources and personnel and, above all, for speed. Instead, they were preoccupied with the implications of the reduced timescale for the demise of the CPA and the prospect of having to establish a bilateral development programme with the Iraqi Government.

My most realistic meeting was with the Foreign Secretary, Jack Straw. He asked for my assessment. I told him that I had detected two schools of thought at middle-management level in London. One, which I supported, wanted to continue to do more. The other seemed to reflect a waning of interest against the prospect of the CPA's early dissolution. But, I pressed, if we did not maintain a momentum, we risked losing the benefits of everything we had done up to now. We needed greater efforts to recruit more personnel for deployment and a more attractive package of remuneration to back them up; we still had serious gaps that needed filling. The need for progress over the economy, infrastructure and capacity building had increased, rather than diminished, as a result of the shorter timescale. Whatever the political imperatives, we now had less time to secure progress which would prove durable. I went on to rehearse the weaknesses of CPA's plan which had been exposed earlier that month.

As always, I found Jack Straw very encouraging. His Private Secretary took a note of my advice and he promised to bear it in mind during his own imminent visit to Iraq. I also told Straw that I did not want to extend my tour in Basra beyond the end of January, when I would have completed the same six-month period as the British military commanders. I had been asked originally to build up an effective capability in the South. By the early New Year, provided my requests were fulfilled, this would have been largely achieved. I would prefer if it fell to someone else to preside over its dissolution over the following five months. That task would need different qualities, which I did not possess.

Straw was sympathetic. He said that he would have preferred me to stay on but he was not going to ask me to do so, since he did not want to put me in the position of having to decide how to respond. I was genuinely touched by his understanding of the way I thought, not least because, conditioned by 40 years of Crown Service, I was not entirely sure what my answer would have been.

*   *   *

In mid-December I attended another Coordinators' meeting in Baghdad. Over time they had become better organised and more productive. Bremer had evidently been advised that his absences from these meetings had not been understood by either the Divisional Commanders or those who answered to him directly – the four Regional and 18 Provincial Coordinators – and he had begun to participate more actively. But we still seemed to inhabit different planets.

Andy Bearpark, who now had devolved responsibility for setting up the 18 Provincial offices, had a meeting with the civilian Coordinators before the full meeting when we would be joined by the military commanders.

We all noted that we were still being pressed to spend money quickly. The four regional headquarters, which had been established earlier and which were the initial focus for new staff as they arrived, were starting to make progress. But it was proving almost impossible at the provincial level: the teams had insufficient staff, inadequate transport and life support, and only skeleton protection teams at a time when the security situation was deteriorating across the country.

The energetic and articulate team leaders voiced their concerns plainly and loudly. Molly Phee, the newly arrived American team leader in Maysan Province, drew attention to the contrast between the provision of armoured vehicles by DFID for use by any member of the CPA in the South, regardless of nationality, and the failure of the US State Department or USAID to do anything similar in the other 14 Provinces. This placed the entire burden of protection on the CPA military forces in those regions, and many of them simply declined to provide any.

Bringing the meeting to order, Andy Bearpark was characteristically frank. He agreed that Bremer's injunctions to spend were unworkable. Nor should we have unrealistic expectations about the speed at which the various contractors would be able to finish building CPA offices in the Provinces to an adequate level of protection: there had been delays already and there would be more to come. That, he said, was life.

After that discouraging but realistic preamble, Bearpark added that everyone's top priority should now be the personal security of themselves and their teams. He heard what everyone had to say about the consequences of the increased threats and the inadequacies of the current level of protection. There was little he or others could do about this. The bottom line, therefore, was that if any of the teams considered that their situation was unsafe, they should pull out. They should not stay in place and subject themselves to undue risk. It was their call.

While this was sensible advice, it also turned the tables. It came down to: 'If you don't like it, you should leave'. This was not what anyone wanted to hear and was truly depressing. We had at last reached the stage when, having previously let the Army carry almost all the burden, sufficient civilian staff were arriving on the ground to make a real impact, to get their teeth into advising Iraqis in a way which the Army could never do. Now we all wanted to get on with the job and be provided with the tools to do so. Yet here was Bearpark telling us that the main priority for the civilian effort had to be their own security and that this could not be assured. The reaction from the provincial teams was voluble and bitter. But Bearpark was right about the difficulty of sustaining the civilian effort which Bremer had envisaged the previous July, and prophetic in suggesting that the situation would deteriorate further.

The following meeting, at which the Generals were also present, made it yet clearer that we had shifted from trying to plan how best to rebuild the country to focussing on how best to salvage the big-picture political issues and then getting out of the place. It was now a month since the 15 November decision to shut down the CPA early, at the end of the following June. Less than two weeks before that we had been given our first sight of the master plan for security, the economy, reconstruction, governance and strategic communications. The young enthusiast who had made that presentation had left Iraq; and there was no sign of any new plan to take account of the shortened timescale. It was not even to be a mopping-up operation, because the mess was getting worse.

A month later, on 20 January, I was visited in Basra by Major General Karl Eikenberry, who had been sent by the US military headquarters in Hawaii to assess the situation. That morning I had already briefed the Chiefs of Defence Staff of Denmark and Lithuania and was feeling over-exposed to military stars. However, the Major General and I had a long conversation over lunch in our canteen. I told him that Baghdad's ambitious proposals for a new political and constitutional process would not work because no one understood them, and I shared my fears about the consequences for reconstruction of the CPA's early withdrawal. An adviser was taking notes next to his hamburger and ketchup. I wished that I had given him more time, because it later became clear that Eikenberry had direct lines back to Washington and that his findings were very influential, much to Bremer's dismay.

The following day, still preoccupied with the prospect that the effects of our work would be lost when the CPA was wound up, I was photographed by the Iraqi press handing over two massive earth-moving trucks to the Iraqi Water Authority. But my mind was full with plans for my pitch to Michael Jay, the top civil servant at the Foreign Office who had asked me to come out in the first place. Since it was still not clear what would happen next, I wanted to inject some ideas which would ensure maximum continuity.

It was not, however, quite true that there was no planning for the next stage. The Foreign Office had decided that a British Consulate should be constructed within the relatively secure perimeter of our own present location. A planning team had come out to inspect. One member of it had the misfortune to consult me for advice about the best location for the putative Consul's swimming pool, to be told colourfully where I thought that should be. Once again the Foreign Office machine seemed to regard me as their representative in Basra, while I felt that there were other considerations which should have a higher priority.

The outline which I put to Jay and subsequently wrote to London was perhaps a bit radical. London appeared to be planning that, after June 2004 and leaving aside the military aspects, the intergovernmental relationship with Iraq at the civilian level should revert to the conventional diplomatic model: an Embassy in Baghdad, with out-stations in Basra and possibly Kirkuk in the North in the form of Consulates or subsidiary offices. Within this structure, DFID would establish a development cooperation programme which would continue to progress those projects which DFID was already funding; and it could no doubt build upon these and develop new ones. The Americans, meanwhile, would do likewise. There was already talk of the new US Embassy in Baghdad being the biggest in the world and of a big new American presence in the South, focussing on development.

To my mind, that was all very well, but it took no account of the very wide range of CPA(South) projects already in train, which were being actively managed by our international team of experts. The Americans in Baghdad had shown scant interest in these, knew nothing of the background and seemed likely to neglect them without expert guidance. I felt that it would break my heart if that happened. But, more importantly, the Iraqis would be mystified by such an outcome; and many of them would be left high and dry, having put in so much work themselves.

My idea in a nutshell, therefore, was to maintain the personnel and structures of CPA(South) as far as possible but to transform them into a multinational development team, under either British or American management. As with any development effort, they would work for the sovereign government of the country – no longer as representatives of a Coalition in occupation.

Jay seemed taken with the idea when I explained it to him. And he seemed impressed by the zeal and effectiveness of our team on the ground. I followed up by telegram within 12 hours. Having heard nothing a week later, I made some enquiries.

'An interesting idea', I was told.

Oh dear. That word 'interesting' always meant trouble. A bit like 'courageous' in a similar context.

'But we are thinking on slightly different lines. Thank you all the same'.

I had another go, in February 2004, when I called on Prime Minister Blair soon after I left Basra. Again, I heard the words 'interesting idea'. I realised that my idea was doomed: Number 10 would have been briefed beforehand and, had they been really interested, they would have asked me to elaborate. This saddened me; not because I had failed to carry what I thought was a good idea, but because I believed that the managers in London had no real appreciation of the extent and value of the activity in train and hence of what would be lost if it were not maintained. And, even if there had been an appreciation in some quarters, it seemed that there was no longer any stomach to face the costs and organisational effort in maintaining such a management structure on the ground.

The post-occupation planning showed every sign of following similar lines to the planning for post-conflict: too little, too late. I have no way of knowing whether my ideas, had they been pursued, would have proved politically or administratively workable; or whether our projects could have been maintained in the deteriorating security climate. But from what I was able to gather subsequently, my fears about the alternative proved justified. DFID did what it could to continue with those projects which it had funded; but the great majority of the many projects which had overcome the obstacle course of conception, approval, tendering and contracting ground to a halt as soon as the CPA(South) team was broken up.

It also turned out that, when additional funds were allocated for new projects under the new management system, they proved almost impossible to spend on the ground. The main beneficiaries were not the Iraqis, but the contractors and consultants hired to do a job which was virtually impossible. Most of those who knew the personalities and how the Iraqi systems worked had disappeared to the four winds.

Further down the line, after the security situation had deteriorated still further, the smart, newly constructed Consulate in Basra was emptied. Its occupants moved to the military headquarters at the airport. Such a remote control operation, with virtually no scope for mentoring Iraqis to take tasks on for themselves, except in third countries, seemed an odd way to achieve the objective of:

> a unified and stable, democratic Iraq that provides effective and representative government for the Iraqi people and is underpinned by new and protected freedoms for all Iraqis and a growing market economy. . .

which formed part of the ambitious Vision which Bremer had set for us in the summer of 2003.

Chapter 11

Promoting Security and the Rule of Law

The only test of generalship is success .... The soldier may comfort himself with the thought that, whatever the result, he has done his duty faithfully and steadfastly, but the commander has failed in his duty if he has not won victory – for that is his duty.

Field Marshal William Slim.

WHEN THE CPA was established, the Americans in Baghdad regarded the four southern Provinces as unproblematic and a low priority for their attention. Bremer had told me that Baghdad was the key to settling Iraq. Initially, Iraqis appeared generally to welcome the overthrow of Saddam. He had, after all, murdered tens of thousands of the Shia population – during the Iran–Iraq war, during the draining of the Marshes in Maysan and Dhi Qar Provinces, and after the Shia revolt which followed the first Gulf War. People were grateful to the Coalition forces for deposing him.

The British in the South had a somewhat different perception. The Iraqis' initial gratitude soon turned to resentment as looting broke out and was not restrained. Law and order deteriorated.

Worrying outside influences started to emerge. An Iranian presence was increasingly detected in Maysan Province in the East. There was extensive smuggling across the three sets of shared but unguarded borders with Kuwait, Saudi Arabia and Iran, as well as across the borders with Jordan, Syria and Turkey, which were outside our southern area.

Meanwhile, organised criminality was growing, unchecked. It encompassed extortion, blackmail, kidnappings and intimidation. Old scores were settled under the pretext that the victims were Ba'athists. Local strongmen flexed their muscles to gain political advantage. Smuggling, which had developed into a sophisticated industry during the years of sanctions, was now a free-for-all, no longer a Saddam monopoly.

In the past, law and order were maintained by the all-pervasive Ba'athist intelligence and security agencies, who dominated the South. They had had no compunction about using brutal methods; and they had a good knowledge of the potential sources of conflict and of the actors. The public knew that they had no scope to express any discontent, either about the general situation or about methods used by Saddam's regime.

The local police had virtually no role in maintaining law and order. They dealt almost exclusively with traffic control and petty crime and were riddled with corruption. After Saddam's fall, they were weakened by the effects of de-Ba'athification on their leadership, demoralised and preoccupied with their own security. Despised by the public, their instinctive reaction to trouble was to take refuge in their police stations. As a result, the Coalition's military forces had to try to deal with the security situation with no effective help from Iraqis.

In the South, where the relatively low intensity of violence allowed for a more low-key and less overtly aggressive approach than in other parts of the country, the British-led military were initially able to make use of tactics which they had employed successfully in other theatres, especially in Northern Ireland.

I accompanied a military patrol to a poor area of Basra city one afternoon. I was squeezed in the back of an unarmoured Land Rover, while the young lieutenant in charge gave me a running commentary about the situation in the town. Apart from the military driver, there were two other soldiers, one of whom stood with his weapon and upper body exposed through the top of the roof at the back. We all wore body armour and helmets during the drive around the city. Once we stopped, the driver stayed with the vehicle and the rest of us emerged, took off our helmets, which my companions replaced with berets, and started to walk around. Carrying automatic weapons at a low port, the soldiers attracted interest and attention. Men and children looked on silently. But I noticed that their faces would light up with smiles as the passing soldiers met their eyes without the barrier of protective sunglasses, grinned and greeted them with 'As-salaam aleikum' in a variety of British accents. These patrols stopped well short of distributing sweets or other ingratiating goodies since, as had been bitterly learned on the streets of Belfast and Londonderry, an ensuing crowd could provide cover for assailants whose violence might kill or wound children as well as the primary targets.

The foot patrols had several functions. They were intended to deter aggression and maintain security in the manner of the once-traditional British 'Bobby on the beat'; and they provided reassurance. But they also presented opportunities for two-way dialogue with the local population and thus a form of sounding board for the current state of opinion. Conversations on street corners could be frank and courteous. Once on the move again, the Land Rovers proved irresistible targets for little boys to throw stones. But a sharp 'Oi!' from a soldier, accompanied by another grin, seemed enough to cause the stone to be dropped and often to have the young offender cuffed over the head by his father.

However, this early, sunny personal experience, though not unusual, was by no means the norm. The fact that other outcomes were possible was brought home to me by the reaction of one of the soldiers in the back of the vehicle to the sound of a burst of gunfire which seemed to originate about half a mile away. Out of his officer's earshot but within mine, the soldier muttered irritatedly that, in his view, we should at once drive off to find out what was happening and be ready to take aggressive action in response. The lieutenant, however, who had registered the sound, carried on with his patrol unperturbedly. I had no idea what his orders were, nor what other patrols might have been in the vicinity, nor did I ask. But it was clear that such incidents could give rise to two radically different sorts of response.

The lack of local knowledge proved to be a major obstacle for the Coalition forces. When fighting broke out in Basra city, it was impossible for a patrol to judge between the conflicting accounts of its cause. If a raid on a property led to a fire-fight, the soldiers had no way of knowing who was the rightful owner and who was the intruder, while this would be immediately known by the neighbours. The arrest of both factions could simply make matters worse.

Seeing the Coalition's obvious difficulties, local leaders sought to take matters into their own hands. Tribal and, later, religious leaders used teams of armed men to project their power and status, which might be real or aspirational. Criminals used gangs of thugs as a matter of course. And community leaders established vigilante squads to thwart attacks on their bailiwicks.

Such groups, despite their diversity, could easily all be labelled as militias. Their formation seemed to present both threats and opportunities and became a source of controversy within the Coalition. On the one hand was the view that any militia amounted to a challenge to the Coalition's responsibility for the security of the state – visible reproaches that the Coalition could not do its job – and would serve as rallying points for all sorts of malign interest groups. If unchecked they would lead to anarchical and violent competition for power and influence. Faced with the emergence of the firebrand cleric Moqtada al-Sadr and his Mahdi Army militia, Bremer was in no doubt that such groups were unmitigated menaces and should be stamped out. If this were true in the Baghdad region, the key to stability, then, in line with Bremer's overall approach, it must be true elsewhere. He ruled that militias of any form were not to be tolerated.

In the South we took a more nuanced view. There seemed to be no absolute need to oppose all such groups head on. To do so could prove militarily impossible and politically unwise. Recognising that some of them had come into being as a result of legitimate concerns, we thought that they might be encouraged into a more positive role. Community leaders were asked to recommend and vouch for men who might help the Coalition to guard the neighbourhoods from which they came. Such carefully selected men could then be given a licence to help Coalition patrols identify interlopers in their locality. If the recruits then betrayed the trust accorded to them, the licences would be revoked, and the community leaders who nominated the man would lose face and the benefits which came from their cooperation. The Army called this arrangement 'Neighbourhood Watch with attitude' and for a while it proved both useful and effective. It did not seem necessary to bother Baghdad too much about the details of the arrangement; the Commander's intent was clear: to maintain law and order. Local commanders were best placed to judge how to secure this objective in practice according to local conditions. Furthermore, Baghdad's response might prove unhelpful. It was only in January 2004 that Bremer's advisers came to the view that 'one size does not fit all'.

But there was more to establishing security and maintaining law and order than military-led peace-making, notwithstanding all the difficulties which that entailed. The ultimate sanction of military force, even if used with care and discrimination, cannot settle citizenry on its own: it is far too blunt an instrument. The panoply of civilian institutions needed to be brought into play: a police force, courts of law, a judiciary, and jails. And, considered more widely, all these instruments needed to be underpinned by progress in the infinitely more difficult task of calming the general mood of the population by offering opportunities for jobs, advancement, well-being and even survival.

By the end of the ground combat in April, all of the security-related institutions were dysfunctional. For the Army, the highest priority for their attention was the police force, since they represented a body of men (no women) who might be induced to make their presence felt on the ground.

In tackling this task, British Army had to make use of the resources at their disposal. In the absence of other means, it initially fell to the Royal Military Police (RMP) to embark on the difficult task of training new recruits or re-training former policemen out of the ways of the Saddam regime. The task was urgent, but there was an early and dramatic setback. On 24 June 2003, six RMP personnel were attacked and killed by an angry mob in the town of Majjar al Kabir, the second largest town in Maysan Province, some 200 miles south-east of Baghdad. This was the greatest loss of life in a single day since late March. It was a profound blow to the British effort in the South and gave rise to much soul-searching and a major official enquiry. It was many months before the Coalition proved able to pursue police training across the country in any significant or sustained manner. But despite this setback, the South was able to make some progress.

The Army took the view that police training should properly fall into the civilian domain. It was a view which I strongly shared. Police forces are not military organisations. They are meant to be servants of the public and subject to civilian direction and management. This is not an exclusively Western concept, but one which is held widely in the developing world. It is when policing is dominated by repressive security and military regimes in pursuit of political or corrupt objectives, as in Iraq previously and in Syria, that its effect becomes more corrosive than beneficial.

The Coalition's leadership had also recognised at once that expertise in civilian policing was desperately needed on the ground. In May 2003, an American team from the Department of Justice had called for the deployment of 6600 international police advisers and the provision of armed and equipped international constabulary units, with a total of 2500 personnel to help Coalition military forces restore stability and to train Iraq counterparts. During a visit to Baghdad in early July, when he had called at a nascent police academy, the British Foreign Secretary, Jack Straw, had told Bremer that he wanted to help. As a result the UK was asked to supply 100 British police officers as part of this wider effort. Allowing for leave and roulement, this meant that some 200 officers would need to receive firearms training to allow them to be deployed. The FCO passed this request on to the Home Office and the British police authorities.

It fell to the FCO in London to take a lead on the policy surrounding all these issues and in monitoring and stimulating progress. A section was set up within the FCO's Iraq Policy Unit to coordinate the roles of the various government departments and deal with the totality of what was called 'security sector reform'. Like every other aspect of the London operation, the section appeared to those in Iraq to be chronically understaffed.

In the South, a two-prong approach was adopted. The British Army had performed wonders in refurbishing police stations. By the end of June they reported that some 5000 policemen were back on the streets, although I was never clear how such seemingly precise statistics could be verified. But these policemen needed to adapt their practices now that they were no longer in effect subordinate to Saddam's security and intelligence apparatus.

The Danish Government despatched a team of Danish police officers with experience of police training in Palestine. They quickly and effectively set about establishing a small training academy in the town of Umm Qasr, outside Basra. For its part, the British Government sent a senior police officer from the Police Service of Northern Ireland with considerable experience in counter-terrorist operations, assisted by two officers from London's Metropolitan Police. Assistant Chief Constable Stephen White was told on being recruited for the job that he was to be in operational charge of the Iraqi police in the South. But he quickly learned from the unit in the FCO and from the CPA headquarters in Baghdad that there was no question of him, or anyone else at this stage, assuming such a direct, hands-on role. This was both a disappointment and a missed opportunity.

The dozen or so Danes were impressive. Lean, fit and wiry, under the leadership of a grizzled dynamo called Kai Vittrup, they were self-starters. By the time I arrived at the end of July they were well on the way to setting up the academy. Vittrup had a great deal of international experience, some of which he had gained in developing countries. His team clearly knew its mission; I had no need to intervene.

But the Danish effort involved more than just the refurbishment of buildings and lecturing to groups of Iraqis. The pre-existing police force were in as much confusion as all the other Iraqi institutions. The Danes had had to track down whoever was prepared to admit to being in charge and persuade and cajole him into cooperating in the selection, vetting and motivation of the potential students. As part of this process, the senior officer concerned had to be convinced that such a role was both worthwhile and in his interests. The latter aspect was boosted by greatly enhanced pay scales. As the balance of interests and the potential benefits became clearer, so the attractions of the job increased and stimulated competition. We had to contend with constant power struggles among senior police officers, involving all sorts of allegations against perceived rivals, the merits of which we were in no position to judge. It was to the Danes' immense credit that their small academy continued to operate without let-up until political developments beyond their control intervened the following year.

Stephen White's over-arching role proved more problematic. If he was not to re-organise the police force in the South, what was he to do, and who would take on the reorganisation task? With all his experience in the front line of policing in a tough environment, Stephen was nothing if not a practical man. Results-orientated, he was determined to make something out of his presence in Iraq. The London team were still exploring options and had no advice or help to offer. So Stephen and I spent many hours together thrashing out options. In need of policy guidance and resources from Baghdad, we decided to call on the recently appointed head of the CPA team which dealt with policing, Bernie Kerik.

Kerik had been Commissioner of the New York Police Department and had become famous for his heroic role after the terrorist attack on the World Trade Center. The trouble was that our emails before our visit received no response and we could not track him down once we reached Baghdad. His team of only six men from the US Department of Justice, to whom we unloaded our problems, did not know where he was. More importantly, they had no advice to give us. They had been given nominal responsibility for reforming the Interior Ministry, creating an Iraqi

Police Service, and re-establishing immigration, customs and border checks. They were overwhelmed. Everything, we were told, was 'still under consideration'. Only one piece of information emerged, namely that plans were being made to establish a police training facility in, of all places, Hungary. The American view was that it was too difficult to undertake such a massive task within Iraq.

The fact that the Danes were already well on the way to inaugurating a training college near Basra, albeit on a small scale, was not regarded as relevant. We pointed out that it would inevitably take a long time to set something up from scratch in Hungary and suggested that we might usefully expand our existing operations in the meantime. No one was able to authorise this.

We left this encounter downhearted and dismayed. It all seemed far worse than we had expected. We had appreciated that everyone had underestimated the size of the challenges; but we had assumed that the senior managers in Baghdad would by now – it was four months after Bremer's arrival – have drawn up a range of contingency plans to make best use of such resources as existed. As it turned out, no such planning started until after Kerik's departure. Even the Hungary plan was dropped in favour of Jordan, causing further delays.

On our return to Basra, we brainstormed again. Stephen recommended that, if Baghdad was to be no help, the UK needed to act alone. He had devised a strategy for rolling out a training programme in the South which built on the Danish activity. It could be presented as a pilot project and would require 91 police officers from the UK to act as mentors for existing members of the Iraqi police. He argued that, notwithstanding the American request to Jack Straw for 100 such officers in Baghdad, the British priority should be to settle the South. I strongly favoured the idea. Blair had told me that he wanted the South to be a model; this would be a step on the way and, most importantly, it would help stabilise the increasingly precarious situation. Stephen and I drafted a proposal for London accordingly.

But I was also conscious that it would be hard for London and the various police constabularies in the UK to deliver, certainly in the timescale which we thought was necessary. I therefore talked the idea through with the FCO before submitting the plan. They reassured me that the issue was being grasped and advised against any recommendation from Basra at that stage. Making use of the time-honoured bureaucratic ploy designed to defer unwelcome initiative, my London adviser suggested that I should avoid 'muddying the waters' at such a delicate stage of policy formulation. I put the proposal on hold.

Still justifiably impatient, Stephen continued to badger Baghdad for guidance and help. He was told that new uniforms would be provided 'in due course', to be supplied by KBR, presumably acquired from the USA. Police vehicles and equipment would also be on their way 'soon'. 'Soon', however, proved to be very much later.

On one triumphant day in mid-September, Stephen returned from one of his many visits to Baghdad bearing $360,000 in a cardboard box. Stephen had convinced Baghdad that, taking advantage of the Danish success, we should construct a Regional Training Academy to service all four southern Provinces. Such an arrangement was certain to be more popular with the trainees than the prospect of going to Jordan and leaving their families behind. This proved to be a considerable achievement. Baghdad's instincts always tended to favour maintaining control themselves rather than allowing others to get ahead. Initially they put up resistance on the grounds that they had not yet developed a curriculum; nor had they decided on the length of the course. But our arguments that the Danish project was already up and running, and that anything was better than leaving a vacuum, proved decisive.

As a starting gesture, we commissioned local tailors to run up some smart winter uniforms at a fraction of the cost to be charged by KBR. It was now too late for any summer uniforms, but these might at least help restore some of the demoralised police force's self-esteem.

By 29 September, the Danish training college was ready. Jeremy Greenstock was paying his first visit to the South after his appointment as the Prime Minister's Special Representative in Baghdad. I took him along to witness its formal inauguration. The

Danes had arranged the refurbishment of an existing building; even the stones at the edge of newly planted flower beds had been painted white. In immaculately clean classrooms the Danish officers were using their accented English and Iraqi interpreters to take forward a pre-prepared curriculum with several classes of burly Iraqi policemen. And now we had a bit more money to expand the operation.

It was Kerik who had asked the UK to supply 100 policemen. The Iraq Policy Unit's enquiries of the Association of Chief Police Officers (ACPO), a central authority which encompasses all Britain's complex constabularies, elicited no enthusiasm. Stephen White, who was not above making use of the media to pursue his operational objectives, had got into a bit of trouble for implicitly criticising the British Government and ACPO for failing to rise to the challenge; but that blew over after I had trenchantly emphasised that what was important was that Stephen's view was correct, not that he had expressed it to the media in addition to our many previous representations through the proper channels.

Despite the American request, there were still no signs of any influx of American police officers. When Kerik left, earlier than expected, he bequeathed no tangible legacy. His mantle in Baghdad fell on a senior British police officer, Deputy Chief Constable Douglas Brand. Brand's tremendous height and imperturbability had earned him the affectionate nickname 'The Tower of London'. He quickly gained Bremer's confidence. As a result, however, he found himself not only having to provide policy advice on how to take forward the challenging task of transforming the Iraqi police, but also having to serve as Bremer's itinerant law enforcer. He had very little professional assistance within the CPA, and neither Washington nor London proved able to produce police boots on the ground.

The military, meanwhile, were getting restless about the patent absence of progress, in contrast to their own achievements in creating a multiplicity of new, security-related organisations such as the Iraqi Civil Defence Corps – later to become the Iraqi National Guard, the Facilities Protection Service and the Department of Border Enforcement.

Something had to give. But when the next development arose, it took me and the British Divisional Commander by complete surprise. One afternoon in late October, I was told that a team of US Army officers had arrived unexpectedly in our offices in Basra. I was invited to come and listen to their presentation.

What followed was another of the surreal experiences which were characteristic of the CPA and to which I was trying to become accustomed. With no prior consultation with anyone in the South, it had been decided – by whom was never clear – that all responsibilities for police training would henceforward be assumed by the Army. I politely enquired about the authority for this step, which seemed at odds with the policy objective of establishing a civilian police force. A US Army colonel read out a FRAGO, or Fragmentary Order as the US military instructions were called, which I and others found incomprehensible because of the jargon and acronyms. But the translation was clear enough, and, whatever our annoyance about lack of consultation and the differences between the British-led and American military resources and dispositions, it was clearly intended to apply to us.

Reactions within CPA(South) and in the military headquarters were varied. The redoubtable Kai Vittrup declared that, since the Danish contribution had evidently not been appreciated, and since the Danish police were not a military force, he and his team would leave forthwith. Stephen White and I lamented our own failures to secure a larger British civilian police presence more quickly. I recalled the famous occasion in 1968 when Prime Minister Harold Wilson had sent a force of Metropolitan Police officers to the Caribbean island of Anguilla, a British dependent territory where some trouble had broken out. Times, it seemed, had changed.

The British Army headquarters went strangely silent for a while as they absorbed the implications of the FRAGO. Up to now, middle-ranking officers had been openly sceptical about our, admittedly humble, efforts to develop the police force. It was obvious to all of us that the resources at our disposal, which were tiny compared with the 8500 British armed forces in theatre with their associated command teams, were far less able than them to make an impact over such a task. But the Army had proved reluctant to provide Stephen or the Danes with any help in setting up the small training academy. Suddenly the tone changed. The Army realised that such progress as we had made could provide them with a lifeline. The fact was that the British military capability paled into insignificance beside the 135,000 US forces. And the Royal Military Police, still suffering from the tragedy at Majjar al Kabir four months earlier, were severely overstretched already. They did not want this additional task thrust upon them and realised that we might help them to secure a special, compromise arrangement in the South.

I was only too happy to oblige the delegation of officers from the General's headquarters who came to sound me out. Yes, I told them, I had always emphasised the importance of the civilian character of the police. Yes, I agreed that this could not be achieved solely by using Military Police as trainers. And yes, I was already pressing London to send out some police officers for this purpose. But, I said, the result of our efforts alone seemed unlikely to match the scale of operations envisaged by the FRAGO. I therefore agreed that we should try to work something out together.

The prospect of a continuing civilian role mollified the Danes. I persuaded Kai Vittrup to agree that his team should stay on until their previously agreed departure date. I was proud to present graduation certificates to a batch of his students just before Christmas.

Although worrying at the time, the Danish ultimatum proved to be an invaluable bargaining counter in our efforts to secure Baghdad's agreement to our plan. I pointed out that it would be a shame to lose the results of the Danish efforts; and it would be an insult to an important and loyal Coalition partner for them to be treated with such disregard. I kept Bremer and Greenstock informed of all these developments, and it would have been characteristic of Bremer to have supported the incontrovertibly strong arguments for our special arrangements. The real problem was to convince the US military chain of command that a clear order, already transmitted, should be capable of subsequent modification.

Fortuitously for our efforts, the head of the British Association of Chief Police Officers passed through Iraq in mid-November. A security scare did not allow him to visit us in Basra, so Stephen and I went to see him at the military headquarters in the airport. We put the case to him personally, contrasting the versatility and resourcefulness of the Danes with what appeared to be the inertia of the British authorities. Did the British police and their administrators really want their contribution of three police officers in Basra to be compared unfavourably with the courageous efforts of tiny Denmark? We all knew, I suggested, that the British copper was made of sterner stuff. So were their administrators being over-cautious? Or simply recalcitrant?

I also put the case to Foreign Secretary Jack Straw, when I called on him a few days later in London. He was entirely supportive and pressed hard to ensure that the prospect of the Christmas/New Year holiday in the UK would not delay deployment. At about this time the ACPO report finally emerged, in favourable terms, although envisaging a deployment on a far smaller scale than we regarded as necessary.

I learned afterwards that I was deeply unpopular among British civil servants for my conspiracy with Straw and was blamed for his daily badgering of hard-pressed officials. I have no doubt, however, that without his personal, ministerial-level engagement, the whole project would have slipped well into the New Year.

The upshot was a combined effort: British police officers and a combination of British and Czech military trainers, physically located at the site of the Regional Police Academy which Stephen had already earmarked. The team of trainers arrived in Basra on Christmas Eve, and on Christmas morning Stephen and I went to see them over a festive lunch. Two days later Judge Wa'el, Basra's Governor, joined us to inaugurate the academy, with the full traditional panoply of speeches and dignitaries. To the best of our knowledge the Academy was the first of its kind in Iraq.

* * *

If an offender was arrested, either by the Army or the police who we were trying to train, then they needed to be brought to trial. This required courts and a judiciary to preside over them. It also required prisons in which to lock up those convicted. These issues fell squarely in the civilian rather than the military domain, although the British Army Legal Services had done valuable work to fill the vacuum. Since I needed to assess what the situation was so as better to judge what needed to be done, I went to visit Basra's law courts. I was accompanied by our single legal expert in the South, Aline Matta, an energetic and highly motivated young Australian woman of Lebanese descent who spoke fluent Arabic. Having been in Basra for a few months before my arrival, Aline had met all the key figures and was evidently already greatly respected by her Iraqi interlocutors; and she got on well with the American judge who led the Coalition legal effort in Baghdad.

I was surprised to be met at what were once the entrance gates of Basra's main law courts, not by a lawyer or a judge but by an architect and a building contractor. I saw that those courts would have no need of judges or advocates for some time. There could be no court proceedings and no court personnel could lodge in these buildings, even temporarily. All that remained was a burnt-out shell. Recognising the importance of the court's role, the British Government had already allocated funds to renovate the place. The architect was keen to show me his plans, but the work would take many months. I asked why the courts, which did not seem a fruitful source of loot, had been so damaged when there must have been more attractive booty to be had elsewhere. The question seemed a silly one when I was told that the court buildings housed the city's criminal records and accounts of previous legal proceedings: it was naturally an early and prime target for destruction.

My next step was to meet the Iraqi judiciary. This greatly heartened me after such a depressing visit to the courts. There was exceptionally good and close cooperation between the CPA in Baghdad, under the leadership of American Judge Rubini, and the regions. Judge Laith Abdel Samad Lifta, who presided in Basra Province, was full of jolly charm and affability. He proved to be an avid fan of Manchester United football club. Having reeled off the names of the entire 1966 World Cup team, he was disappointed that I did not share his passion for either the team or the sport. But he seemed to accept my excuse that my limited interest in English football was a result of my ancestry: my Irish forebears had probably pursued other interests, including the ejection of what they regarded at the English oppressor from their homeland.

Judge Laith and his colleagues were operating from a very basic building with minimal amenities. But this did not seem to put them out. Judge Laith took me to witness two hearings then in progress, where I met two other judges, who were dressed in Western-style suits and ties. One described the case with which he was dealing as 'unimportant'. It involved the death by accident of the son of a weeping lady who described the circumstances to me. It may have been unimportant compared with the many iniquities over which the presiding judge had witnessed, but of course it was not to this mother. I was impressed that, despite all the difficulties of the city, such cases were able to be dealt with, and that Coalition staff had been able to facilitate the process.

I learned that, even under Saddam's regime, the training of judges was thorough and professional. Unusually, the senior judiciary were not required to be members of the Ba'ath Party, which Judge Laith was not. Nonetheless, some were, and the Coalition was helping the Iraqis with a review of all the judiciary to establish who should remain and who should go. I also learned that Saddam had once allowed women to enter judicial training, but that this permission was withdrawn after only one year. Two women had entered the system during that period and, having completed the full training process, they were still practising.

In December 2003 there were some 52 judges and prosecutors in Basra and 160 in total in the South. In Basra Province, plaintiffs generally had recourse to State Law. But in the rural Provinces the old and hallowed tribal law was still applied, just as I had witnessed in my diplomatic postings in Pakistan and Jordan. The judiciary therefore had to be conscious of, and sensitive to, both systems; and so did we in the CPA.

* * *

The third pre-requisite for the maintenance of law and order, a prison system, proved to be an unholy mess. In early September, conscious of the desperate shortage of expertise in the South, I had requested the urgent despatch of someone with experience of prison management and procedures. None of us in CPA(South) had yet visited any prisons in the four southern Provinces – they fell under US responsibility – but I was hearing worrying rumours from sources in Baghdad.

In mid-December we were reinforced by the governor of Pentonville prison, Gareth Davies, who had taken leave of absence for the purpose. His arrival was an enormous relief because it coincided with the departure of Stephen White who, like so many others, was leaving without a successor. I desperately needed someone to take charge of all our small but important and specialised Law and Order 'Pillar', for which Stephen had been responsible. I could not possibly add such a portfolio to that of one of my existing managers; and I could not take over such day-to-day management issues myself. Gareth, whose burly frame and battered ears bore witness to an earlier participation in rugby football, made an immediate impression as an experienced and measured administrator and manager. I thought him ideal for the task, even if his lack of experience of the local situation and non-prison issues caused him to be modestly diffident about taking it on.

Gareth's visits to the prisons in the South brought disturbing reports. A British official had been attached to the prisons section in the Baghdad headquarters and, worried about what was going on, had asked to be transferred to Basra, to back up Gareth. The Americans were content to let him go and I was delighted at the reinforcement of our team. Gareth had a solid knowledge of international norms and was shocked by what he saw during his tour. He wrote me a full report. In view of the sensitivity of both the subject matter and the alleged actions of our American Coalition partners, I decided that it should be brought to London's attention at once. I despatched it in January, shortly before my departure from the CPA.

The story of the appalling mistreatment of prisoners in the Abu Ghraib detention centre first appeared on the US television news channel *60 Minutes II* some four months later. Gareth Davies told me some time after I had left that, despite his further enquiries, he had no response to his report and that he, like myself, was not aware whether any action had been taken on it. I was delighted, however, that the Crown subsequently recognised his contribution to the Coalition's effort by the award of an OBE.

*   *   *

As we struggled to encourage the Iraqis in the South to establish and reinforce their damaged institutions, the deterioration of the security situation in Baghdad and elsewhere was reflected in the southern Provinces. The Army were encountering increased criminality, insurgency and violent attacks. Our contacts gave us accounts of intimidation, extortion and murders within their working environment. Hospitals were particularly affected: pharmaceutical drugs were stolen for onward sale at great profit; doctors were blackmailed or murdered.

The first murder of an Iraqi working for us was of a man who was helping us open up the ports. We speculated that one of the criminal gangs who ran mafia operations there wanted to ensure that we did not meddle in their business. But our colleague's death could have simply been a punishment for associating with the 'occupiers'. Other murders, later, were more clearly for this reason. They included the two women who ran our laundry and the very efficient Chief Assistant to the Governor, who seemed to organise the business of the Basra Council entirely on his own. Many more were to take place later. Such were the costs to patriotic Iraqis who were genuinely trying to help their country by making our own operations more effective.

Faced with such challenges, we continued to try to forestall further opposition through political activity. Our objective was not to ensure that local leadership was put into the hands of supporters of the Coalition. We knew that we were quite incapable of controlling day-to-day political management: we had neither the knowledge nor the resources. Instead, we wanted to promote a process which allowed for as great a consensus as possible in determining the membership and leadership of local bodies. This in turn might allow competent and trusted representatives to engage in local governance, which might then lead to stability and equity.

Sometimes this meant heading off tribal leaders or others who seemed disposed to monopolise power. In Basra Province, for example, Sheikh Muzahim al-Tamimi, whom the Army had appointed to head the Basra Council in April 2003, started increasingly to favour his own tribes people and associates over the broader community, and was less and less open to cooperation with the CPA. Had he not been removed by the edict that Ba'ath party members were to be excluded from public office – his party membership had come along with his career as an Iraqi naval commander – we would probably have had to find some other way to remove him to avoid jeopardising the fragile progress towards some sort of representative institutions.

I met Tamimi as a guest at one of my Iftar dinners during Ramadan. Every inch the former officer, with a vice-like handshake and a proud demeanour, he wryly mentioned his deposition but seemed to bear no ill-feeling about it.

Tamimi's replacement by Judge Wa'el followed wide-ranging consultations about his acceptability. This of course fell well short of elections, which were not practicable at that time, but the process was as open and consensual as was feasible. The result proved effective and relatively long-lasting.

The process of consensus-building was, however, far from easy for the Coalition and for Judge Wa'el. The fact was that the South was not going to unite itself politically, religiously or tribally behind a single cause or figurehead. Each group was divided within itself: Islamic political parties versus democratic; radical religious groups versus moderate; traditional sheikhs versus Saddam's sheikhs. Even the radical religious groups had difficulty cooperating with each other: they followed varied routes to the personalities who influenced them in Najaf. The Sadr and Fudala groups, for example, would only cooperate when expedient, such as when their leaders in Najaf were arrested or harassed. Followers of Sistani considered Moqtada al-Sadr's activists as upstarts.

As Moqtada and his Mahdi Army, the Jaish al-Mahdi, became increasingly threatening, Bremer summoned a group of civilian Coordinators to a meeting in Baghdad in mid-October to discuss how to deal with him. Robert Wilson and I had gathered with Scott Carpenter, the head of the CPA's Governance Directorate, when Bremer and General Sanchez, the head of the military Task Force, came in. Bremer was determined to cut Moqtada down to size. An Iraqi judge had prepared an arrest warrant against him for murder: this was to form the basis for action. There was little opportunity for discussion during this hasty meeting and the outcome was confused. Sanchez indicated concurrence of some sort. There was some reference to taking people out, but it was not clear what decision had been taken, still less what we were all supposed to do about it beyond the idea that Moqtada's henchmen should be progressively arrested so as to start to isolate him. If it were necessary, Moqtada should also be arrested, but since he was holed up in a mosque this would be problematic. I was glad that at least there was no question of storming the mosque directly, since this would have caused a furious and widespread backlash.

Bremer and Sanchez left the meeting as hurriedly as they had arrived. Carpenter, whom I had incorrectly assumed had advised Bremer beforehand, appeared as confused as the rest of us. After some further discussion we parted, agreeing that we in the South would reflect further and offer Carpenter some thoughts about the implications for our region.

I went from that meeting immediately to consult the senior British general in Baghdad, Sanchez's deputy, to see if he had a better idea what was going on. I needed to know whether the military chain of command had developed an operational plan which would affect our political activity. I was reassured to be told that there was no question of any imminent military action against Moqtada, but left even more confused about the reasons why we had been summoned to Baghdad and what might happen next.

Robert and I thought it would be deeply unwise to start taking drastic action against Moqtada if we had not first done everything possible to prepare the ground with potentially sympathetic opinion leaders. We therefore drew up a plan of political action in the South and suggested to Baghdad that they should prepare a note which made the case against Moqtada in terms of the damage he was doing to Iraq and other Iraqis. The CPA could then use this note as the basis of a consistent approach across the country. The main purpose would be to persuade selected religious leaders of the supremacy of the law and to disassociate themselves from Moqtada. It would be essential that Iraqis themselves were seen to take a lead and that there should be minimal evidence that the CPA were trying to orchestrate opposition, although that of course was exactly what we would be doing. Therefore the approaches should be limited to a small number and conducted with great discretion. We hoped that, knowing that Moqtada was not popular in the South and that other Iraqis were concerned about him too, this might leave him high and dry.

We were under no illusions about the difficulties. Even in the South, the region was divided. Basra and Al Muthanna provinces had no sympathy for Moqtada. But a successful rally in his support had occurred in Dhi Qar Province. And Abu Hatem, the Lord of the Marshes in Maysan, was carefully hedging his bets; he had enough opposition to contend with already.

The magnitude of the task was brought home to me a few days later, at the end of October, when I called on the elderly Mohammed Bakr Nasri, a leading cleric in Nasiriyah, in Dhi Qar. On arrival at his house I was told that he did not receive visitors during Ramadan. I therefore met his son, also a cleric, whom I found mediating between the leadership of two rival groupings. This incidentally reinforced my view that local leaders were likely to be more effective in maintaining peace and security than either the civilian or the military arms of the Coalition could ever hope to be.

After some conversation in which the cleric responded positively to my account of our objectives in the South, I asked him for his opinion of Moqtada. I remember the conversation well, for its subtlety and courtesy.

'His father', replied the cleric, referring to Muhammad al-Sadr, 'was a great man'.

'But what of Moqtada?'

'He is still young'.

This conveyed a lot, but was not getting me very far. I asked whether the violence associated with Moqtada's Mahdi Army was not a matter for concern.

'He is a young man. Young men make mistakes'.

'But he has been charged with murder'.

'Young men make mistakes'.

In view of such mistakes, would he consider making it clear publicly that they were indeed mistakes? And that he did not approve of them?

'Ah', came the reply. 'You must understand that Moqtada al-Sadr has a large following. His supporters are mainly young people. They do not think that he is making mistakes. They believe that he is right to take such actions. If I were to speak out against the son of the revered Ayatollah, then such people would no longer come to my mosque'.

The message could hardly have been clearer and was a reasoned one. The cleric was certainly no supporter of Moqtada al-Sadr. He probably thoroughly disapproved of Moqtada's violent ways, which were starting to cause problems in his area and which threatened to reduce his influence. But he would lose still more influence, and income, if he were to speak out.

I changed the subject. Even in a region where the religious leaders had no affinity with Moqtada's leadership and disapproved of his methods, Baghdad's ideas for isolating him were going to be thwarted by on-the-ground realities which had greater weight than the upholding of a CPA notion of the rule of law.

We never received any further instructions from Baghdad on how to take the matter forward nor, despite our suggestion, any speaking note for use with selected contacts. It looked as if the headquarters would simply carry on regardless of any opportunity to influence opinion or generate support.

But perhaps the efforts had not been in vain, at least for the moment. Word evidently got round that the CPA were planning a crack down. In early November, Moqtada proclaimed that it was Saddam Hussein, not the Americans, who was the enemy of Iraq, and described the American Army as 'guests of Iraq'. That seemed sufficient to vent the CPA's pressure – and to allow Moqtada's forces to fight another day.

* * *

Our hopes about the security situation rose in early December 2003, when Saddam was discovered in his foxhole hideout. Correctly anticipating that the Basrawis would be loosing off feux de joie, Pete Duklis instructed all CPA(South) staff to wear helmets and body armour on the basis that what goes up must come down. Pete and I went along to the outside bar later that evening for a celebratory beer to find most of our team elated by the news and punctiliously wearing their full protective kit. But, being close to Christmas, they had adorned themselves with festive decorations, including illuminated bobbles stuck to their tin hats. The next morning we discovered that a falling rifle bullet had penetrated the aluminium roof of one of the hooches and embedded itself in the floor. Despite the frivolity, the helmets had been necessary.

A few days later a senior British general on a visit from the UK gave me an account of what he said was the 'real story' of Saddam's capture which he had picked up in Baghdad. Acting on reliable intelligence, members of General Ray Odierno's Fourth Infantry Division had swarmed into the target location but had been quite unable to find any trace of Saddam. They picked up a suspect whom they found on the site and, certain that their quarry was there somewhere, pressed him to reveal his whereabouts. Not wishing to betray his master verbally, the man said nothing. Instead he stamped his foot upon the ground. Directly underneath where he was standing, and covered with a layer of sand, was the trapdoor which covered Saddam's 'spider hole' hiding place.

Predictions by even the highest level of the British Army that Saddam's arrest would lead to immediate improvements in security unfortunately came to nothing. By December, constant alarms and intelligence reports of imminent threats were seriously disrupting our operations. It became very difficult to travel to Baghdad. We needed armed escorts for the road journey to Basra airport, and then we had to find room on one of the increasingly stretched RAF Hercules aircraft. We faced similar logistical problems on arrival. One or more links in such a complicated chain would inevitably break, which entailed delay or cancellation of the trip. Frequently, intelligence reports dictated that the road to Basra airport could not be used, which meant that the only way to travel between the two locations was by helicopter. This could be managed for senior visitors such as Ministers and Generals, but it was hard to get approval for a helicopter for a specialist in infrastructure, even if a successful mission allowed him to return from Baghdad with a suitcase containing a couple of million dollars. I had to miss several of Bremer's meetings with the military commanders and Provincial and Regional Coordinators simply because I could not get myself to Baghdad.

When we were all woken at 2.30am in the last days of January by four crumps, evidently mortars, new concerns emerged. This was the first significant mortar attack on our civilian operation – until then such attention had been reserved for the Army. But even this incident seemed barely significant. Two of the impacts proved to have fallen 500 metres outside our compound; and the statistical chances of the other two causing damage in the very wide area seemed slight.

Nonetheless, the next morning I reviewed our contingency plans for mortar attacks. Someone suggested that we should dive under our beds if we were attacked again, since the mattress would be good protection against shrapnel. Someone else observed that the design of the beds allowed space only for the ubiquitous dust balls which seem to breed in such places, and certainly not for a human. But KBR had already constructed a mortar-proof shelter into which we could all huddle in the event of a sustained assault. We should be safe to carry on our work for a good while yet.

In April 2004, when the US Marines stormed the city of Fallujah in what was widely interpreted by Iraqis as a revenge attack for the bloody murder and mutilation of four American contractors, there was a further vicious lurch down the spiral. The main challenge for the CPA was now confined to hanging on until the end, when, finishing as it had begun, it would leave the task to the Army.

Chapter 12

Repairing the Wreckage:

The Realities of Reconstruction

Better let them do a poor solution than you presenting the best. For theirs is the land and the future and your time is short.

A quote from T.E. Lawrence, posted in Rory Stewart's
office in Amarah.

'WINNING THE PEACE', announced the headline in *News&Views*, the Foreign Office's in-house magazine. Beneath it was a photograph of a young man who appears to be hoisting a flag on the roof of a building. He is wearing a blue body-armour jacket. The flag is an Iraqi one. The city is Basra and the roof on which James Roscoe, my private secretary, is standing was our headquarters, the Electricity Accounts building.

The impression conveyed by the picture is one of a valiant endeavour to help the people of Iraq. But a closer examination of the photograph reveals some oddities. There is a stick of some sort protruding above the flag, while the flag itself is attached to what is clearly a metal pole which is stuck in a mound of sand and cement. And why is James fiddling with a piece of string at the bottom of the flag?

The reality was very different from the impression. In the autumn of 2003 the Foreign Office wanted to publicise what we were doing and asked us to provide some stories and photographs. The front page picture of *News&Views* was one of the results. But far from representing valiant endeavour, the occasion was one of mourning. The day before the photograph was taken, Aqila al-Hashimi, a member of the Iraqi Governing Council, had been assassinated. I decided that we should lower the Iraqi flag at the top of our building to half mast in a gesture of respect. So James and I went up to the roof to see how best to do this.

As the photograph shows, our makeshift mast was only about six feet tall and the flag already took up half of its length. If we were to lower it any further it would be quite invisible from the city. So what James is really doing is attaching a broom stick to the top of the mast to give the impression that the flag had been lowered.

This makeshift solution entirely met the purpose. But to me the incident spoke volumes about the nature of our mission, the resources available, and the story which governments chose to convey about the situation – although, to be fair to *News&Views*, the small print inside the magazine does make clear that the flag is being lowered, albeit with no mention of the clearly visible broomstick.

*   *   *

I had been neither shocked nor surprised by my first impressions of southern Iraq. Of course Basra city had none of the brilliant, shiny and grossly expensive perfection of Kuwait city, which I found myself reacting strongly against. But neither did it reveal any of the poverty and deprivation which were such common sights in parts of Pakistan and India. Despite its deep troubles, it still looked like a city of a middle-income developing country. There were plenty of cars on the roads; shops were open; Basra city's tea shops were busy and there was a general air of bustle.

But these superficial impressions were deceptive. Lurking below the surface were two practical challenges of leviathan dimensions which threatened the CPA's objectives from the outset and until after its dissolution a year later. They may have been more apparent in Basra than in Baghdad's Green Zone simply because we were able to get closer to them.

The first was a consequence of the nature and extent of Iraqi expectations. People constantly told us, and I had no doubt that they genuinely believed, that the Coalition ought immediately to make life better for ordinary Iraqis: the prosperity and technological advances in our own countries showed that we had the capability; and we clearly had the resources. The privations to which we had subjected Iraqis as a result of the UN's sanctions regime imposed a moral obligation on us to repair the damage we had caused, so we should get on with it.

The second challenge arose from the fact that neither the Coalition nor the Iraqi citizenry had any idea about the parlous state of the country's infrastructure and manufacturing capacity. The causes of this went back a quarter of a century, not just to the start of the international sanctions as many Iraqis maintained.

Iraq had been at war with Iran for eight years in the 1980s. This was followed by Saddam's invasion of Kuwait in 1990 and his defeat in the First Gulf War. These two adventures and 12 years of international sanctions expended most of Iraq's oil wealth. A once-prosperous country was reduced to the poorest in the Middle East; poverty and malnutrition became widespread.

Before the Second Gulf War, in 2003, Saddam controlled the economy and levers of government by means of three instruments: provincial Governors underpinned by the intelligence and security services; subordinate offices of the central, Baghdad-based ministries; and all-pervading state-owned enterprises whose senior officials and managers had to be members of the Ba'ath party. The system worked after a fashion, but it was creaking badly.

Saddam's fall caused the whole edifice, such as it was, to collapse altogether. The once all-powerful Governors and top managers vanished: they fled, were deposed or were assassinated in settlement of old scores. The ministries ceased to function; the subordinate offices were paralysed. The security services evaporated. The CPA, which had assumed all responsibility for the country, found itself presiding over a management system which was not simply weak, under-resourced or inefficient; the state's institutions had imploded. Like so many other aspects of the occupation, the contingency had not been planned for, although, as is explained in Chapter 10, it had been predicted.

When I had taken up diplomatic postings in the past, I had started by reading as much contemporary literature about the country as I could find. I was able quite quickly to build up a picture not only about the politics and the economy, but also about customs, norms of behaviour, cultural attitudes and the currents of popular thinking. This was simply not possible in the case of Iraq.

The long absence of foreign observers – journalists, diplomats, businessmen and aid agencies – combined with the regime's secrecy meant that very little was known about the true condition of the country. Reports from international weapons inspectors gave only a partial picture. Iraqi exiles, claiming to be well informed and wishing to encourage outside intervention, suggested that all would be well once Saddam was disposed of. Such testimony was welcome to British and American governments and was disseminated with embellishments in support of their policies.

But the exiles' self-serving accounts were totally unfounded. When the Army engineers in the South came to assess the infrastructure there, it was immediately clear that large parts of it were on the point of collapse. Power generation and distribution systems and water-pumping, filtration and distribution networks were prone to massive failures and were being held together by makeshift repairs and the ingenuity of Iraqi engineers. Collapsed sewerage systems were threatening public health. Civil engineering works such as canals, drainage channels and bridges were crumbling. Basra's six canals were blocked by noxious effluents. The several ports in Basra Province were silted up and unusable. According to a British senior military officer, the whole place was 'held together by chicken wire and chewing gum'.

As our civilian experts started to trickle into the country, the deeper, structural problems over agriculture, health, education, and legal systems emerged. The infrastructural problems were probably worse in the South than in the Baghdad region. Because of the Shia opposition to the Sunni domination by Saddam and his regime, and especially after the failed Shia revolt in 1991, the South had been methodically squeezed and deprived of an equitable share of available resources in favour of Saddam's supportive heartland, around the Tikrit region of his birthplace. The only infrastructure which received special attention was that which was of benefit to areas further north. Anything intended primarily to serve the South was left to decay.

The looting which erupted soon after the ground combat made matters much worse. I saw for myself how the main university in Basra had been pillaged. The Dean lamented to me that his friend, the Head of the Engineering Faculty, had been murdered. Like many other Iraqis, he pressed me to agree that looters and other criminals should be shot on sight, to deter others. The British Army were conscious of this point of view and of the damage caused by the looting; but such summary executions would have been unlawful. And they certainly would have further undermined the legitimacy of the occupation internationally and impeded the objective of winning consent. The only real way to have prevented the looting would have been the presence of more troops on the ground, who were not available.

By the time the looting was eventually got under control, much of Iraq's infrastructure had been targeted by saboteurs and exploited by criminals and smugglers. Power lines were stripped; copper and aluminium cable were smelted into ingots and sold on in neighbouring countries. As a result, whole swathes of the country were without electricity, even when generators were brought on stream by the joint efforts of the Coalition and Iraqi engineers.

I received up-to-date reports each evening at my regular meetings with the heads of sections. One day our Northern Irish water specialist reported that the banks of one of the water canals had caved in and the surrounding area was flooding and polluting the rest of the canal. The next day I heard that it had been fixed. Our health specialist reported a spate of extortions and murders of doctors in the main hospital: in one case a man wanted revenge for the failure to cure a sick relative; in another a blackmailer had wrongly assumed that any doctor must be rich and had demanded money. Other reports came in of damage to power supply cables causing blackouts, opportunistic burglaries in the dark, the disruption of water pumps and the failure of domestic water supplies with consequential health hazards.

No one expected me, 'The Boss', to solve such intractable lists of problems – all concerned quickly learned how to deal with them, perhaps by mobilising and mentoring the Iraqi technicians, perhaps by calling on military help. But such shared information allowed us all to develop an overall picture of the state of the region and to monitor the extent to which our efforts to build indigenous capacity were working. When, as was frequently the case, we lacked the capacity ourselves to tackle the daily income of challenges, we discussed how best to prioritise them and whether we needed support from Baghdad.

Bremer had made absolutely plain to me that his focus would be on Baghdad – the key to Iraq as a whole, as he described it. But Basra was the country's second most important city, and the Province was home to a significant stock of infrastructure which fed into the nation as a whole. The problems in the South therefore had implications which extended well beyond its own area.

The Americans had made certain to secure the southern oilfields and, unlike the northern oilfields which were constantly sabotaged and largely out of operation, these were never directly under threat. But Basra Province also contained Iraq's only ports, of which three or four had great potential if they could be made fully operational. The only international airport outside Baghdad, which currently housed the main military headquarters in the South, had been fitted out to high international standards by a German company: marbled halls resonated to the sound of army boots and solid, highly polished hardwood tables were decorated with ubiquitous plastic cups of tea. Basra Province also contained major power stations which fed into the national grid; petrochemical, steel, cement, plastics and fertiliser plants; and a major oil refinery. Many were now largely derelict. In addition to the airport, the South's communications included an excellent road system in good repair, a rail link from the south of the country to Baghdad and beyond, and the Shatt al-Arab waterway. The Marshes offered inestimable potential for high-value agriculture and employment.

Despite Baghdad's clear priority for the capital region, my own view was that the redevelopment of the southern region was also essential – for the sizeable population who lived there and for the country as a whole.

For a period, the CPA in Baghdad gave the impression that the Coalition would be able to take on this reconstruction task on its own. The leadership broadcast a confident message which reflected the political imperative that the Coalition's mission was bound to be a success. The task was to be achieved by means of massive contracts let out to major external companies, almost exclusively American, which would provide both the equipment and the management.

I tried hard to find out what these companies were up to and asked around in Baghdad. However, I and my small team could not establish any detail and it proved impossible to determine the rationale for whatever planning was going on. I was given the impression that I should not concern myself: the situation was well in hand; contracts were under way; funding was already available, particularly from existing Iraqi sources; and more funding was to be expected from Congress.

Meanwhile, London was similarly exercised, but for a very different reason. While I needed to assess how the American plans might affect my area of responsibility and try to mesh my Regional Plan into Baghdad's larger plan, London had gained the impression that all the contracts, even those to be paid for by Iraqi funds, were going to American firms. They wanted a tendering process for contracts which was open for competition by all the Coalition countries. London therefore asked me to press the traditional plea for a level playing field and to advance British commercial interests.

I was not interested in that game, whatever the state of the playing field. I was in the country to make progress over its reconstruction, governance and security, not to tout for British business. I responded sniffily that this was a matter for the (tiny) British Embassy which had just been established in Baghdad, not for an arm of the CPA.

I reflected later that my difficulty in finding out what was going on was not just because CPA(South) was regarded as irrelevant. Indeed, when I called on Lewis Lucke, the head of the American development organisation USAID, he could not have been more helpful and friendly. His equally affable representative in Basra made a point of maintaining close contact with me and we regularly shared perceptions. But the briefings were all about 'metrics', which seemed to reflect a peculiarly American fixation with quantifying results in terms of, for instance, the number of schools refurbished, kilometres of roads re-surfaced, pipelines repaired and the like. These were the figures which our governments liked to publicise. But they conveyed nothing of the reality. It proved impossible to discover a rationale for the choice and prioritisation of projects. I was always glad to hear that a particular town's generator had been repaired. But I also wanted to hear whether there were any plans to sort out the problems of another town; and if not why not.

I eventually concluded that the reason I could not find out the information I wanted was not because it was deliberately withheld but because my interlocutors were struggling to make sense of it all themselves. It would be imprudent for anyone to reveal these dilemmas. Anything short of success could not be countenanced. The emperor could not be seen to be naked.

The consequences of such a Panglossian approach worried me. The contractors hired by Baghdad or Washington had not consulted either our team in the South or any local Iraqi engineers or administrators. If it was the imploded Baghdad ministries who provided advice, we were quite certain that they did not know the true picture and were not able to take account of local political factors such as the effects on individual cities which might be deprived of services while the wider network was being established.

After discussion with the Army and my own specialists, I became convinced of the need for a two-prong approach: long-term replacement of outdated plant in tandem with short-term make-good-and-mend. Development specialists tended to favour the former approach; it was no use trying to stitch things together, they would just break down again, and time and money would have been wasted. But those on the ground, and especially the Army, wanted some quick and visible results and to generate employment for the crowds of men who had nothing to do. As the security situation deteriorated, the need to show progress, albeit on a small scale, assumed greater importance, even if it would be more costly in cash terms in the long run.

To be fair to the Baghdad headquarters, we were not alone in reaching this conclusion. Andy Bearpark, the Operations Director, would spread his hands in acknowledgement of the analysis and of the fact that there was little that the CPA bureaucracy could do about it: events must take their course. Bremer continued to press for instant expenditure, anywhere and everywhere.

General Lamb and I grumbled to each other that this was no way to run a railroad. He observed that 'We are where we are'. I occasionally and uselessly remarked that 'If I wanted to get there, I wouldn't start from here'. We both resolved to proceed as best we could.

* * *

Our efforts, however, would depend on involving the Iraqis and especially their managers. The Ba'athist regime was not popular anywhere in Iraq outside the Sunni triangle in the central part of the country. It was particularly reviled in the South, where so many who had opposed Saddam had been oppressed or killed by his agents. Active Ba'athists, frightened for their lives, left the scene very quickly. The CPA's misguided de-Ba'athification Order removed the top four levels of the party from whatever offices they held, whether or not they had been Party activists.

Had the country's management systems not already imploded, these departures would have caused it to do so. All senior positions in the many state-owned enterprises in the South, the managers of hospitals, the deans and senior faculty members of universities and technical colleges, all had to join the Party if they were to be eligible for such positions. Those who remained after de-Ba'athification had never had senior management experience and had been accustomed to working on instructions from others. Because of the authoritarian nature of the regime, they tended to be cautious and shunned initiative. In the uncertain political situation after the conflict, many were reluctant to cooperate with the CPA when it was becoming increasingly unpopular and they might put themselves at risk if they did so.

We were painfully aware of the Coalition's limitations. Because we all travelled widely and were not constrained by the limitations of the Green Zone in Baghdad, we could see that Baghdad's top-down approach was having no practical impact; and we made our own judgements about the credibility of contractors' promises. We were mindful that private commercial companies had no moral obligation to ensure that Iraq was rebuilt on workable lines. Their responsibilities were to their shareholders, while the responsibility for the future of Iraq rested squarely with the CPA and the governments of the two occupying powers – the US and the UK.

But we could not fulfil this task on our own, with or without assistance from contractors. Iraqis had to be brought into the process at the earliest possible stage; they had to be consulted and feel that they were an integral, if not the leading, component of the effort. Where individual managers did not have experience in running the organisations for which they worked, our specialists could offer guidance and add value. 'Capacity building' of Iraqi managers would have to be one of our prime objectives.

We needed more information, about the state of the infrastructure, about management systems and about the competences of the workforce and remaining managers. Our teams permeated the Iraq offices and factory headquarters. I held meeting after meeting around plastic tables in a hot room in the Electricity Accounts building, under the glare of fluorescent lights, where we offered warm water in plastic cups for refreshment. Iraqi officials who dealt with water declared that water was the top priority, as did power engineers, sanitation experts and fuel distributors. The truth was that each of these sectors faced urgent needs. But the middle-managers concerned had no tradition of discussion among themselves or of prioritisation – a process which is difficult enough in highly developed governments including, as was apparent every day, our own. I tried to get past the insatiable lists of demands and our Iraqi counterparts' irritation and on to operationally useful information and advice.

As the provincial councils were formed and started to mature, it became possible to benefit from the wider visions which they were developing and which we were trying to encourage. This was particularly the case in Basra Province, under the firm leadership of Judge Wa'el Abd al-Latif. Of the four southern Councils, the Basra provincial Council was the first to realise that the Basrawis' own interests would be better served by cooperation than obstruction. But for many Iraqis there remained a question mark about the advisability of working with the CPA. We therefore had to build up credit; to earn trust and be viewed as an asset rather than as an interference; to be regarded as liberators rather than occupiers. To this end, and to a great extent as a result of military effort, the Coalition produced some quick wins, some equipment which could be put into service at once, as a token of more to come.

Speaking a common professional language, bonds of cooperation and respect started to develop between the Iraqi and Coalition specialists. Soon the wish-lists were replaced by specific priority areas, which were themselves refined into projects which included specifications of new equipment which might be most compatible with existing resources and with the expertise of the operators.

This close cooperation between specialists was the key to capacity building, across a whole range of disciplines from engineering to agriculture and health care. What the experts had in common became more important than the ideological or cultural differences of their respective countries.

'The Synnott Plan' – Actually the Army's

MND(SE) military headquarters had arrived at similar conclusions about the need for quick wins, but from a different angle. Riots in the streets of Basra in early August 2003, following temporary fuel shortages, had highlighted the linkage between the provision of essential services, and the safety and security of the local population and of the Coalition forces. People's expectations were high. They wanted results at once. And CPA Baghdad's plans were not going to provide these.

Motivated by security concerns, the Army Engineer Branch hired a British firm of contractors and in August came up with a plan for a package of quick-impact, carefully targeted infrastructure projects. The purpose was to turn public opinion round by producing a range of small-scale results of visible benefit to as many people as possible. The concentration would be on electrical power, fuel distribution, water and sanitation – services which everyone needed. The aim was to complete over 50 such projects in two or three months. The plan was called the Emergency Infrastructure Plan, or EIP, and was robustly backed at the most senior military level.

When they started drawing up this plan, the energetic Army engineers were still deeply unimpressed by our civilian capability. They wanted to get on with it themselves, without the complications and delays caused by involving any civilians outside their direct control. Understandably, but nonetheless sneakily, they had kept their project under wraps, without consulting or otherwise involving us at all. But once the plan was ready, it could no longer be kept hidden.

I needed no time to realise its implications. It would have to be financed; the various funds at the Army's disposal were intended for individual projects, not a whole programme such as this. Approval for funding would only come about if the plan could be shown to be compatible with what we knew about longer-term plans – otherwise it would be rejected on the grounds of duplication and waste. We in CPA(South) knew more about Baghdad's thinking than the Army. Since the plan did not originate there, it would be a human reaction on Baghdad's part to be suspicious; they would be pre-disposed to oppose it and would therefore need careful handling. The political and technical reasons for absolute urgency would need to be clearly spelled out: if they were accepted, then we could justify adopting unconventional, fast-track approaches to tendering and contracting.

In addition, the furtive manner in which the plan was conceived amounted to a challenge to the civilian role in the South. Some of my staff were furious at having been sidelined and wanted to block the plan in favour of one of our own. I took a different view. I understood the Army's frustrations and shared their wish to get things done. But while they and their contractors had been laying their plans, we had strengthened our pool of expertise. And, ultimately, we civilians effectively had a power of veto: the plan would not get past Whitehall or Baghdad if we were to oppose it. The Army needed our support.

Rather than stand on our honour, therefore, we now had an opportunity both to advance a good plan and to demonstrate to the sceptical military that we could add value to their own efforts, showing that cooperation between us would be beneficial to everyone.

I asked Brigadier Bruce Brealey, who was the Division's Chief of Operations Support and the principal military liaison officer with my team, to chair a meeting to hammer out a joint paper. I made clear that they were to keep working until they had come to an agreement. I held myself in reserve in case of deadlock and for any final presentational glosses which might be necessary.

By the time the participants emerged late that night, sustained by the inevitable plastic cups of unpleasant coffee but exhausted, they had worked through their earlier differences and exuded that air of exultation that follows a tough but successful negotiation.

We put the cost at $127 million. But the CPA's contracting and accounting procedures would not allow Baghdad to provide even a first instalment of such a sum in the timescale which we felt was necessary. So we suggested that DFID should kick-start the project with a down-payment of $30 million. If we could then show progress, we might be able to leverage the balance out of Baghdad by the time it was needed to come on stream.

Such sums of money were peanuts compared with what the Americans were already spending in Iraq and the costs of military operations. But I knew from experience that they were exceptionally large amounts in terms of the usual way in which British Government departments did business. It would have been unheard of for any normal British development programme to plan, commit and disburse $127 million in the space of two or three months for anything other than basic humanitarian relief. The CPA headquarters, which regarded the South as a side-show, would normally have balked at such additional funding, which was well above our usual allocations for individual projects.

Before we launched the plan, therefore, we needed to prepare the ground and gather support to ease it through the various bureaucracies. Luck lent a hand. A group of development specialists from DFID and Andy Bearpark, Bremer's British Director of Operations, fortuitously came on separate visits. I immediately diverted them to talk through the plan and secured their agreement to support us. But Bearpark was cautious over the financing. There could at that stage be no promise, or even hope, that Baghdad would provide the $97 million balance after any DFID funding had been spent. Available funding was fully committed, new accounting procedures were being introduced and future availability of funds remained uncertain.

I was disappointed by this reaction, but in Bearpark's position I would have done the same. The main point, however, was that he was not blocking the idea. So we decided to go ahead anyway, in the hope that Baghdad could be brought to come up with the funding when the time came.

I immediately despatched an outline of the proposal, with a colourful description of its rationale, to Number 10 Downing Street, the FCO and DFID, even before we had fully completed the fine detail. A meeting of the ad hoc Ministerial Group on Iraq Rehabilitation, under Jack Straw's chairmanship, was due to take place two days later. I wanted to warn London that the final version would be arriving just beforehand and that we needed decisions there and then.

Within hours, I heard that the Prime Minister had instructed Ministers to support the plan in its entirety and find the necessary $30 million to get it started. Blair had proved as good as his word to me six weeks earlier, on the day that I had first set out for Iraq.

Back in Basra we were jubilant. We had shown to each other that joint civil–military cooperation could produce an exceptional result. And we had thwarted any potential bureaucratic obstructionism. I was confident that, once we had got going, we would find the missing $97 million from somewhere: if Baghdad proved obdurate, we could shame DFID into providing it on the grounds that failure was not an option.

To my embarrassment, the military briefings thenceforward referred to 'The Synnott Plan'. I never established whether this was an example of the highly developed military sense of irony since there was no doubt that it was all their original idea. I continued to use the original label.

The Emergency Infrastructure Plan became one of the highlights of the Coalition's reconstruction activity in the South. Its concentration on small-scale projects rendered it doable and allowed for flexibility if obstacles should arise, which of course they did. It proved feasible to proceed with and protect small projects, even in a deteriorating security environment. And, since local people could readily see that they would benefit from the projects' completion, they actively helped maintain security: potential saboteurs realised that they would be deeply unpopular if they prevented the repair of, say, a water pumping station or a generator providing lighting and air-conditioning for several thousand people. Also, the activity entailed in implementing the Plan motivated and stimulated those of us involved in it, at all levels.

I chaired weekly progress meetings personally. DFID provided an experienced professional project manager; and the Army was represented by the Colonel of Engineers. Sometimes I had to hold the ring between these exponents of two different schools of thought. But my main objective was to maximise Iraqi engagement.

We invited all the relevant Iraqi departments to send representatives to attend our progress meetings and provided interpreters. It was only on the day I left, when the Colonel of Engineers had asked for my curriculum vitae so that he could say some words of farewell, that he discovered that, albeit 30 years previously, I had once been a Chartered Engineer, as was he.

By the end of January 2004, my weekly coordinating meetings included more Iraqi engineers than Coalition personnel. And these Iraqis, of different disciplines, were talking to each other in a way that they had never experienced before. Also present were an increasing number of American visitors from Baghdad, interested in observing this, to them, novel way of doing business with Iraqis.

As I had anticipated, the optimistic two- to three-month timescale for the Plan slipped. But, also as anticipated, our progress had successfully levered the additional $97 million out of Baghdad.

By January, too, the deteriorating security environment and the prospect that the CPA would be wound up in less that six months had all but destroyed the momentum of the bigger, Baghdad-led projects. Much of the investment in Baghdad's holistic, root-and-branch approach, which had been so optimistically advertised six months earlier, proved to have been wasted. Security-related costs of some of the major projects came to exceed the basic costs; and often these projects failed altogether, benefiting no one apart from the contracting companies.

The lessons to be drawn from this experience were essentially traditional ones, based on common sense and conventional wisdom. They relate to the importance of inclusive consultation and the development of a sense of ownership; to the 'art of the possible' and to the cliché that 'the best is the enemy of the good'. At $127 million, the sums involved in the Emergency Infrastructure Plan were tiny compared with other expenditure in Iraq, although they were greater than the other sources of expenditure available to local Coalition managers, as described below. Yet the positive effects were out of all proportion to the outlay.

A couple of years after I left Basra, while reading Bremer's memoir *My Year in Iraq*, my eyes were caught by his description of the difficulties which he had encountered with the bureaucracy in Washington over their 'overly rigid interpretations of the regulations on letting contracts, which usually required long lead times'. He recorded:

> Our budget staff developed the project plans required for contracting federal moneys, and in a meeting on December 8, I instructed them to come up with a minimum of $500 million in 'quick-dispersing' (sic) projects that we could have under way by spring.

The brief paragraph which surrounded this sentence seemed to correspond exactly with the rationale for our Emergency Plan, albeit on a four times-greater scale and intended to cover the country as a whole. But what really struck me was that the date of this instruction was three whole months after the conception of our Plan. Could it have been that our progress in the South had eventually had an influence on the great supertanker of state in Baghdad?

Counting Beans: The Complexities of Funding, Contracting and Accounting

It was a sultry weekend in September when we received a visit from Baghdad's Deputy Director of the Office of Management and Budget – an impressive title for a personable 30-year-old seconded from the US State Department called Sherri Kraham. Her visit coincided with one of my regular meetings with our provincial teams who, pending the arrival of civilian reinforcements, consisted mainly of energetic young British Army officers supplemented by a few civilians. They all sat where they could in the largest room of our decrepit building to hear what Sherri had to tell us. Despite the half-hearted efforts of a lazy fan hanging from the low ceiling, the ambient temperature rose to boiler-room levels. The last to arrive, I found that my colleagues had kept a chair free for me: a high-backed, heavily carved wooden sort of throne, with a padded seat and ornate arms which made note-taking almost impossible, especially when clutching a plastic cup full of tepid water. From this vantage point I listened attentively.

Sherri embarked on a PowerPoint presentation which purported to explain new rules that we should follow in tendering, contracting and accounting for our project expenditure. It was an impressively professional performance and was followed by total silence.

In Sherri's subsequent testimony to the US Institute of Peace, she remarked, frankly, that it was hard for the civilians in Baghdad to coordinate with the Army, because, she said, 'I don't think we speak the same language'. So far as we were concerned, however, Sherri herself might have descended from the planet Vulcan. Perhaps we had not yet made enough progress in learning American English, because her message to us was incomprehensible. The audience of young Army officers may momentarily have been tempted to respond with some flirtatious banter. If they were, they sensibly thought better of it. Instead they turned to me, on my throne, to see my reaction.

Whatever I may have thought, I did not want to undermine the authority of this highly intelligent young woman. After a deep breath, I observed that we British unfortunately had no experience of American accounting procedures, and hence we were unfamiliar with the various regulations and acronyms to which Sherri had referred. Indeed, most of us had no experience with accounting procedures of any kind; therefore, it might prove difficult for us to conform to the Office of Management and Budget's wishes. I hoped that, in view of the CPA Administrator's repeated exhortations to us to spend quickly, the Office might be lenient towards us if we failed to conform precisely to its rules.

The response was uncompromising: no conformity, no money. It all belonged either to the Iraqi people or to the American taxpayer. There could be no way round the procedures. If we had a problem with that, then Baghdad would send us some American accountants to help us out.

It was gracious of Sherri, in her same testimony to the US Institute of Peace a year after this presentation, to acknowledge that Basra and other parts of the South had been neglected in the allocation of funds and had needed more.

In the circumstances which prevailed in 2003–4, there was bound to be an inescapably high level of corruption. Under Saddam Hussein, Iraqis had been accustomed to being allocated funds for specific purposes, within a Soviet-style command economy. Over the previous decade, however, central control had weakened and the state-run economy had come to resemble a mafia-style criminal operation. We in the Coalition had no means of breaking into the well-established cartels, tribal links and extortion rackets which had become an integral part of economic activity.

Added to these hazards was the fact that Iraqis believed that they had every right to benefit from Coalition largesse, which they regarded as no more than their due. Nor were we to be feared like Saddam's regime, in which the risk of reprisals and violent summary punishment acted as some restraint. Many Iraqis were therefore of a mind to take full advantage of the opportunity to improve their families', or their own, welfare. The Coalition's need for rapid results became an invitation to corrupt practices.

There was little that the Coalition could do to change this, in such special circumstances, except cease to employ contractors who were found to charge too much. Tightened accounting procedures, which amounted to a paper trail within the CPA, would have little effect on reducing local corruption.

The passage of time has revealed allegations of corruption on the part of Coalition administrators as well. No doubt the opportunities could have been and were reduced by better internal procedures. That I was not aware of any cases of corrupt practice among any of the CPA international staff in the South is not to suggest that our team was inherently more honest than elsewhere. But we were a much smaller outfit than Baghdad, with tighter and more transparent management lines. Any gossip about sharp dealings would most likely have surfaced very quickly.

But it was not just the new accounting regime which caused us frustration. Just as we started to get our heads around the new procedures, they would be changed again. We eventually managed to impress upon Baghdad that we simply could not realistically fulfil US accounting procedures with which our multinational team were completely unfamiliar. They sent us American military accounting officers to help out, but they had no flexibility to deviate from the rules, so bids were constantly being returned for revision.

It was hard to judge what happened in other Regions. I compared notes with one of the other Regional Coordinators whom Bremer had publicly praised for his high levels of expenditure. He blithely confided that he ignored the rules: he had a two-man American–Australian team who 'made things happen' and who were evidently very good at doing so. The US military commanders would also have been adept at working the system. And they had the benefit of 3500 Civil Affairs reservists under their direct command, who were employed in units which reflected their civilian skills – an asset which would have been useful for the British Army.

The consequences of this 'Best being the Enemy of the Good' practice were evident from our statistics. By early March 2004, the Army in the South, which had greater operational discretion, less rigid accounting rules and many more staff, had accounted for a total of $88 million on quick-impact projects. The equivalent figure for CPA(South) was about $35 million. But a closer look at our figures reveals that $35 million was the total value of projects for which expenditure had been allocated. The sums committed, that is, for which contracts had been concluded was about a third of this, at $12.5 million. The sums actually spent were a mere $6.7 million.

What the evidence also suggests is that, after a frustrating start which slowed down initial expenditure, the pace picked up to such an extent that there was a sizeable pipeline of projects which had been approved, authorised and on the point of commencement. This was borne out by the fact that at the end of May 2004, a month before the CPA was wound up, CPA(South) had committed over $54 million of funds and had spent $33 million of it. Sixty per cent of committed funds had been spent as against less than 20 per cent four months earlier; and the commitment figure had shot up too.

The main problems which we faced, therefore, were not about any shortage of funds. They stemmed from the fact that we had to set up procedures from nothing against the background of constantly changing rules. Having done that, there were serious difficulties over our ability to disburse funds – a phenomenon which is common to even the most advanced development assistance programmes. In view of these obstacles, it was fortunate that we had succeeded in launching our Emergency Infrastructure Plan, without which local initiative our practical contribution would have been very limited.

But these figures convey an incomplete picture of the CPA(South) team's actual contribution. Any projects which we recommended whose cost exceeded our devolved funding allocations were funded separately by Baghdad and figured in their overall expenditure, even if they were conceived, administered and overseen by the southern team. We had no means of establishing the grand total.

Nor was project finance the only means of injecting finance into the Iraqi economy. As early as September 2003, our civilian Finance Department was disbursing $30 million a month in salaries for 119,000 employees and $40 million in operating budgets for the provincial directorates. It was these massive sums which caused the local markets to flourish.

Rebuilding Management

For a mix of practical and political reasons, the finance sector was one of CPA's highest priorities. In the South we were again fortunate in having some unique expertise at hand. Andrew Alderson, a major in the Territorial Army, had previously been a director of Lazards merchant bank in London. Finding himself on a lowly rung of the military ladder and regarded as a non-professional soldier, he exercised his entrepreneurial skills in identifying a gap and filling it himself. The Army confessed that they knew little about finance, while Andrew made plain that he knew a lot more than that. His book, *Bankrolling Basra*, recounts the many bizarre aspects of his efforts to impress upon his military chain of command and the custodians of funds in Baghdad that

Iraqi state employees needed to be paid; and that he needed millions of dollars for this purpose. His attachment to our civilian outfit proved invaluable to us, as well as for him, since, much as he enjoyed his long-standing relationship with the Army as a reservist, he had more initiative to follow his instincts than would have been possible within the military hierarchy.

Andrew's book describes how, just before I arrived, he had somehow managed to acquire responsibility for an astonishing range of specialist sectors. When I discussed his realm with him and asked about his objectives, it was clear that he was both vigorous and content with his lot, so I saw no reason to change the arrangements I inherited. Over the following weeks he would tell me of the seemingly irresolvable crises which faced him each day. But most proved to have been settled by the following day. This experience, and the knowledge that I had no one else on hand with any knowledge of finance and banking, persuaded me that I should continue to give Andrew his head. I was glad that I did so.

One of the areas which Andrew kept me closely informed about was Baghdad's ambitious plan to replace Iraq's entire stock of banknotes. Politically, it was desirable to remove all these representations of Saddam Hussein's image. In practical terms, the currency urgently needed to be stabilised – exchange rates were fluctuating wildly. The issue had become a touchstone of the CPA's effectiveness. Huge resources of personnel, funding and attention were allocated to it. But there were massive obstacles to be overcome.

Andrew reported that all the banks in the South had been looted; vaults had been blown up and the walls had gaping holes. They needed to be renovated and made safe and secure. Thousands of tons of new banknotes had to be transported all over the country, at a time when convoys were being intercepted by insurgents and criminals. The notes had to be distributed to local banks whose security and integrity were suspect. Local police, of doubtful reliability, were required to guard premises, since such a task required numbers on the ground which were far greater than anything the Coalition could provide, at least in the South. And complex arrangements had to be put in place for the equitable exchange of old notes, against a background of wholesale corruption.

The deadline for this task was 15 October. The Army got to hear about it from Baghdad before we did and promptly demanded to know what I was 'going to do about it'. They were rattled because the preparatory plans were not impressive and it seemed likely that, if things went wrong, they would be left to deal with the security aspects. While the Americans, with some 150,000 troops on the ground, could throw troops at any obstacle, this would be beyond the capabilities of the 11,000 personnel in the British-led Division in the South. Representatives of the private contracting firm hired for the distribution process had turned up at the Army's headquarters and, despite receiving generous payments to do the job, were trying to squeeze additional resources from the Army. This had ruffled a lot of feathers.

One story which did the rounds was that a British ex-serviceman, among the many employed by such firms, had tried to trade on his former links to cadge materials from Army units which his firm had neglected to supply. Among these was toilet paper. When the Americans got to hear about this they unaccountably found it immensely amusing. Their British counterparts did not.

Since I shared the Army's concerns, I made some enquiries during a visit to Baghdad. Although I was truly impressed by the planning for the operation, I could not be confident that Baghdad had fully thought through the implications for the special situation in the South, about which Baghdad knew little.

An opportunity arose to make a pitch at a high level at one of the first meetings of Divisional Commanders and Regional Coordinators on 30 September, a fortnight before the deadline. I was determined not to appear as a lone whiner: I needed to make clear that the military and civilian arms in the South spoke with one voice. So by prior agreement, Graeme Lamb and I both spoke out and offered a list of questions which did not seem to have been addressed.

We received some support. My counterpart at Hillah, Mike Gfoeller, gently observed that he had received no briefing on the subject. The US General in charge of the Baghdad region confessed that the operation 'scared the hell' out of him.

A retired American Brigadier, Hugh Tant, who had arrived in Baghdad just two weeks earlier to take charge of the operation, sought to deflect our points light-heartedly. Graeme and I were not consoled, and I said so.

'What are you going to do, for instance', I demanded petulantly, 'about the fact that the counting machines which you have just introduced are unable to detect counterfeit banknotes? How can you be sure that the local police will keep order when so much currency is moving around the country? A training programme for bank managers only started a week ago'.

The outcome of the discussion was a humiliation. The embarrassed silence which followed my outburst was broken first by the redoubtable General Petraeus, Commander of the 101st Airborne Division.

'Tant's one of The Screaming Eagles', he declared. 'We're glad to have him with us. When The Screaming Eagles say they'll do a job, they get it done'.

That was all we needed. The elderly brigadier had once been a member of the 101st – a Screaming Eagle – and American tribal loyalty kicked in. Petraeus was followed by the massively built General Odierno, Commander of the 4th Infantry Division.

'If our British friends find that they can't manage what they have to do', he boomed, 'the 4th would be only too glad to help with some helicopters'.

Brigadier Tant had the last word.

'Teamwork that Works', he intoned: his catchphrase which we southerners thereafter found constantly maddening.

While I would have liked either to strike back (but with what?) or disappear into the ground, I did not feel as bad about these put-downs as did Graeme. I felt that we had made our points and that they were valid, even if no one would ever have admitted the possibility. Despite the bluster with which they had been received, they would be considered and this might even make a difference to the outcome.

But Graeme, who was very familiar with US military steamrollers and did not always sympathise with their style, was furious at the encounter, which had implied both that the Brits were whingers and that we were badly equipped. On our flight back to Basra that evening, the air was blue with his imprecations.

As a result, we had mixed reactions when it turned out that the currency exchange was effected on time and without incident. It began on October 15 and ended three months later, during which period the value of the new dinar rose by 25 per cent. Almost 4.5 trillion new Iraqi dinars or $3 billion were put into circulation. Transporting the money to Iraq required 28 747 aircraft loads of about 100 tons each.

It was one of the CPA's few major successes. According to the CPA's official 'List of Achievements', the introduction of a new currency had taken three years in post-war Germany, as against three months in Iraq. But even that success came at a cost. It will never be known how many of the new notes were exchanged for counterfeits. And large sums of the old dinars had been looted from the banks during the post-combat chaos. The currency exchange in a sense legitimised this looting and allowed the culprits to launder their ill-gotten gains.

But it was the more prosaic day-to-day organisation and management of financial issues which took up most time and effort. For some time, crucially important projects, for which funds were available, could not be started simply because the Basra Finance Directorate, which was controlled by the Baghdad Finance Ministry, would not sign the necessary authorisations unless or until instructed to do so by the Ministry. The local Director's main concern, not unnaturally, was to keep his job rather than to facilitate expenditure. This log-jam was only resolved when Andrew Alderson persuaded the CPA in Baghdad to intervene with the Ministry.

Such wrangles lay at the heart of the challenge facing the CPA. No one in Iraq could be confident about how the management of the country would turn out. Despite being the paymaster, albeit also using Iraqi resources, the CPA was seen as a temporary phenomenon. Iraqis had to survive in their country after the

Coalition had left, so it would not be prudent to bend to the CPA's will if that meant offending those who might ultimately once again become their bosses.

For many months a container stood inside the Brigade headquarters in Basra. It was secured by two padlocks; the Basra Finance Directorate held one key and we in the CPA held the other. It was full of banknotes ready to be used but awaiting the necessary authority. Fortunately it was never the target of attack.

*   *   *

Not long after the start of school term, at the end of October, I paid a visit to a secondary school in Basra City. I arrived during a break amid a tremendous din of small children at play. This stopped instantly when a bell rang and everyone returned to their classrooms. The headmaster greeted me courteously and introduced me into several classes, where I was glad to see that a 'Schools in a Box' package supplied by the Coalition was being put to good use. I was about to leave, having seen all that I thought I needed, when the headmaster ushered me into another classroom. The teacher, a man in his mid-forties, introduced me to his class, which he was teaching chemistry. He then turned to me and told me, politely but with barely concealed anger, that foreigners such as myself had not been invited to Iraq. We were not welcome, and should leave.

Such a reception was unusual in Basra, although more common in the eastern province of Maysan, and took me aback. I said humbly that I realised that we were sometimes perceived as occupiers, but our intention was to liberate the country from the legacy of Saddam. For my part, I simply wanted to help to rebuild the damage as best we could. We would leave as soon as our help was no longer useful.

The teacher's tone changed. His anger gave way to deep emotion as he explained that his brother and eldest son had been killed in crossfire during the occupation of Basra seven months earlier. When we finished our conversation, which turned into a long one, he shook me warmly by the hand. As I looked into his eyes which were brimming with tears, it was hard to hold back my own.

The astute headmaster must have been aware of his colleague's grief. And he may have felt that, as one of the occupiers, it would be beneficial to me to be exposed to an example of the human consequences of our actions. He was right. It was clear that the chemistry teacher had suffered personally and was in a turmoil of anger and grief while at the same time being glad, albeit at a different and less personal level, that Saddam had been removed. The grief and anger would remain: it was up to us now to demonstrate that the removal of Saddam would go some way to compensate for them.

With no education specialist in our civilian team, the Army lent us a Territorial Army reservist who was an experienced senior teacher at a British private school. Charles Monk, who single-handedly liaised with the local Iraqi authorities and universities about almost every aspect of education, took me to visit Basra's main university. All the computers and furniture had disappeared, as had every piece of equipment, whether or not bolted to the structure. Electrical fittings and light switches had been removed, and cabling had been torn out of the plaster. Worse, walls had been smashed and all the windows broken. When I visited again, after DFID-sponsored contractors had made some progress in renovation, students had brought in their own home-made desks. The thirst for learning was immensely strong and classes continued throughout.

The most senior lecturers, being also senior Ba'athists, had gone. Staff who remained had been promoted into more senior positions. With the Army guarding against disruption, Charles managed to ensure that the annual exams took place even in the turbulent year of 2003, only a few months behind schedule. Had they not taken place, a year's intake of tertiary students would have wasted that time; and their demoralisation, or worse, would have infected many others.

Similarly, with the help of $500 to every school which had not received Schools in a Box, primary and secondary teachers were able to make a start in the autumn term. Had they not been able to do so, parents, teachers and students would have taken to the streets in protest.

It was in Basra University in mid-January that I witnessed what was perhaps that place's first formal and open debate among its students. An energetic young British FCO official, Nikesh Mehta, had organised students' groups and invited me to attend the start of the debate which was being held in a large lecture room. I opened the proceedings with a few carefully rehearsed words in my imitation of Arabic. I was so fascinated by what followed that I stayed until the end.

The subject was Federalism and the motion was that Iraq should become a federal state, with a high degree of autonomy accorded to its various regions. There were three speakers in each of the two teams. The debate proceeded on traditional Western-style lines. The participants expressed themselves confidently, clearly and politely, and confined themselves to about five minutes each. The issue was then opened to the floor, where the contributions, of which there was no shortage, were similarly clear and to the point. The big difference from the Western tradition, however, at least as regards an exercise in dialectic, was that every one agreed with each other. Each of six short, final contributions amounted to the answer: 'Yes, but not yet' – although any comparison with St Augustine's alleged attitude to chastity would have been quite inappropriate. There was no concluding vote. But the event was universally regarded as a success.

* * *

There seemed to be scope for similar progress in the health sector. Like the schools, hospitals had been looted, senior medical staff had gone, and there was a chronic shortage of equipment. Highly dependent on a single state-owned company, Kimadia, which distributed all medical supplies, the health sector was prone to extortion, blackmail and criminality; medical supplies went astray and many doctors were murdered.

The human tragedies were poignantly described in an article written for the *British Medical Journal* by Dr Celia Duff, one of three British specialists who assessed the situation in mid-2003:

> There are no drugs; hospitals have run out of oxygen and have been looted of beds and equipment; there are no laboratory reagents; elective and diagnostic procedures impossible with intermittent power and no essential clinical supplies. There is a public health crisis. Water is contaminated with sewage; there is not enough fuel; food, previously supplied on ration, is scarce and expensive; the cold chain has broken down and immunisation programmes suspended for over six months. We have cholera, typhoid and whooping cough. On street corners children take water from pipes deliberately broken because their homes are not reached by the supply – the pumps are not working.
>
> Three of us. Where does one start? The British military here have done a wonderful job. Our medical colleagues, young regimental medical officers and senior medical command staff, have made huge strides in understanding the key structures, personalities and immediate problems facing this region. Together we have a plan which covers immediate and longer term issues. Much of this rests on leadership emerging from the profession locally, a tall order given the political unrest and undercurrent of corruption. Self determination is the key, an imposed health economy will neither work nor is it for us to decide. We can only try to support, guide and advise. But in the transition our leadership is essential.
>
> In the midst of the current chaos we must stay focussed on the long term objective, an Iraq that gives its people choice and provides those basic needs for all: health, employment, shelter, adequate nutrition, security. That there is no service now must not distract us from the task. But this is difficult when faced with inevitable personal tragedies. People come to our office hoping for help, for a gift that might transform their lives. One morning, a five year old boy and his loving, gentle father came to the gate. The boy has thalassaemia, common here, and needs a blood transfusion. Nothing is free, even blood comes at a price. The price is unaffordable for a man with no job. The blood transfusion service has been destroyed. The boy, yellow under his dark skin, will die without treatment. One day, hopefully sooner than later, we will have identified the way to replace this essential service along with all the other life saving services that are lost. Other children may

then live. This boy cannot wait that long, he needs a solution now. I cannot offer hope. His papers tell me his blood group is B+, the same as mine. If I offer my blood, how many more children might need it? That is no way to solve the problem even though it might make me feel better today. Later, in my office, I cry uncontrollably with impotent rage.

As a result of Dr Duff's mission, another team of four health administrators joined us in Basra for a three-month tour. They visited hospitals, built up trust with senior Iraqi administrators and doctors, and drew up recommendations for follow-on work. I wrote personally to the Permanent Under-Secretary at the Department of Health, the highest official level, pleading that the administrators should be replaced so as to retain a continuity of our knowledge of this important sector. I received no reply. Perhaps in London's eyes it was clearly a losing battle – there was little or nothing that we could do to help; and out of sight would be out of mind.

*   *   *

I tried hard to convince Baghdad of the importance of agriculture, which employed some 20 per cent of the population and supported a rural population of 7 million souls. A succession of emails remained unanswered so, in mid-October, I decided to put my points personally to the CPA's head of the Agriculture Ministry. The Australian Government had pressed hard to secure this post as a part of their contribution to the Coalition's effort. I had therefore expected to meet someone who was truly engaged in problem-solving and helping those provinces where agriculture was an important part of their economies, as was the case in the South.

Perhaps it had been a bad day for both of us, but my encounter with Trevor Flugge, a former chairman of the Australian Wheat Board, was one which caused me to become more angry than at any other time in my stay in Iraq. Judging by the tone of our exchanges, witnessed with open mouths by James Roscoe, my Private Secretary, and Flugge's own small staff, the feeling was entirely mutual.

I explained to Flugge that, in troublesome Maysan Province, farmers had sold the wheat seeds which they would normally have kept aside for winter sowing because in the summer of 2003 the Coalition was paying unusually high prices for wheat. In the past they would have received a top-up of healthy, treated seeds through Baghdad's central administration. But no such provision was now available. Without the seeds, there would be no sowing, which would lead to massive unemployment. Without the sowing, there would be no winter crop, which would lead to further unemployment and food shortages. The provincial authorities, who were fully conscious of such consequences, were understandably pressing us hard to arrange for supplies. If we did not do this, we would have a major security problem on our hands.

To my mind, which was at one with Graeme Lamb the military commander, the case was incontrovertible. But Flugge did not want to listen. He responded bluntly that the CPA policy was to do away with such subsidies. The Iraqis had to learn to stand on their own feet. They should not have sold their seed grain, so it was their fault if they had no winter crop. As I persisted, making much of the security implications, the temperature rose.

Security was not his concern, yelled Flugge. Well, it should be, I yelled back. We broke away from each other with none of the reconciliatory gestures which are customary with Arabic people after a good argument. This had been a bad one.

In the face of this opposition, I raised my sights and sought assistance from Jeremy Greenstock and Pat Kennedy, Bremer's ever-helpful Chief of Staff. Supplemented by persuasive pressure from Rory Stewart's team in Al Amarah, we secured funding to arrange the purchase of healthy seeds from Mosul, where there was a surplus. This solved the problem, albeit right at the last moment. Rory's team arranged transport and the grains were sold at reasonable market prices, thereby avoiding the additional trap of distorting the market.

I was saddened later to see that the section on agriculture in the official document 'CPA's Achievements' was one of the shortest. In less than a page, it listed just four 'achievements', one-eighth as many as the section on Foreign Affairs which, important though they might be, had little effect on ordinary lives. The four items included the less-than-breathtaking announcement that six Iraqi students had been selected to study agriculture at the University of Hawaii, and a note that the price of wheat in Iraq had risen from $105 per metric tonne in 2003 to $180 in mid-2004. Why this should be regarded as an 'achievement' escaped me. I could not see how such a price rise would benefit ordinary Iraqis, though I supposed that foreign wheat producers and exporters who did business with Iraq might have welcomed it.

I was also saddened to see reports in the Australian press that the same former chairman of the Australian Wheat Board, having been embarrassed by the publication of a photograph of him, half-naked, brandishing a pistol while in CPA service in Baghdad, had become the subject of allegations about kick-backs in connection with the controversial 'Oil For Food' programme. In March 2006, ABC News On Line reported: 'The former WA (Western Australian) farmer was labelled the "million-dollar man" by the Federal Opposition when it was revealed the Government paid him $1 million for less than a year's work in Baghdad'. In contrast, a report from the US General Accounting Office in June 2004 reported that of the $22 million allocated for agriculture infrastructure projects, only $12 million had actually been disbursed.

I had one other encounter with the Australian administration. In early autumn of 2003, a ship load of 50,000 live sheep were on their way from Australia to Saudi Arabia when a skin disease called scabby mouth broke out on board. Saudi Arabia declined to receive the sheep and the Australians magnanimously offered to unload them in Iraq for use as part of the rituals at the end of the holy month of Ramadan. Australian diplomats in Baghdad engaged in frantic lobbying. As the Australians' generosity increased and they offered to provide the sheep free of charge, messages became confused.

If the shipment were to land, it would have to be in one of the ports, which were all in the British-led sector. I had told an Australian diplomat who had approached me during one of my visits to Baghdad that, in my view, the Iraqis would take it seriously amiss if they were presented with a consignment of diseased sheep which no one else would accept. But, for some reason, the British military headquarters had come to believe that I had approved such a delivery, which they too opposed. I had to make clear that this was not the case. In doing so, my email pointed out that, anyway, the unfortunate sheep would all first need to be subjected to 'de-baa-thification'. I counted it as a compliment when I heard an Army major at a military briefing some days later recount the same poor joke as if it were his.

The last I heard of this saga was that, unable to slaughter the animals on the high seas and stymied by international quarantine laws, the Australian Prime Minister had declared that they would be returned to Australia for disposal there. The Australian opposition leader had the final word: 'They went out as lambs ... they're coming back as mutton'.

The famous Marshes in Maysan and Dhi Qar provinces offered enormous agricultural potential. A group of American scientists briefed me about the ecological implications of Saddam's malicious draining of them during the war with Iran. They explained that, when the water level dropped, so the soil had become saline and useless for agriculture. Re-flooding would be beneficial because it would increase the available stock of agricultural land, provide employment, and attract the traditional dwellers back to the land and away from the over-crowded cities. But, if re-flooding were rushed, the salinity would be washed into other more productive soil and make matters yet worse. It would have to be carefully controlled and taken very slowly.

I listened to such calls for caution impatiently. I shared Bremer's enthusiasm for rapid and visible results, and knew that the Iraqis would not understand and have no patience with such a prudent approach. I was convinced that the Marshes offered great scope for high-value agricultural production and employment. And, in the colder months, the warmer climate gave the southern provinces an edge in cultivating winter crops which were consumed throughout the country.

The winter tomato crop in Basra Province was such an example. The relatively warm South supplied 75 per cent of the country's demand for this staple component of the Iraqi diet, and a failure would again have had far-reaching consequences. But, even in Basra's relatively mild climate, the crop had to be protected by plastic sheeting; yet the factory which manufactured the sheeting had collapsed. With much help from the British Army, we secured funding for a supply from other sources and arranged transport for it just in time. I inspected the resulting crop with our Danish agriculturalist, Ole Stockholm Jepson: the tomatoes were a bit gnarled by an early cold snap before the sheeting arrived, but they survived; and they tasted all right.

Jepson's single-handed achievements illustrated the importance of individual contributions in such challenging environments. Well past his first bloom of youth and with deep and long experience of working in developing countries, he forged close professional ties with agricultural managers throughout the South and held regular regional meetings to arrive at common ground. When, predictably, the Marsh Arabs started to re-flood the Marshes and brought in livestock to graze on the new pastures, Jepson was able to provide desperately needed advice on animal husbandry and the establishment of dairies.

* * *

By about October 2003, once established in our new premises, our multinational team included experts in trade, industry and business, many with prior experience in developing countries, who methodically called on the managers who presided over idle industries such as cement, oil, petrochemicals, iron and steel, and fertilisers.

The port of Umm Qasr to the south of Basra, which I visited with one such specialist, was an example of a key strategic asset suffering from neglect. The British soldiers guarding the place developed a hand-picked squad of fast runners who specialised in chasing after the local young men who surmounted the perimeter walls to make off with stolen goods. Each morning the soldiers would compare notes about how many 'Ali Babas' they had caught the night before. But, once caught, the young men were invariably

freed and the fastest of them came to be recognised as special
challenges when, inevitably, they returned to have another go. It
was only when the US Army was faced with the challenge of a
massive troop rotation at the end of the year, when they realised
that the port would be essential for shipping military equipment in
and out, that they focussed on making it operational once again.

The thrust of policy from CPA Baghdad, reflecting Washington-
based ideology, was to encourage privatisation and hence to resist
the restoration of industries on their existing basis. Conscious that
great hardship had occurred in other developing countries when
external models had been applied without regard to local
considerations, I spoke up against the privatisation policies at
successive coordination meetings in Baghdad. I argued that
potential investors would have no interest in such uncertain and
high-risk investment ventures in any foreseeable timescale. It
would therefore be better to deal as best as one could with what
remained; to get plants running again and thus increase
employment and save the foreign exchange costs of imports; and
to promote links with similar industries in other countries.

Ultimately the accelerated timescale for the demise of the CPA
put paid to any CPA-engineered privatisation schemes, as has been
explained in Chapter 10. In retrospect, the Coalition's misplaced
policy caused major opportunities to be lost.

* * *

Pursuing the fifth objective in Bremer's original vision
statement, military and civilian press officers in Baghdad and
Basra did the best they could to disseminate good news and scotch
false stories. But the Coalition seemed always to be on the back
foot. It was difficult enough for CPA administrators to establish
policy and facts over a wide range of activity. It was yet more
important that Iraqis should receive information and gain
confidence in what the CPA was up to. The British and US
governments and Bremer personally attached a high priority to
establishing a successful and credible nationwide television
network, not least to compete with Al Jazeera and other satellite

stations. Washington and London wrestled with the problem and successive Directors of Strategic Communications tried and failed to meet the challenge.

But this challenge went much wider than a television channel. The industrious CPA bureaucracy in Baghdad had busied themselves in drawing up a plethora of Orders, Regulations, Memoranda and Public Notices. Once approved, they were despatched to the Regional offices with instructions that we should disseminate them and ensure compliance. But only rarely were they translated into Arabic. Each region therefore had to arrange for its own translation, which inevitably differed.

Many of these instructions were fiercely contested by Iraqis. Having no explanation of their rationale, we could do little to deal with objections. Most of them therefore were just ignored. In December, I informed Baghdad that, since our efforts had become destructive, we would cease to circulate any untranslated and unexplained directives. I had no response, no doubt because there was no available answer. But the directives kept coming.

There remained only one effective way of trying to convince the southern Iraqis of the sincerity and effectiveness of our efforts, and that was to get out into the streets, schools and public utility centres and tell them, having first invited all the local media to come along too. That is why I had found myself in front of a television camera nervously tasting the first product of a newly constructed water purification plant.

*   *   *

Over the long term, the re-establishment of viable infrastructure in Iraq would only have been possible if the imploded supervisory ministries and their directorates in the provinces were themselves made to function. Only this would ensure adequate funding flows for running repairs and maintenance of newly installed equipment, without which it is liable to break down within months. But the imperative at the time was to make rapid and visible progress over reconstructing Iraq's broken infrastructure in order to influence the security environment. The CPA failed to achieve this. Its concentration on large country-wide and US-led contracting projects, based on the false assumption that the CPA would remain in being for more than two or more years, distracted from the need for small and feasible projects which benefited and created jobs for large numbers of individuals. These fundamental deficiencies were exacerbated by accounting procedures which did not allow for the CPA's shortage of staff and lack of expertise.

In terms of approach, the elimination of top managers through the de-Ba'athification process accentuated the importance of capacity-building to enhance middle managers' skills and confidence, and so increase Iraqi ownership of the reconstruction process. Such success in this as there was demonstrably increased support for the CPA's efforts.

By the end of 2003, after Washington's decision to wind up the CPA prematurely in June 2004, Baghdad had established a new Project Management Office under the leadership of Admiral (Retired) Dave Nash. Nash and his Deputy, Larry Crandall, paid their first visit to Basra in May, a month before the whole operation was to disappear. They concluded: 'This is the only CPA organisation in Iraq that is appropriately structured and equipped'.

They may have been right. But their views were scant consolation for those who were part of it.

Chapter 13
Big-Picture Politics

Politics and the pulpit are terms that have little agreement.
Edmund Burke, *Reflections on the Revolution in France.*

WITH THE PASSAGE of time, the common perception of Iraq has increasingly focussed on the idea that the country is divided between three blocks: Kurdish, Sunni and Shia; and that these blocks are geographically distinct: the Kurds live in the North, the Sunnis in the area north of Baghdad, and the Shia, the majority, from the middle down to the South. With the growth of sectarian violence, the murderous tit-for-tat between Sunni and Shia has progressively worsened since 2004, so some commentators from outside Iraq have advocated that the country should be allowed to split into its supposed three component parts. This, it is suggested, would immediately remove the sources of sectarian tension.

The reality, as ever, is far more complex. It is part of the tragedy of the Iraq conundrum that it has proved so difficult to identify the various strands of influence in the political and social scene and keep abreast of their development. Even in the once-peaceful South, it has been virtually impossible since early 2004 for Westerners to sit down with tribal or religious leaders and political figures at the provincial level in order to assess what is really happening on the ground. It is all too tempting to rely on generalisations and simplifications.

The absolute priority which CPA Baghdad assigned to the establishment of central governmental institutions led to some bizarre anomalies. As 2003 wore on, so the pressure from within Iraq for early direct elections grew. Grand Ayatollah Ali al-Sistani, in particular, vocally advocated elections to establish a legitimate government at the earliest opportunity and thus free the country from both the Iraqi Governing Council, which he regarded as having no legitimacy, and the 'occupation' by the CPA and Coalition forces.

The CPA's considered position, drawn up by Washington, was that the complex pre-requisites of transparent, free and fair elections could not be put in place quickly. Nor would it be possible in short order to establish any appropriate constitutional arrangements to determine the parameters on which elections could be held. The subtext of this position was that early elections might be hijacked by undesirable strong-arm factions and thereby thwart the Coalition's objective of establishing democracy. Open elections were likely to provide the 'wrong' result. As in Algeria in January 1992, democracy might be used to abolish democracy.

Pressures grew when the date for the CPA's departure was brought forward to June 2004, instead of late 2005 as had been originally envisaged. But, at provincial level, some Provinces had already conducted apparently successful elections on the basis of ration cards in lieu of up-dated electoral rolls. And the process was proving infectious. This risked giving the lie to the CPA's position or, more accurately, it risked providing political ammunition to those who wanted to argue against it.

As a result, Regional and Provincial Coordinators found themselves at one point being instructed by Baghdad to discourage any further elections at local level, in the interests of higher and supposedly over-riding objectives. Since CPA staff at local level had taken the CPA's democratic objectives at face value, and having judged that democratisation would do well to start at the grass roots, they were not surprisingly dismayed by these directives, about which they had not been consulted. And, of course, it was difficult if not impossible to present such a position convincingly to the Iraqis.

The CPA in Baghdad faced another dilemma. Many of the Provincial Councils were patently flawed. Not only had most of them not been the product of any quasi-democratic consultative process, but some were corrupt and in the pockets of self-serving or ineffective leadership factions. Somehow they needed to be legitimised if they were to become reasonably credible and authoritative.

The proposed solution to these conundrums was to 'refresh' the Councils, by reviewing them all and having the Governors submit to a reasonably uniform, transparent process of selection or confirmation by representatives in their Provinces. The originators of this idea initially conceived that such 'refreshment' should be very widespread, in the interests of uniformity and harmonisation. But arguments came from the field that the best would be the enemy of the good: some perfectly effective governors were likely to resent the apparent humiliation, and risk, of submitting themselves to such a trial. They might therefore either withdraw from the process altogether, and possibly bring their Councils down with them; or they might work against the idea, which would encourage those who were trying to undermine the Coalition's efforts more generally.

The compromise, which saved face all round albeit after some painful controversy, was to refresh only a small number of Councils. This allowed the Coalition to take the line that a review had taken place and, where difficulties had been discovered, remedial action had been taken. This was to a great extent a true statement. But it was also a fudge and a step back from the CPA leadership's more ambitious objectives.

Contrary to appearances, however, these complex machinations over the Provincial Councils were not stimulated primarily by a belated recognition of the importance of grass roots democracy. In fact, they were motivated by an attempt to set up a indirect election process before the Coalition departed. The objective was to enhance the legitimacy of the Transitional National Assembly, which was to be successor to the Iraqi Governing Council when it and the CPA dissolved, while at the same time meeting the concerns of Grand Ayatollah Sistani halfway. Instead of the direct elections, as Sistani advocated, the CPA proposed that prospective Assembly members should emerge from an immensely complex consultation by means of 'caucuses' drawn from a range of representative groups. Such groups clearly had to include the Provincial Councils. And if the process was not immediately to be rejected by its opponents on the grounds that many of the Councils were simply CPA appointees (as was indeed the case), then their credibility had to be enhanced.

On instructions from Bremer, it fell to Basra Province in December 2003 to arrange the first public meeting which, it was hoped, would explain and advocate the caucus concept and stimulate a debate about it. The idea for this, which made good sense if one agreed with the concept in the first place, was characteristically covered in CPA fingerprints. We in Basra were instructed to set up the meeting, select a group of Iraqi panellists, and ensure that they explained and advocated the reasoning behind the caucus ideas. The meeting was to be televised nationally, but only the CPA official media people were to be allowed to record and edit the broadcast.

We quickly pointed out that such an arrangement would not be credible, because it would be clearly seen as engineered by the CPA, and was likely to do more harm than good. It would be essential that senior Iraqis were visibly in the lead. The broad idea had been endorsed by the Iraqi Governing Council, so it should be for its members, not the CPA, to be seen to be the advocates. We therefore put the ideas to the Basra's Governor and to Izzedine Salim – both members of the Iraqi Governing Council who originated from Basra.

I put the case to Salim myself. He proved to be most reluctant. It became clear the he did not himself fully understand the complicated proposals. I genuinely sympathised. But, more importantly, he did not want to risk setting himself up in opposition to Grand Ayatollah Sistani and thus cause himself immense political damage. Both he and the Governor flatly declined to express support for the proposals, whatever they may have agreed in the Council as a whole. But we eventually persuaded them that no harm could come from a debate about the ideas, with no commitment to supporting them.

This was not at all what Baghdad had in mind, but it was the only possibility in prospect. And, if there were difficulties in Basra, they would have been a lot worse elsewhere.

After massive lobbying efforts by Henry Hogger, the Basra CPA provincial team leader, Robert Wilson and their teams, a suitably impressive panel of debaters was identified. The debate took place on 26 December 2003 and was broadcast nationally.

At one level it was a breakthrough and an enormous success. This was the first occasion in Iraq that there had ever been a free and open political debate on television. The discussion itself was well informed, lucid and considerably more polite than many debates in the Western media. In terms of gathering support for the CPA caucuses idea, however, it made no headway. But it had the unintended merit of reinforcing the advice offered by CPA officers in the field, namely that the proposals suffered from being too complex to be readily understood and from a lack of legitimacy, because they so clearly emanated from the CPA's, rather than the Iraqis', concepts of democracy.

Soon after my first meeting with Izzedine Salim, whom I liked and respected, he made contact again. This was to lodge a request for accommodation, for funds to pay office rent and the unlikely figure of $3000 for car repair. Salim was killed in Baghdad by a car bomb a few months later, on 17 May 2004, when, as that month's president of the Governing Council, he was being driven on his usual route to his office.

* * *

Three weeks after the 'Town Hall' meeting in Basra, the city acted as host for what was possibly Iraq's first ever major, peaceful public political demonstration. A rally had been called by Grand Ayatollah Sistani and was supported by Sunnis, Christians and political parties, as well as the Shia who formed the majority of

Basra's population. It seemed to have the potential to turn into a major confrontation with the Coalition and its thinly spread military forces in the South. If it were to become violent, it would be impossible to control and major bloodshed would follow.

On hearing of the plan, Henry Hogger's team approached the Iraqi religious leaders and asked whether the event was likely to remain peaceful. Thankfully they were assured that it would be. Taking the instigators at their word, and mindful of the risk of provoking an outcome which we desperately needed to avoid, the military leadership decided to maintain a low profile and keep at a distance. As we had been assured, the demonstration passed off without incident.

A similar event took place in Baghdad a few days later, where, influenced by the experience in Basra, Coalition forces adopted a similarly low profile.

These events offered several significant lessons. First, it was now incontrovertibly clear that Ayatollah Sistani, for all his reclusiveness, was a powerful political force. Second, he and the Iraqi people had demonstrated that they were capable of massive, direct political action while maintaining peace. And third, the caucuses idea was a non-starter. The idea was dropped altogether in the rush to broker compromise arrangements before the CPA's dissolution in June 2004.

With the benefit of hindsight, it may be judged that much of the Coalition's, and hence the CPA's, considerable effort to introduce a lasting and durable political system in Iraq was wasted. It was simply not possible to devise such arrangements on the basis of insufficient or unrepresentative consultation. Nor could the Iraqi people be persuaded or cajoled to accept that the Coalition should impose an external notion of governance against their will. They had had enough of that under Saddam.

In consultation with Washington and London, Baghdad hurriedly devised an alternative plan, which involved a multi-stage process. When the CPA dissolved, the Iraqi Governing Council was to be replaced by an Interim Government whose Ministers had been selected beforehand, during the CPA's tenure, and whose legitimacy was therefore limited. Elections would follow in December 2004 or January 2005 to form a Transitional Government, which would preside over the establishment of a draft Constitution. The draft Constitution which emerged from this process would then be submitted to a referendum and, if it received the necessary endorsement, it would become the basis for another round of elections which, hopefully, would then result in a truly democratic constitutional government.

This still-complicated process was followed successfully and, in doing so, exceeded many expectations. The first set of elections duly took place in January 2005, the referendum on 15 October, and the constitutionally-based elections occurred on 15 December 2005, with a turnout of nearly 80 per cent. The Iraqi people went to the polls three times in 12 months, with turnouts which put many Western democracies to shame.

Coalition governments subsequently portrayed this as a great success. In some respects, mainly theoretical, it was. But in practice the country made very little progress towards governance in the following few years and instead slipped unsteadily downwards, together with the Coalition's hopes for it.

The constitutional outcome was also a very long way from what was envisaged by Coalition leaders in April 2003. One of the less visible costs of this failure of ambition arose from the disproportionate political effort and attention expended within the CPA, and by the American and British Governments in attempting to engineer inappropriate political outcomes. Since high-level attention is finite, there were also tragically high, albeit unmeasurable, opportunity costs in terms of lost achievements in other areas of activity where quicker and more effective wins might have been possible.

Epilogue

In years to come, people here in this country, and I believe around the world, will look back on what you have done and give thanks and recognize that they owe you a tremendous debt of gratitude.
Prime Minister Tony Blair, Basra, 4 January 2003.

There can be only one purpose in Iraq: to support the Government and people of the country to attain the necessary capability to run their own affairs as a sovereign independent state. ... Now in Basra, over the coming months, we will transfer more of the responsibility directly to Iraqis. ... The UK military presence will continue into 2008, for as long as we are wanted and have a job to do. ...
Prime Minister Tony Blair, 21 February 2007.

We could have done it a lot better. We should have done it a lot better.
Prime Minister Gordon Brown, *Today Programme*, Radio 4,
3 September 2007.

Just a few words long, Tony Blair's articulation in February 2007 of Britain's purpose in Iraq says a lot. But it also leaves out a lot. There is no reference to democracy, or to peace and stability, or to Iraq no longer posing a threat. His statement as a whole refers to support, but it announces that this was to be reduced; it refers to a long-term military presence, but it says nothing about the size or function of any such presence. It is a far cry from the objective which was meant to guide the civilians working for Blair's government, and the soldiers serving the British Crown, in Iraq's long, hot summer of 2003. In July that year, the Coalition Provisional Authority (CPA), under the leadership of the two 'occupying powers' designated by UN Security Council Resolution 1483 of 22 May 2003 – the USA and the UK – had declared a very different and much more ambitious aim:

> '... a unified and stable, democratic Iraq that provides effective and representative government for the Iraqi people; is underpinned by new and protected freedoms and a growing market economy; is able to defend itself but no longer poses a threat to its neighbors or international security'.

Nevertheless, it quickly became apparent that that objective, however desirable, was both over-ambitious and unrealistic. Seven months later it had become compressed into:

> '... to establish a secure, peaceful and democratic Iraq that will stand against terrorism and no longer threaten America, the region or the world'.

Even that, however, is a lot more than what in late 2007 seems attainable in the foreseeable future. On 14 September 2007, during a Senate hearing, Senator John Warner asked the senior American soldier in Iraq, General David Petraeus, whether the mission in Iraq made 'America safer'. Petraeus responded. 'Sir, I don't know actually'.

After years of spin and unsubstantiated optimism, this honest, soldier's statement of fact was long overdue. To many of those who have been engaged in Iraq, if that answer had been given at almost any point since April 2003 it would have rung true or seemed understated. For American law-makers, the main objectives for Iraq may well have centred around the reduction of threat to the USA's homeland, as reflected in Senator Warner's question. But, for the civilians working in the South, their mission was less directly concerned with threats and more about Iraq itself. While it was primarily for the military to provide and maintain security as a means of settling the country down and hence reducing its latent threat to others and to its own citizens, the civilians in the Coalition considered that they too had an essential contribution to make to such an objective, and that this needed to involve the Iraqis themselves. True security, which went beyond the threat from insurgents or criminals, entailed the broad stability of the country as a whole. This in turn could only be brought about by improved living conditions, by employment opportunities, by systems of governance which took account of public opinion, by an informed knowledge of what was really happening and, above all, by a well-founded sense of hope.

To achieve all this called for civilian, not just military, engagement in encouraging, advising and assisting the Iraqis to reconstruct their own country, to foster sound government systems at the local and regional levels, as well as at the national level, and to facilitate the establishment of free and accurate media. Without progress in these fields, there could not truly be any more definite answer than that given by General Petraeus to Senator Warner's question.

By 2007, and in fact well before this, it had become clear that the civilian-oriented challenges were not being met. The hospitals, the supply of medication, and public health generally, declined rapidly from the already low levels under Saddam. The enormous potential of agriculture to provide employment was neglected as it became too dangerous for Coalition civilians to operate in open country, and the military understandably lacked the skills to fill the gap. The re-establishment of opportunities for education became limited to trying to rebuild schools and providing some basic hardware and textbooks, while management and curricula were perforce neglected. The essential services of power, water and fuel could to some extent be provided by the Coalition's military forces, but the development of economic and other management systems, replacing the centralised arrangements which had imploded after Saddam's fall, required civilian rather than military skills.

Leaving aside the immense consequences of inadequate planning and preparation and of some ill-advised initial decisions, however, it was immediately apparent at the time that the greatest single deficiency of our civilian operation was the shortage of human resources and expertise.

It is now clear that there were two main reasons for this. Partly, it was a result of the excessive priority which was, and still is, placed on the security of civilian public servants. Unlike those of the armed forces and private security companies, the terms of service of civilian officials do not allow them to be exposed to significant risk of death or injury; and, if either were to occur, their managers or parent organisations risk being sued. This leads managers to take a very cautious approach to deploying staff for whom they are ultimately responsible, even if they are volunteers, while pressing non-volunteers into service is out of the question. It was no doubt such considerations which led the small team of British diplomats based in the relatively benign Kurdish region to be protected by a very much larger number of private security contractors, as I discovered when I visited there in the summer of 2007.

But a more fundamental reason for the short supply of personnel and other resources stemmed from a lack of political direction. Seen from Iraq and notwithstanding Blair's rhetoric, there was little evidence that the British Government as a whole saw itself as being at war. Management and oversight at ministerial and senior official level was essentially ad hoc and bore little resemblance to the highly organised arrangements for post-conflict reconstruction which had been put in place, for instance, some four years before the end of the Second World War. Blair put a constant public emphasis on the importance and urgency of making progress in Iraq. But, seemingly little interested in the processes within Government by which this might be brought about, he proved unable to mobilise Government departments to produce the necessary results. The Army could, as always, be relied upon to find solutions for themselves, albeit cut according to their overstretched means. But in the civilian domain, Blair's exhortations and verbal commitments were not reflected in exceptional measures such as identifying and encouraging volunteers by means of trawls of Embassies around the world, fast-track recruitment procedures, or new management and coordination systems across government departments.

It was for such reasons that, even well after I arrived in Basra in the summer of 2003, the British Army was engaged in tasks which should have fallen squarely in the civilian domain. This was not because they wanted to do so, but because there was no one else. And several areas of activity, essential or not, were being neglected because the necessary expertise was not available.

So far as I could see from my outpost in the South, the Americans had similar problems over marshalling suitable civilian personnel. Like the British, their civilian contribution also suffered from a lack of numbers, expertise and experience, but the reasons were somewhat different. Since overall responsibility had been devolved to the Pentagon and, to all appearances, the managers there placed little value on the skills and resources of the State Department, it was hardly surprising that there should be difficulties in attracting volunteers from that source – although at a later stage American officials were encouraged in a way which never occurred with their British counterparts. The fact that other parts of Iraq were more dangerous than the South, which was then relatively quiescent, also impeded recruitment, which has remained problematic and inadequate ever since. But the American effort was greatly strengthened by the deployment of some 3500 Civil Affairs personnel, reservists under military command, whose civilian experience and expertise were recognised, valued, organised and put to good use. Civilian expertise also existed among the British Territorial Army reservists. But these quasi-military personnel seemed to be regarded within the Army as second-class soldiers, who were often used to fill in gaps, albeit in the face of danger, while their civilian skills were seldom either recognised or put to systematic use. In the cases where individuals' skills were recognised and their comparative advantage was put to good use, generally by seconding them to our civilian organisation, their contribution was in some instances beyond price.

Looking back on it all, the experience for the civilians working in the South in trying to make progress over all the varied challenges was a mixture of frustration and irritation – even anger and, thankfully not infrequently, exhilaration and mirth. There were never enough resources, human or financial, to meet the needs. Progress was bedevilled by bureaucracy, incompetence and sometimes plain obstructionism; and that was before trying to deal with the Iraqis themselves.

However, despite the obstacles and the pressures, progress did occur. At the end of each week, the prospect of what needed to be done could seem overwhelming. But, at the same time, it was apparent that many of the previous week's issues had been resolved. Occasionally, the balance appeared to be positive, which provided great encouragement to carry on. At a personal level, in the face of common discomfort and danger, it was the best side of people's characters which showed itself. Moments of stress were often relieved by moments of relief and humour. Was it not astonishing that throughout the CPA's 13-month existence, despite the violence and the risks, no single member of its staff in the South was killed? Tragically, however, the same was not true of the Iraqi staff who worked with us or of the Army with whom we worked so closely and who provided much of our protection.

In the more troubled times which followed the demise of the CPA in June 2004, the already under-resourced civilian contribution in the South all but evaporated. The multinational team of expert volunteers, some of whom had carefully built up links with individual Iraqi managers for more than a year, was replaced by more conventional, bilateral development cooperation programmes, managed by aid agencies – primarily USAID and DFID. The USA and the UK predictably paid greatest attention to new or existing projects which they had themselves funded directly. Many of the large body of multinationally managed projects in train or in prospect simply withered away. There was no way in which the greatly reduced number of aid officials, many of whom had had no prior exposure to the South and knew none of the Iraqis involved, could continue to manage projects which had been conceived and set in train by the now-vanished Coalition experts, hand in glove with those whom they had been trying to mentor. Radical ideas for avoiding such an outcome, such as by maintaining the previous CPA team and management structure on a different basis – not as part of an occupying/liberating power, but with full Iraqi consent – found no favour in either Washington or Whitehall.

In practice the Americans set up a small Embassy office in the CPA(South) compound in Basra, and the British sought to administer their aid programme from what became their consulate there. As a result the impetus behind the previous reconstruction effort collapsed. A year or two later efforts were belatedly made to re-establish what came to be known as Provincial Reconstruction Teams in the provinces. These too suffered from the inter-departmental squabbling within the American and British government systems which had characterised so much of the earlier efforts.

Later, as security deteriorated further, it became too dangerous to maintain any foreign civilian aid administrators in Basra or the other main towns in the South. The American team, which had taken over the bulk of the reconstruction effort after the CPA was wound up, moved away, while British officials and contracted experts moved out of Basra city to the relative security – and isolation – of the military base at the airport. Some efforts were made to train Iraqi managers in outposts such as Dubai and Amman, well away from the projects on the ground. The reconstruction teams covering the other three provinces – Maysan, Dhi Qar and Muthanna – took shelter in the massive US base at Tallil, in Nasiriyah Province. In an effort to show results quickly, the British government concentrated ever more on short-term projects, linked to the relatively short military and civilian tours in the country, at the expense of the deeper and more fundamental capacity-building needs.

In such circumstances it is hardly surprising that a close mentoring relationship with the Iraqi managers, or even half-effective project monitoring and management, becomes well-nigh impossible. Attempting to make the best of it, the British and American governments have taken to publicising 'Factsheets' and 'metrics' listing: for example, kilometres of water pipes laid, completed electricity projects, schools which have been refurbished and even the planting of date palms. Such statistics indeed indicate activity but, without being presented in the context of the economy as a whole, they convey little meaning; and their relevance to the security of the Iraqis, in its wider sense, must be at best uncertain.

Sadly, it is clear from the experience at the time and the testimony of subsequent events that our mission as the southern arm of the CPA in Iraq failed to meet the unrealistically high standards which the Coalition leadership had set for us. If, however, it is now proving difficult to meet even the much less ambitious 'purpose' put forward by Tony Blair in February 2007, this must in part be due to a failure to build on the albeit limited progress that was made in the early days, the decision in June 2004 to reduce the pace of the then-existing reconstruction effort, and the subsequent flip-flop approaches to the Provincial Reconstruction Teams coupled with short-termism and chronic under-manning.

Whose fault was all this? To what extent was it a consequence of a lack of political will or a lack of understanding? What would have been the effect on Iraq as a whole if Washington and London had been better prepared to deal with the situation in the country as it really was, rather than what they had hoped to find? And what if the 'occupying powers' had not sought to conjure a new-model capitalist democracy out of a proud nation which had never in its history experienced either democracy or a free market? Would Britain now be withdrawing from a stable, prosperous and democratic southern Iraq? More parochially perhaps, would it have made any difference to the ultimate outcome of the war and its aftermath if the civilian effort in the South had been a success?

Such counterfactual questions cannot of course be answered with any certainty. It is quite possible that, even without the terrible failures of planning documented here and in other books, without Rumsfeld's attempt at an 'Invasion Lite', without putting over 200,000 Iraqi soldiers out on the streets with no employment, without removing all the senior civilian managers, and without all the other deficiencies of foresight and execution, Iraq would still have spiralled into internal conflict and ungovernability.

Although arguments can be made for it, the notion that Iraq was lost from the start, whatever the Coalition did, carries great risks. Such a line of thinking, if it leads to a concentration on the failures of judgement of the political leadership who took the decisions, distracts attention from the myriad shortcomings surrounding the operational activities in the field. The key decision-makers, and especially Bush and Blair, must inevitably bear ultimate responsibility, both for the war itself and for the failures surrounding the process by which success might be achieved. But many important lessons will be neglected if the focus is exclusively on the fundamental decisions. The deficiencies of process and planning need to be examined in detail: the inability quickly to mobilise adequate numbers of appropriate experts or sufficient financial resources and support materiel; the restrictive 'duty of care' impediments to civilian deployments; the bureaucratic accounting and contracting procedures; the failures of communication and understanding – between the hub in Baghdad and the regional and provincial spokes, as well as between the key Coalition partners; and, perhaps most important, the failure to motivate and organise the Coalition's central government departments so that they were each required and able to contribute their particular skills and resources to an effort which needed to be a truly comprehensive one. Only by careful analysis of such failings will it be possible to decide to what extent changes need to be made and then – easier said than done – ensure that they are brought about.

Understanding the causes and consequences of what went wrong in Iraq should not therefore be regarded as just an academic or historical exercise. Nor would the implementation of institutional changes which should follow on from sound assessments simply be a case of 'fighting the last war', without relevance to the present or future. Despite the unpopularity of the Iraq war, Britain and America seem likely to be involved in more, not fewer, nation-building efforts in the coming years. International experience since the end of the Cold War and the trend of uncertainties arising from migratory pressures, climate change, demographic expansion, weak governance, insurgency and terrorism suggest that the need for external assistance to fragile states will increase rather than diminish. Even in Afghanistan, after more than six years of operations, the challenges show little sign of abating, and several of these are, yet again, being examined from first principles – police training and the role of Provincial Reconstruction Teams being significant examples. Many of the shortcomings in that country have similarities with those in Iraq and still need to be properly assessed, with appropriate conclusions drawn.

There are also more contemporary political implications surrounding the interpretation of events in the South. Much of the USA–UK debate in the autumn of 2007 about a supposed 'British defeat' in Basra was based on serious flaws of understanding and invalid comparisons between the different circumstances in Basra and the Baghdad region. The American surge in 2007, involving an increase of some 30,000 troops on the ground, was able to capitalise on the dissent in, especially, Anbar Province between the indigenous Sunni and the Al Qaeda fighters, also Sunnis. As a result, sectarian violence, by which Al Qaeda aimed to gain ascendancy over the Shia majority in the country, declined. This development, coupled with a more sensitive and targeted American military approach in that troubled region, has justifiably been portrayed as progress, even if it was not sufficient to allow General Petraeus honestly to claim that America had been rendered more safe.

The successes of the surge coincided with a move by the British out of their small garrison in Basra city and the reduction of troop levels which had been foreshadowed by Blair in February 2007, some six months earlier. This led to accusations that the British, reducing their military presence, had somehow 'lost' Basra, while the Americans, increasing theirs, were at last gaining ground – although only the most optimistic of commentators went so far as to suggest that 'victory' was close at hand.

Such allegations were no more soundly based than the self-indulgent assertions by some British ministers in 2003 that the apparent British successes in the South should be a model for others. Now, as then, the two situations bear little comparison. Unlike in the Baghdad region, sectarian violence has never been the main problem in the four provinces in the South, where the great majority of the population is Shia. There, the main challenge in the last few years has been the rivalry between three Shia political groupings, each of which was competing for the title of having driven the Coalition out of the city. Their ultimate objective, however, is less to get rid of the so-called oppressor than to have the field free for them to do battle between themselves and gain political ascendancy. The rewards for the winners go well beyond the political domain, and include the profits of organised crime and kickbacks from oil revenues and smuggling. Such activity, while it may and does involve violence and criminality, is, however, essentially political in nature, in the hands of Iraqis themselves, and seems unlikely to be capable of resolution by the use of external force. Interventions by outsiders in the disputes by rival political factions would be of dubious legality in a country where the Coalition purported in 2004 to have transferred sovereignty back to the Iraqis themselves; and, more pragmatically, they would probably direct yet more concentrated fire on to the external interveners. In the absence of any other alternative, there is little option but to let such tendencies work themselves out, leading to Iraqi solutions, of a sort, to Iraqi disputes.

In a similar vein, in the autumn of 2003, when the South was quieter, some optimists – generally British – suggested that the progress which was then becoming evident might have a beneficial effect on other regions in Iraq: that the relative stability of the South might spread through the Iraqi body politic like a curative anti-biotic. Again, however, this was self-serving, wishful thinking.

In practice, the problems and issues in the various and complex components which make up Iraq are to a great extent special to the particular regions and sub-regions; yet the mood in these regions can also be affected by events outside them. Thus the attack in February 2006 on the Shia mosque in Samarra had the effect of inflaming sectarian animosity which had long lain relatively dormant. And the CPA's attempts in 2003 to impose a complex, and ultimately unworkable, system of governance on the country, its espousal of free market economics, and its failure to deliver improvements on the ground, mobilised all segments of society in favour of the earliest possible elections and led directly to the occupying authority's early demise.

In the wider context, therefore, it was never possible to 'win' in the South except as part of the establishment of stability in the country as a whole. The best that could be hoped for was to hold the line and if possible improve conditions there so as to avoid adding to the overall challenge. For a period that temporary result was indeed almost achieved. It is possible, but unprovable, that more sustained and more intensive interventionism would have maintained that relative stability for a longer period. But it would have been unrealistic ever to suppose that the South, or any part of the country, could remain immune to the infections which surrounded it. The passage of time has allowed these infections, and new ones, to gain hold. This in turn has rendered what should be the political objective of war – peace, not victory – an even more distant prospect, increasing the possibility of anarchy and the break up of the country.

While the experience in Iraq has highlighted major errors of judgement at the highest level as well as systemic shortcomings within the US and UK administrations, there remains the possibility that events might have turned out differently, and better, had governments taken different approaches. Such a possibility is of course unknowable. But what is certain is that the failures in these various domains made the already slim chances of success in administering Iraq almost if not entirely impossible.

It would not, however, be entirely true to suggest that governments have taken no steps to learn from the civilian-related lessons of Iraq. But such attempts as there were have proved half-hearted. The British Government created a Post-Conflict Reconstruction Unit, based in and dominated by the Development Ministry, but including representatives from the Foreign and Commonwealth Office, the Ministry of Defence and the Armed Forces. The US State Department established a Coordinator for Reconstruction and Stabilization. Both arrangements have been, to be charitable, disappointments. They have so far exercised little influence and, notwithstanding some successful operations, have done nothing to break down the fundamental tensions, rivalries and differing policy priorities between the government departments concerned.

Much more effort is needed. And nation building does not come cheap. It will not be enough simply to 'tweak' existing government structures. Management systems and financial and human resources have to be provided and designed for the long term. The techniques involved differ from conventional humanitarian relief, development cooperation and diplomacy, although expertise in each is essential. The main requirement is to be able to deploy at short notice teams of civilians with appropriate training, experience and aptitude to work in difficult and hazardous environments, and then to resource and manage them effectively once they are on the ground. This need not conjure up a vision of a standing force of dark-suited bureaucrats ready to deploy at a moment's notice, like some civilian special forces regiment; that would be to exaggerate the nature of any 'civilian expeditionary force' to the point of absurdity and beyond what could reasonably be resourced.

The need could be met in several ways. Appropriate adaptation of the British Territorial Army, which occurred on an ad hoc basis to some extent in southern Iraq, would be a major step forward. But this relatively easy task would not suffice. The Territorial reservists' contracts already allow them to be deployed in war zones and to carry weapons. The provision of such possibilities for other Crown Servants and the lifting of the dead hand of senior managers' 'duty of care', which bedevilled the civilian operations in southern Iraq, has complex organisational, legal and managerial implications. These need to be examined and not dismissed as being all too difficult.

There have nonetheless been some improvements. For example, the procedures for recruiting experts on a consultancy basis, albeit at a price which greatly exceeds the remuneration of any civil servant with similar qualifications, have been streamlined after the appallingly slow results in 2003. In the autumn of 2007 the Chancellor of the Exchequer announced that the Development Ministry would make a renewed effort to deal with conflict stabilisation and prevention. But the sad history of such efforts hitherto give good grounds for scepticism. And the Army is still justified in complaining about, even resenting, the delays in deployment of civilians in parts of Afghanistan after they have cleared the ground. It may be sound developmental practice to proceed in a measured fashion, drawing up needs assessments and canvassing opinion. But the challenges in places like Iraq and Afghanistan go well beyond developmental orthodoxy and call for quick results to help pacify a suspicious population. Less conventional civilian methods are therefore needed as well. If such methods were to involve high costs, or waste, it is doubtful that either would be commensurate with that incurred by the Army's expenditure of blood and treasure.

* * *

I was aware of none of these complexities and constraints when I was politely and unexpectedly told, in mid-July of 2003, that it would be 'nice' if I were able to get myself out to Basra by the end of that month. Nor did I expect to find myself, in my late fifties, living in conditions which bore comparison with my experience in diesel-electric submarines in my early twenties, but without a submariner's nutritious rations.

But I was right in my initial instinctive judgement that I would for ever kick myself if I did not agree to go. In practice, the dangers faced by our civilian contingent in the South in those early days were not nearly as severe as was portrayed by the Press or as was perceived by our managers in London.

The variety and complexity of the challenges stretched every facet of my experience – of the armed forces, of developing countries, of Islam, of management and leadership, of the machinations of governments and of political expediency – which brought its own peculiar gratification. On bad days, memories of the frustrations and failures re-emerge and inflame in me an irritation which is perhaps a characteristic of someone in their 'third age'. But the most lasting recollections are positive ones and reflect the stimulus and satisfaction of working closely with highly motivated people, from Iraq and many other countries, including my own, who sincerely wanted to do the best they could in a task which, whatever its appalling and misguided genesis, they felt to be worthwhile.

Appendix One
CPA(South):
Its Role and Purpose

(A paper by Hilary Synnott issued to all CPA(South) staff after their move to new premises in November 2003)

HAVING MOVED TO our new location at Al Sarraji in mid-October, we and the Governorate teams are starting to receive additional staffing and physical resources. It is time to take stock and to consider how we should adapt to the new opportunities and challenges. This note sets out some thoughts about a way forward. We must be ready to adapt further as new resources arrive and our capabilities increase.

What are we Trying to Do?

There are four main challenges. The most important at present is *security*, for the people of Iraq and for ourselves in setting about our tasks. The other three play into this, just as security plays into the other three. The primary responsibility for the maintenance of law and order, in the broadest form, rests with the military in MND(SE), following the direction of their Headquarters, CJTF-7, in cooperation with CPA Baghdad and Ambassador Bremer. CPA(S)'s activities can also have a direct bearing on security.

The *reconstruction* of Iraq and *economic reform and development* are essential if a new Iraqi government is able to provide adequate services for the Iraqi people after the Coalition has left. The state of Iraq's infrastructure proved, once the Coalition was able to examine it, to have been in an even worse state than many expected. Arrangements for power, water and fuel were particularly poor. Social services such as health care and education had deteriorated under Saddam's regime. Literacy rates, which used to be relatively high when compared with similar countries, had declined. Improvements are needed and will be welcomed; by reducing dissatisfaction they should enhance security.

Saddam did not allow the people any say in their own *governance*. Now, however, many different centres of power are seizing the opportunities which are opening up to them. At the national level, a process of constitutional reform is under way; Ministries are exercising authority and a degree of independence, under the umbrella of the CPA and the Interim Governing Council. At the Provincial level, there is a vigorous 'bottom up' process in train. Provincial Councils have been formed and, in many cases, interim Governors. Local Councils are developing. Tribal Sheikhs remind us of their traditional role of influence and patronage. Political parties are springing up. And religious parties are also in the field. This process is developing almost without restraint, but with as much input from CPA as has proved feasible. The picture varies greatly around the country and from Province to Province. Such developments can have both stabilising and destabilising effects. The situation is unlikely to become any simpler as people enjoy and exercise their new-found freedoms. We should encourage constructive trends.

Linked to all these considerations is the *perception* of the Iraqi people. Even if things are getting better, the people will not be impressed unless they can perceive this for themselves. We must all ensure that progress is publicised. The fact that lights stay on for longer than previously makes less of an impact than when they go out.

Our Task

Under the broad direction of CPA Baghdad and working to CPA's Strategic Plan, our task is to work on each of these areas so as to enable an Iraqi government to have the best possible chance of managing the country, politically and technically, when the Coalition leaves. This means, most importantly, that we must help Iraqis help themselves, building up their own capacity. It is no use supplying massive capital equipment, for instance, if it breaks down through lack of management or maintenance when the responsibility for it shifts. Nor must we end up doing the job entirely ourselves. This means some hard and often counter-intuitive choices, requiring Iraqis to do things for themselves even when we are closely exposed to real poverty and want to secure results quickly. Fortunately the quality and resourcefulness of the Iraqi people is one of the country's most valuable assets, especially in the South where they were oppressed by Saddam for so long.

Resources, Human and Financial

Both CPA(S) and the Governorate Teams have felt short of human resources to deal with the tasks in hand.

CPA(S) will soon have some 200 staff of eight different nationalities, including many military personnel. Some have considerable expertise in their fields; others are generalists. There are many other support staff as well – security, life support, etc – so the total number at Al Sarraji is quite large. What is unusual about CPA(S) when compared to other regions is the absence of large numbers of US Civil Affairs Officers, who have been heavily engaged in such tasks as project identification and implementation which has been an area of particular difficulty for us until recently. That is why we have more civilians than other regions. But UK, Italian, Danish and other forces working at the coalface here have thrown themselves into civil reconstruction work no less enthusiastically than their counterparts elsewhere, with results out of all proportion to the numbers deployed. This activity is an integral and vital contribution to their main task of consolidating the security situation.

CPA(S) is currently organised into seven 'Pillars' which cover several sub-pillars of specialist subjects. Many of these have been under-resourced. As more people arrive, they will bring real technical expertise to replace the 'sticking plaster' and 'common sense' approach which we have had to adopt up to now. Once here, these experts will be able to help us adopt a more strategic approach than hitherto, with better appreciation of potential problems which may arise in the future and, crucially, a greater capability to offer expert advice and assistance to the GTs.

But the Coalition's effort involves many more than the staff at CPA(S) Headquarters and the military. The massive USAID and contractors' resources, the work of the US contractors RTI, the Iraqi IRDC contribution, all need to be meshed in with our own. We have established mechanisms to do this and are now elaborating detailed Action Plans consistent with the CPA's overall Strategic Plan. I shall be reorganising CPA(S)'s management structure soon to reflect the new situation.

The *GT's* are due to be fully staffed and equipped by the end of November. In the interim they have received support from military Governorate Support Teams, to a greater or lesser degree, and some, but not nearly enough, support from CPA(S). This has not been tidy or altogether satisfactory, but that situation has been largely inevitable. When fully up and running, the GTs should each comprise between 70 and 80 staff all told. The relationships between the GTs, Baghdad and CPA(S) are complicated. But I see no reason why they should not become workable and mutually advantageous.

Until recently we have been plagued by inadequate *flows of funds*: from Baghdad and from CPA(S) to the ministerial departments and to the Provinces. Resolving this problem has been time-consuming and painful. New parameters have constantly arisen. I am optimistic that we are just about there now. Funding is flowing as never before. But the new procedures must be understood and conformed to, bearing in mind also that they are subject to change. The bottom line is that outflows are rapidly growing, and that they need to grow further.

Baghdad

My top operational priority since I arrived has been to improve the flow of information and expertise between the South and Baghdad. This may sound easy, but the difficulties in the relationship between the GTs and the Regional Centre pale into insignificance beside those involved in mastering what is going on in Baghdad. This is not a criticism. It is inevitable. Which means that the task remains essential. In several cases Baghdad has solved a problem once we informed them of it. In some cases, we have brought genuine and important problems to Baghdad's attention when their attention was elsewhere. And in some cases Baghdad have proved unable to solve a problem which we judged to fall to them, leaving us impotent. We have to keep working at it. The better we know the system, such as it is, the more effective we shall collectively become.

Priorities

We have recently drawn up a draft plan to guide us in the selection of projects. Hitherto, and particularly in the light of the experience last August, we have majored on *Power, Water and Fuel*, and have addressed these in a holistic way through the Emergency Infrastructure Plan. This is proceeding well: contracts are being approved in weekly meetings under my chairmanship. Results are becoming visible. After that has come *Education* and *Agriculture*. The former is coming along quite well. Schools are being refurbished and materials have been supplied, with more on the way. Universities are being repaired. There have been no significant demonstrations of protest. Agriculture is potentially more difficult since we lack both expertise and data; and Baghdad is evidently in the same position. But it is important because it provides jobs and food; and it is a potential source of unrest.

Other sectors must not be neglected. *Financial activity* must shift from sorting out routine payments to economic development. *Health* is doing well, partly because we have a team of experts in sufficient numbers to make a difference. Similarly over *Police Training*, where the Danish contribution has been inestimable. The *rehabilitation of buildings* is progressing. We have gaps in *trade, industry, customs, prisons, fire services, judicial reform* and elsewhere. And we need to do more on *capacity building*, and take better account of *civil society, gender issues and sustainability*. Our *media efforts* need better centralised media which Iraqis will want to read or watch. These all require the special expertise, which is on its way.

I have focussed on CPA(S)'s sectors of activity. But in the longer term, it is the big national-level projects which will have the greatest impact: multi-million dollar activity under Projects RIE (electricity) and RIO (oil), especially when the additional US $20.3bn starts to get on stream. It remains to be seen how effective these will be in terms of capacity building. If they are not, then we must be even more so.

Perspectives/Managing Expectations

In the South especially, the population's expectations after the fall of Saddam were very high – unrealistically so. Conditions were expected to improve immediately and visibly after Saddam's yoke was lifted. If the US could put a man on the moon, then they should be able to give us electricity, was a frequent refrain. A greater degree of realism is already apparent. But there is still a tendency to subject us to lists of demands. Of course we shall do what we can. But we cannot do everything. Nor should we strive for perfection. We must concentrate on capacity building and try to discourage a dependency culture according to which the Coalition becomes a sort of benign Saddam. This may involve disappointment, protests and disorder on occasion. If we cannot do the impossible, then we must plan for the consequences, while all the time trying to minimise the dangers which they may entail. The key is to build up understanding, a cooperative approach, consent and support.

Security

In fulfilling our tasks, we must take proper care for our own security. The environment in the South is more permissive than elsewhere. But that does not make it risk-free. There are people who want the CPA's endeavour to fail. On the other hand, as was all too evident in the former Electricity Commission Building which housed us until October, intensive security measures can directly impede our operational effectiveness. If they are too strict, we might not be able to contribute at all. So some balance must be struck. I am therefore trying to ensure that advice from elsewhere takes full account of all the relevant factors, including different conditions in different parts of the country, is well-informed, is sensibly balanced, and is reviewed whenever necessary. Most important, however, is that everyone conforms to the procedures which are laid down, even if you do not necessarily agree with them.

Hilary Synnott
Al Sarraji
12 November 2003

Appendix Two

The CPA Vision Document

(July 2003, Extract)

Introduction

This progressive plan is an overview of the strategy necessary for early restoration of full sovereignty to the Iraqi people. The strategy is driven by more detailed action plans (e.g., plans for the New Iraqi Army, the police, restoring electrical power, etc.).

Our strategy has four principal objectives or 'core foundations' :

- **Security** – establishing a secure and safe environment
- **Essential services** – restoring basic services to an acceptable standard
- **Economy** – creating the conditions for economic growth
- **Governance** – enabling the transition to transparent and inclusive democratic governance

These objectives are intertwined: none can be pursued in isolation. Political and economic progress depends in part on security, but should itself help to create a safer environment.

L. Paul Bremer, Administrator
Coalition Provisional Authority

Summary

Now that Saddam Hussein's regime has been removed, the Iraqi people have the opportunity to realize the President's vision of a stable, prosperous and democratic Iraq. The Coalition Provisional Authority (CPA), in close partnership with the Iraqi Governing Council, the United Nations, and the international community, has a key role to play in the next stage of rebuilding Iraq.

This document describes the CPA's strategy for carrying out its role in this historic process. While the CPA remains the legally sovereign power in Iraq, we now have a significant partner in the Governing Council (GC) of the Interim Administration. That Council represents the voice of the Iraqi people to the CPA, and to the world. Together the CPA and the GC will forge a partnership that will guide the nation forward in its transformation.

This document is designed to direct the work of the CPA and the coalition militaries in a flexible manner that recognizes the need to retain the support of the Iraqi people in all that we do, knowing that their support is vital to our success. It is also aimed at the international community whose political and financial backing will be essential if our overall objectives are to be achieved. The plan recognizes the need for further planning in coordination with the GC as the process of rebuilding Iraq evolves. While full economic recovery will take years, the economic reform program provides a vision of a future of freedom and prosperity towards which we and the GC will work in the short term.

The plan describes key action steps within the various core elements that determine the CPA's priorities in the short, medium and long-term. From this, we can review what we have achieved and where we need to adjust. Finally, the plan will assist us and the Governing Council to allocate our resources and those of Iraq. It will also assist in attracting critical resources and capabilities from the international community.

The CPA Vision

After decades of a ruthless dictatorship, the Iraqi people can at last control their destiny and establish the conditions for a free and stable future. With the international community, the CPA will help the Iraqi people achieve the President's and Prime Minister's vision for Iraq – a free Iraq governed by a representative government chosen through democratic elections. At the core of this new Iraq is the development of a democratic, accountable, and self-governing civil society respectful of human rights and freedom of expression. The future prosperity of Iraq's citizens depends on the use of Iraqi resources to foster the development of a market-based economy. This needs to be done in a manner that is economically, socially and environmentally sustainable for the long term benefit of all Iraqi people. Furthermore, our goal is an Iraq at peace with itself and its neighbors, once again able to play a responsible role in the international community. The Coalition is firmly committed to the future of Iraq. The CPA succeeds when Iraq succeeds. Hence we will stay as long as necessary, and not a day longer. But we will not leave until we have succeeded in carrying out the President's and Prime Minister's vision. Our foundation of authority is firmly embedded in international law and in accord with United Nations Security Council Resolution 1483.

The Mission

The CPA will work with the Iraqi people and the Iraqi Interim Administration to establish the conditions for a free, sovereign, democratically-elected representative government. We want to work with Iraqis to establish an Iraq that uses its resources for the benefit of its people. It should be an Iraq that is stable, united, prosperous, at peace with its neighbors and able to take its rightful place as a responsible member of the region and the international community. This Iraq must be free of weapons of mass destruction and terrorists.

The End-State

The ultimate goal is a unified and stable, democratic Iraq that: provides effective and representative government for the Iraqi people; is underpinned by new and protected freedoms for all Iraqis and a growing market economy; is able to defend itself but no longer poses a threat to its neighbors or international security.

ACHIEVING THE MISSION

Taking Forward the CPA Strategic Plan for Iraq

Goal

The primary goal of the Coalition Provisional Authority (CPA) is the early restoration of full sovereignty to the Iraqi people. We seek:

"a unified and stable, democratic Iraq that provides effective and representative government for the Iraqi people; is underpinned by new and protected freedoms and a growing market economy; is able to defend itself but no longer poses a threat to its neighbors or international security."

A major step towards that goal was taken on 13 July, with the establishment of a Governing Council of 25 Iraqis representing all major strands of Iraqi society. The Council will have substantial powers. It will appoint Iraqi Ministers and approve budgets. It will be consulted on all major policy issues and on our planning for the transfer of power to a sovereign Iraqi government.

Strategy

Our strategy has four principal objectives or 'core foundations' :

- **Security** – establishing a secure and safe environment
- **Essential services** – restoring basic services to an acceptable standard

- **Economy** – creating the conditions for economic growth
- **Governance** – enabling the transition to transparent and inclusive democratic governance

These objectives are intertwined: none can be pursued in isolation. Political and economic progress depends in part on security, but should itself help to create a safer environment.

Security

Coalition forces will help Iraqis to eliminate the threats to their security and will remain in country for as long as they are needed. **Over time the transfer of security responsibilities to local military and police forces will determine the speed with which we can advance reconstruction and build up institutions of good governance.**

The Iraqi people are already contributing to that effort but must acquire the ability to assume full responsibility for meeting the country's security needs as soon as practicable - thus enabling the draw-down of coalition forces. Our priorities therefore include:

- Development and training of Iraqi security forces, including a new Iraqi army, new civil defense corps and an effective police force
- Development of national security and civilian oversight mechanisms
- Measures to ensure border security
- Measures to build the justice system and improve the penal system
- Ensuring that Iraq is free of weapons of mass destruction.

Essential Services

Effective delivery of basic services is a major priority for the Iraqi people and the CPA. Our program involves:

- Reconstituting the power infrastructure
- Improving water resource management
- Ensuring food security

- Improving health care - quality and access
- Rehabilitating key transport infrastructure
- Improving education and housing - quality and access
- Reconstructing the telecommunications system.

The Economy

To realize the country's full potential for economic growth, Iraq will need initially to:

- Build financial market structures
- Promote private business
- Determine the future of state-owned enterprises.

Policy work is also in progress on:

- Monetizing and phasing out subsidies, while building a social safety net
- Designing an oil trust fund
- Reform of the tax system.

Governance

Iraq has suffered from decades of tyranny. **Effective representative government, sustained by democratic elections, requires the rapid development of new frameworks and capacities,** including:

- A constitution drafted by Iraqis and approved by Iraqis
- Institutions and processes to conduct free and fair elections
- Open and transparent political processes
- Measures to improve the effectiveness of elected officials, including strengthened local government systems
- Effective and fair justice systems
- Respect for the rule of law and human rights
- Creation of a vibrant civil society.

Information

Strengthening the media is essential for the development of healthy democracy in Iraq. This will require legislation to protect free speech as well as to regulate broadcasting and promote responsible journalism. Professional bodies have a role to play in setting journalistic standards.

The transitional administration in Iraq must ensure that our policies are communicated accurately and effectively at all times to the Iraqi people. **The CPA's communications strategy is designed to get our message out in an honest, clear and timely way -** and then to take account of the responses of the Iraqi people, including their expression through the media.

Resources

It is difficult at this point to quantify the external assistance needed to support Iraq's transition to representative government and a market economy. Eastern European experience suggests that a substantial international commitment will be needed. But Iraq starts the process at a lower level of economic and political development. Its energy resources have been badly mismanaged for decades, leaving the country unable from its own resources at present to provide an acceptable living standard for its people.

Clearly, the United States and the international community and institutions must take the lead. **Only a co-ordinated international effort can bring prosperity and stability to the Iraqi people and contribute to a lasting peace in the Middle East.**

Planning

Our planning, which is a dynamic and iterative process, involves:

- An unprecedented joint civilian and military CPA/CJTF7 planning process to produce a joint strategic plan - the military contribute vitally to all key objectives
- A comprehensive and evolving plan for the short, medium and longer term, but
- Necessary flexibility to change, and to learn from experience.

Attached charts give further details of the sectoral plans being taken forward in military and Ministerial plans.

Appendix Three
CPA Organisation Chart

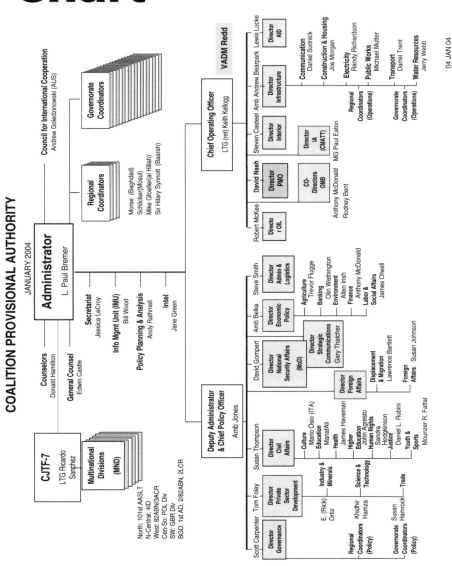

COALITION PROVISIONAL AUTHORITY

JANUARY 2004

Administrator
L. Paul Bremer

Counselors
Donald Hamilton

General Counsel
Edwin Castle

Council for International Cooperation
Andrew Goledzinowski (AUS)

Governorate Coordinators

Regional Coordinators
Morse (Baghdad)
Schlicker(Mosul)
Mike Gfoeller(al Hillah)
Sir Hilary Synnott (Basrah)

Secretariat
Jessica LeCroy

Info Mgmt Unit (IMU)
Bill Wood

Policy Planning & Analysis
Andy Rathmell

Intel
Jane Green

CJTF-7
LTG Ricardo Sanchez

Multinational Divisions (MND)

North: 101st AASLT
N-Central: 4ID
West: 82ABN/3ACR
Cen-So: POL Div
SW: GBR Div
BGD: 1st AD, 2/82ABN, 2LCR

Chief Operating Officer
LTG (ret) Keith Kellogg

VADM Redd

Steven Casteel   Amb Andrew Bearpark   Lewis Lucke

Robert McKee   David Nash

Directo r OIL

Director PMO

CO-Directors OMB
Anthony McDonald
Rodney Bent

Director Interior

Director IA (CMATT)
MG Paul Eaton

Director Infrastructure

Director AID

Regional Coordinators (Operations)

Governorate Coordinators (Operations)

Communication
Daniel Sudnick
Construction & Housing
Joe Morgan
Electricity
Randy Richardson
Public Works
Michael Mutter
Transport
Darrel Trent
Water Resources
Jerry Webb

Deputy Administrator & Chief Policy Officer
Amb Jones

Scott Carpenter   Tom Foley   Susan Thompson   David Gompert   Amb Belka   Steve Smith

Director Governance

Director Private Sector Development

Director Civil Affairs

Director National Security Affairs

Director Strategic Communications (MoD)
Gary Thatcher

Director Foreign Affairs

Director Economic Policy

Director Admin & Logistics

E. (Rick) Ortiz
Industry & Minerals

Khidhir Hamza
Science & Technology

Susan Hamrock — Trade

Culture
Mario Osio (ITA)
Education
Mana'Ali
Health
James Haveman
Higher Education
John Agresto
Human Rights
Sandra Hodgkinson
Justice
Daniel L. Rubini
Youth & Sports
Mounzer R. Fattat

Displacement & Migration
Lawrence Bartlett
Foreign Affairs
Susan Johnson

Agriculture
Trevor Flugge
Banking
Olin Wethington
Environment
Allen Irish
Finance
Anthony McDonald
Labor & Social Affairs
James Otwell

Regional Coordinators (Policy)

Governorate Coordinators (Policy)

04 JAN 04

Selected Bibliography

Alderson, A., *Bankrolling Basra* (London, 2007).

Allawi, A., *The Occupation of Iraq* (London New Haven, CT, 2007).

Allen, M., *Arabs* (London, 2006).

Aylwin-Foster, N., *Changing the Army for Counterinsurgency Operations* (London, 2005).

Baker, A. and Hamilton, L., *The Iraq Study Group Report* (New York, 2006).

Barnett, C., *Post-conquest Civil Affairs* (London, 2005).

BBC News, *The Battle for Iraq* (London, 2003).

Bremer, L., *My Year in Iraq* (New York, 2006).

Burke, J., *On the Road to Kandahar* (London, 2006).

Campbell, A., *The Blair Years* (London, 2007).

Chandrasekaran, R., *Imperial Life in the Emerald City* (New York, 2006).

Chehab, Z., *Iraq Ablaze* (London, 2006).

Dobbins, J., *America's Role in Nation-Building: From Germany to Iraq* (Santa Monica, 2003).

Dodge, T., *Inventing Iraq* (London, 2003).

Etherington, M., *Revolt on the Tigris* (London, 2006).

Fink, N., *One Bullet Away* (London, 2005).

Fukuyama, F., *State Building* (London, 2004).

Herring, E. and Rangwala, G., *Iraq in Fragments* (London, 2006).

Hiro, D., *Iraq* (London, 2003).

Ignatieff, M., *Empire Lite* (London, 2003).

Kampfner, J., *Blair's Wars* (London, 2003).

Keegan, J., *The Iraq War* (London, 2004).

Lawrence, T.E., *Seven Pillars of Wisdom* (London, 1935).

McCarthy, R., *Nobody Told Us We are Defeated* (London, 2006).

Phillips, L., *Losing Iraq* (New York, 2005).

Rathmell, A., *Planning Post-conflict Reconstruction in Iraq* (London, 2005).

Ricks, T., *Fiasco* (London, 2006).

Stewart, R., *Occupational Hazards* (London, 2006).

Synnott, H., *State-Building in Southern Iraq* (London, 2005).

Thesiger, W., *The Marsh Arabs* (London, 1964).

Tripp, C., *A History of Iraq* (Cambridge, 2002).

Woodward, B., *Bush at War* (New York, 2002).

Woodward, B., *Plan of Attack* (New York, 2004).

Woodward, B., *State of Denial* (New York, 2006).

Index